Immigration and American Popular Culture

NATION OF NEWCOMERS
Immigrant History as American History

Matthew Jacobson and Werner Sollors
GENERAL EDITORS

RACHEL RUBIN AND
JEFFREY MELNICK

Immigration and American Popular Culture

An Introduction

NEW YORK UNIVERSITY PRESS
New York and London

NEW YORK UNIVERSITY PRESS
New York and London
www.nyupress.org

Rubin, Rachel, 1964–
Immigration and American popular culture : an introduction /
Rachel Rubin and Jeffrey Melnick.
p. cm. — (Nation of newcomers)
Includes bibliographical references and index.
ISBN-13: 978-0-8147-7553-0 (cloth : alk. paper)
ISBN-10: 0-8147-7553-5 (cloth : alk. paper)
ISBN-13: 978-0-8147-7552-3 (pbk. : alk. paper)
ISBN-10: 0-8147-7552-7 (pbk. : alk. paper)
  1. Immigrants—Cultural assimilation. 2. United States—Ethnic relations.
3. Popular culture—United States. I. Melnick, Jeffrey Paul. II. Title.
III. Series.
JV6465.R83 2006
304.8'73—dc22   2006017648

New York University Press books are printed on acid-free paper,
and their binding materials are chosen for strength and durability.

Manufactured in the United States of America

c 10 9 8 7 6 5 4 3 2 1
p 10 9 8 7 6 5 4 3 2 1

In memory of Joshua Rubin (1962–2002)

CONTENTS

ACKNOWLEDGMENTS

The authors would like to thank Werner Sollors and Matthew Jacobson, series editors of *A Nation of Newcomers,* for the invitation to undertake this rich and rewarding investigation. Eric Zinner and Emily Park, at New York University Press, have been ideal editors—patient, challenging, and supportive—and for this we offer our deep thanks.

We would also like to thank the Joiner Center for the Study of War and Social Consequences and the Institute for Asian American Studies at the University of Massachusetts Boston, as well as the Faculty Research Facility and the Board of Research at Babson College, for their material support of this project. Deep thanks are also due to Lynn Weiss, Charlie McGovern, and the American Studies Colloquium of the College of William and Mary; Reed Ueda and the urban history seminar of the Massachusetts Historical Society; Paul Watanabe and the John F. Kennedy Library Summer Institute for Teachers; Mary Jane Treacy and her class "Multicultural Women's Studies" at Simmons College; Marc Lee Raphael and the other panelists at the " 'Jewishness' and the World of 'Difference' " symposium at the College of William and Mary; and Fred Gardaphe and the other participants at the "Gangster Life and Violence in America" symposium held at the Humanities Institute at Stony Brook, for the helpful feedback they provided.

In addition to being our role model in her own scholarship and so many other things, Judy Smith carefully read this book and offered us a remarkable mix of powerful support and the challenge to think it all through in new and different ways. Her intellectual guidance made this book so much better than it would otherwise have been and her friendship over the years has been so important to us both. Jim Smethurst's influence on this book will be apparent to anyone who knows his fine work in African American and ethnic expressive arts. We thank him for his meticulous readings, his productive leads, and his consistent intellectual generosity. Gary Wilder helped us immeasurably as he commented on drafts and kept us focused on the world history framing our investigation. Aaron Lecklider is a trusted colleague and friend, and over time it has become impossible to think of doing academic work without him around as a co-conspirator.

Vijay Prashad, Murray Forman, and Joe Kraus all read and commented on individual chapters and shared their expertise with us. Thanks are also due to Lois Rudnick and Shauna Manning at UMass Boston, and Mary Driscoll and Kate Buckley at Babson College, for all of their support. Daniel Rodriguez of UMass Boston did fantastic work in helping to assemble illustrations and our timeline, and Malinda Polk also helped track down some crucial images. Katrina Ranum helped us to understand the swing revival scene. We also want to send a deep message of gratitude to the zine writers who shared information (and zines) that made it possible to write chapter 6.

Finally, we want to send a message of love to Jacob Rubin and Jessie Rubin, both acute critics of popular culture.

Introduction

Aliens, Inc.

The popular movie *Men in Black II* (2002), which, along with its 1997 predecessor *Men in Black,* is one of the turn-of-the-century's most widely circulated reflections on immigration, finds its protagonists in a jam even *after* they have won the movie's climactic battle against the bad guys. The heroes, known as Agent J and Agent K, work for a secret government agency that both regulates and hides the presence on earth of "aliens"—in short, for an intergalactic immigration bureau. In a fight that raged all around and over the Statue of Liberty (Agent L?), they have just saved at least two worlds from destruction and bundled off Agent J's love interest in a spacecraft so she can become a leader of her people. But it has been a conspicuous business. Thousands of people have seen at least some part of the flashy battle—and J and K's job is cover-up as much as it is public safety. Normally, they use an essential tool/weapon called the "neuralyzer" to erase the short-term memory of eyewitnesses with the mere flash of a green light. But this time, so many people have been exposed that the tiny green light could never reach them all.

We have chosen to start our book with this movie scene because of its impressive success at setting up a number of important fields of inquiry crucial to the study of immigration and popular culture. Popular culture in general, and science fiction in particular, has long been an important collective processing site for questions concerning the politics and ethics of immigration: it's very easy to see how "aliens" operate as a stand-in for, well, "aliens," that is, immigrants. The casting of *Men in Black II* includes Michael Jackson and rapper Biz Markie in cameos as aliens, further reminding us that popular culture is an arena where "Americanness" and "otherness" are constantly being negotiated.

In addition to mimicking the immigrant experience, *Men in Black II* reminds us that within immigration narratives, even ones written late in the 20th century, certain frameworks and stories are invoked over and over, so that they remain recognizable while being reworked to suit the needs of the latest immigration culture. In the case of *Men in Black II*, for instance, there is familiar emphasis on the trip to the United States, which has evolved over time from a trans-Atlantic ocean liner to Ellis Island, to an airplane landing at Kennedy Airport, to various spacecraft touching down at a hidden government site somewhere in Manhattan. Likewise, the significant presence in the final scene of the Statue of Liberty serves as both a reference to the statue's significance in earlier immigration narratives—many of which describe seeing it for the first time or quote from its famous inscription from an Emma Lazarus poem about immigration—and a very pointed revision of that significance.

Finally, and perhaps most important for our purposes, the ending of *Men in Black II* raises the question of what the act of immigration requires Americans to forget. Quite a lot, the movie seems to conclude: the remarkable solution to J and K's dilemma is to bounce the green rays of the neuralyzer off the Statue of Liberty so that her torch sends waves of forgetfulness to the "huddled masses" it is held aloft to welcome, with the result that once again, the "real" immigration wars fail to disturb the sleep of Americans. With the Statue of Liberty's role as enforcer of forgetting, *Men in Black II* reinvigorates the old idea of America as a haven for new migrants, while making clear that the cost of coming to the United States might be a complete renunciation of all things "Old World."

But the movie has earlier comforted us with the fact that deep down inside, even after you've forgotten, something "real" about who you "are" is there for the tapping—as J is able to do with K to bring him out from voluntary neuralyzer-induced retirement. In short, this movie deftly and humorously connects immigration, identity, memory, and American myth, all from a self-reflective position inside the popular culture industry—and all the while asking: what are immigrants going to "do" to American culture? And what is American culture going to "do" to immigrants? And also: what will American popular culture producers do "about" immigrants?

The most important word in our title, *Immigration and American Popular Culture*, might just be "and." The premise and structure of the book rely on a few different ways we have of understanding the centrality of "and" to the study of cultural history. To begin, our decision to use a case study method in the pages that follow stems from our sense that a traditional historical survey of the subject would be doomed to superficiality. The richness that we think we have found in six clusters of cultural activity that we immerse in over these chapters allows us—requires us, really—to make plain what the major questions facing scholars of immigration and popular culture are, as well as to begin to suggest a number of major approaches currently used to answer those questions. Taken together the six case studies are meant to be decidedly historicist and aim to give readers a clear idea of how the culture industries have incorporated immigrants—both institutionally and on the level of representation—over time.

The "and" is tricky though—it cannot signify a straightforward method or body of knowledge. We could simply "add" immigrants and popular culture and develop a neat chronicle of how one clear activity ("immigration") engaged with another ("popular culture"). The problem, as we define it in this book, is that you cannot separate "immigration" from "popular culture": if we agree that immigrants were at the very heart of popular culture imagery and production (as we begin to argue as soon as chapter 1 and continue to argue throughout the book) and popular culture helped produce and define various moments of immigration history (see especially chapters 2 and 5 for this), then it starts to come clear why our "and" is more than a little unstable.

Ultimately, the biggest problem with our "and" is that it hints that what really matters is the boundary separating "immigration" from "popular culture." But what *Immigration and American Popular Culture* will truly argue is that "immigrants" and "American popular culture" have created each other.

The "and" also anchors (and, we hope, challenges) a powerful allegory about American life, an allegory about the supposed "ordinary"

goodness of certain immigrants. Judith Smith has recently demonstrated in convincing detail how a cohort of American writers and filmmakers in the post–World War II era converted the immigrant family
story into *the* story of proper American modern life, and in doing so
wrote African American families out of the category of the "healthy."
Writers as diverse as Betty Smith and Arthur Miller began to insist that
groups of immigrants formerly seen as "racialized outsiders" (Smith,
Visions of Belonging 4) must now be understood as leaders of a new plu-
ralistic reality. But this cultural work was rooted, of course, in a set of
ideas about "race" that are always in a state of flux: one of the problems with our title is that it cloaks a crucial process whereby "immigrants" have continually been measured against the defining presence
of African Americans.

"Race," then, is the barely hidden term that accompanies our title.
A large portion of *Immigration and American Popular Culture* is about
how immigrants entered a nation constructed around a black and white
divide. Since the first decades of the 19th century, Americans have
habitually (one might even say obsessively) processed a variety of concerns about racial difference and likeness through popular culture
vehicles. None has been more important than the foundational American popular culture form, blackface minstrelsy. The practice of "blacking up" or "acting black" in front of an audience dominated American
popular culture in the 19th century and continued to exert a shaping
influence throughout the 20th. Scholars from diverse disciplines are
still discovering all the many traces that stage traditions of blackface
minstrelsy left in American popular culture over all the decades that
the United States has supported an organized entertainment industry.
As early as 1931, when Constance Rourke published her book *American
Humor,* it has been impossible for historians and other cultural critics
to sidestep the central place of minstrelsy in American popular culture.
From its most important home in theater, through its rearticulation in
vernacular writing, to the central role it played in early Hollywood
sound film, to its later role on the radio and television, minstrelsy has
never left the stage for long.

Blackface has habituated American audiences, producers, and performers to the idea that the most serious conversations surrounding
racial and national identity in the United States can be properly hosted

on popular culture stages. The various "stages" of American popular culture—be they in actual theaters or not—have relied on the masking strategies that energized 19th–century blackface practice. Those strategies were, as contemporary scholars of minstrelsy have demonstrated, full of complex and sometimes contradictory meanings. The mask has signaled many things—racist derision, cross-racial sympathy, sexual attraction, misogyny, confusion about modernity, and so on: perhaps more important than any single meaning that has been produced by the minstrel mask at any one moment is how it has come to serve as a kind of national symbol of trauma.

Traumas of race in American history undergird our study of popular culture and immigration. The "founding traumas," to borrow a phrase from historian Dominick LaCapra, include the original European colonization of Native American lands, and the ensuing centuries of slavery and violent racism that followed. LaCapra explains that "founding traumas" often become the basis of identity for individuals or groups; if nothing else, they present a stable source of identity (23).

Blackface minstrelsy, with its central proposition that the complex challenges of racial identity could be profitably turned into entertainments, gave birth to a popular culture in the United States that has never been able to shrug off its responsibility to process racial (and later) ethnic identity as a central task. To the contrary, one major story we aim to tell here has to do with how often the denizens of America's popular culture stages have put masks on and taken masks off—sometimes ruefully, sometimes gleefully, but almost always with focused purpose.

Michael Rogin usefully noticed in his 1998 book *Blackface, White Noise* that the Jews who created Hollywood in the 1910s and 1920s utterly depended on blackface to make their mark, and also oversaw the demise of the form. But the demise of blackface has been greatly exaggerated. Even as "blacking up" ceased to be a significant mainstream practice after World War II, minstrelsy continued to act as a shadowy and deeply felt presence in American cultural life. "Masking" has been both a symptom of and a remedy for the injuries of racial and ethnic persecution in the United States. LaCapra explains these two modalities by describing the difference between traumas that are "acted out" (a kind of automatic and helpless repetition) and those that are "worked through" (21, 23). In this book we will plot a dynamic in which Americans of the dominant culture and those in marginalized immigrant and ethnic groups wear masks as emblems, as weapons, as apologies. From the all-purpose white ethnic slang of the classic 1930s gangster movies (chapter 1 here), to the now-you-see-it-now-you-don't rebellious spectacle of the Latino zoot suit of the 1940s (chapter 2), up through the white hippies wrapping themselves in "holy" Indian dress (chapter 4) in the 1960s and the Asian American pranksters playing with all kinds of "yellowface" ironies in cyberspace around Y2K (chapter 6), the mask will be a frequent object of our analysis. While this book will only occasionally write directly of African American life in the United States, *Immigration and American Popular Culture* takes it as a given that black-white relations is the frame inside of which immigrant life comes into sharpest focus.

It is important to indicate from the start what *Immigration and American Popular Culture* hopes to accomplish—and how. We offer here a road map of what we might call the "cultural imaginary of immigration." The cultural geographer Michael Laguerre has offered as an axiom that "in order to have ethnic minorities one must also have a minoritized space" (4). Laguerre is interested above all in actual immigrants and their neighborhoods: in his estimation, location is the "elementary" aspect of marginalized identity because it is what "fixes individuals to specific niches where they get their early socialization, where their memories are buried, and from where they read the outside world and interact with it" (97).

We have no quibble with Laguerre's insight as it applies to immigrant settlement in the United States, but simply want to emphasize his final phrase here ("from where they read the outside world and interact with it") and suggest that much of this "interaction" with the "outside world" takes place through the multiple vehicles of popular culture. In this book, we are concerned with real immigrants and what they have made, as well as with how they were processed in and by the American popular cultural industries. As Sandhya Shukla says in her recent work on Indians in the diasporas of America and England, we don't want to choose between "the work of the imagination" and the "everyday cross-border activities of migrants" (12). Instead of offering a "logically" unfolding narrative history of the title's implicit equation (immigration + popular culture = x), our approach is to explore what we take to be particularly rich moments when a key development in immigration history was "acted out" or "worked through" in the context of American popular culture. One guiding principle is that many of these "key developments" were in fact produced—at least in part—through the agency of the popular culture industries. Chapter 3, for instance, will argue in part that the incorporation of Puerto Ricans into mainstream American life has been dominated by the work of *West Side Story*, a Broadway show and later movie. Chapter 5 will explain how Jamaicans were "prepared" for immigration to the United States by the music they heard beamed from American radio stations and on American records.

Each case study will start from a time and place in which the relationship of immigrants and popular culture was being worked out in an especially focused and sustained way—the zoot suit riots of 1943, or sitar master Ravi Shankar's adoption by young white people at the Monterey Pop Festival in 1967. In orienting our case studies around a particular time/space nexus we are borrowing a crucial theoretical insight from Russian literary theorist Mikhail Bakhtin: Bakhtin called this organizing principle a "chronotope," by which he meant to indicate a "means for materializing time in space" (250). For Bakhtin the chronotope is where "the knots of narrative are tied and untied." While Bakhtin was interested in narrative form, we are adopting his approach to the novel for our own purposes: our historical "chronotopes" work as Bakhtin's novelistic ones did, to create a "center for concretizing representation" (250).

But as will soon become apparent, each chapter ranges over time as we trace out the implications of this theme, or that strategy. Chronological simplicity was never a goal: our operating principle is that popular culture texts operate in a fluid field of influence and innovation, that, in short, they constitute an area of cultural activity poorly served by simple attempts to construct unified narratives of development.

That said, there is a concrete history of immigration to (and migration within) the United States that frames this project. As the book progresses it should become clear that it is organized around three major eras of immigration. The first chapter of our book, on white ethnic (particularly Jewish) gangsters in Hollywood movies, is meant to act as a review of sorts: the immigrants who were central to gangster films—as producers, subject, and audience—were the Irish, Italian, and Jewish Americans who had played such a crucial role in the immigration waves that populated the United States from around 1850 to 1924. These immigrants and their children operated in a social milieu in which the purported differences separating African American people from white people was often proposed as the *only* meaningful way to understand the demographics of the United States. But our next two chapters, concerned as they are with Mexican immigration and Puerto Rican migration, demonstrate how a complex set of midcentury actions and ideological claims redrew the racialized American landscape. From here, and keeping in mind the crucial role played by a 1952 immigration law and its 1965 revision, we will turn our focus to the newer immigrants coming from South and Southeast Asia and the Caribbean.

At many times in the book the crucial history will be a legal history. While *Immigration and American Popular Culture* does not intend to offer a narrative history of immigration restriction, it does take into account how the United States government has attempted to manage the flow of people coming into the country, from the first congressional act to legislate naturalization and citizenship (in 1790), to the Chinese Exclusion Act of 1882, the Barred Zone Act of 1917, the Jones Act of 1917, the Immigration Restriction Act of 1924, and the Immigration and Nationality Act of 1952 and amendments made to it 1965. Other federal programs, from the bracero program of the World War II era (which brought Mexican workers to the United States in huge numbers) to Operation Bootstrap (which in the years after World War II was aimed at incorporating Puerto Ricans into mainland life), have also helped define how the United States has come to be populated as it is.

The 1924 law restricting immigration might be the pivotal one here. Mae Ngai has recently made the case in her book *Impossible Subjects* that the very language we continue to use to describe and debate "immigrants" and "immigration" to the United States was codified in that act. To begin, this act was, as she explains, the first ever "comprehensive" immigration restriction law—with a "racial and national hierarchy that favored some immigrants over others" (3). This immigration law treated "race" as obvious and visible as it split the world up into "colored" and "non-colored" races, and into European and non-European

(27). And, in addition to excluding Chinese, Japanese, and Indian people, the act profoundly marginalized Mexicans, turning them, in Ngai's words, into the "single largest group of illegal immigrants in the 1920s" (7). With this one piece of legislation, then, the United States government set the agenda for a huge percentage of future discussions about American immigrants. In the most basic terms, this act organized a long-standing obsession with "good" and "bad" immigrants into a form that would dominate immigration policy for the rest of the century.

Focused social engineering by the United States government has played a major role in the immigration "moments" we are concerned with. Major migrations usually have obvious and direct causes, and government policy is usually a good place to look first. But as *Immigration and American Popular Culture* moves through time, it will be important to note that official government actions have often been augmented (and then supplanted) by less centrally organized geopolitical entities. As this book makes its case, the way that war produces unforeseen and sometimes "unwanted" migrations takes a central role in the drama of immigration and popular culture production. The complex of economic, social, and political connections that ring the world—what we have come to call "globalization"—will also come to define our subject matter and approach as we move from Hollywood film of the 1930s to the Internet of Y2K. Of course, as Laura Briggs has explained, the word "globalization" itself is "a placeholder, a word with no exact meaning that we use in our contested efforts to describe the successors to development and colonialism" (1).

Immigration and American Popular Culture wants to encourage readers to think about the changing nature of immigration in the 20th century. After the first case study, which focuses on "white" ethnics (Jewish Americans, mostly) and gangster movies, the remaining chapters will explore categories of immigrants often classified as non-white: Mexican Americans, Jamaican Americans, Puerto Ricans, Indian Americans, and East Asian Americans. In tracking the ways that these various migrant groups have intersected with American popular culture, a sort of informal history of 20th-century U.S. immigration history will emerge.

The trajectory of the book invites readers to question the very usefulness of the term "immigrant" itself. As Sandhya Shukla has noted, post-1965 patterns of migration to the United States have challenged the accepted notion that it is possible to study immigration and racial minorities as separate subjects (11). It barely suffices to note that over the course of the 20th century the meaning of immigration to the United States and of the category "immigrant" have changed countless times and in complex ways. The Statue of Liberty reference in *Men in Black II* rests on a mythology that tells stories of "good" immigrants— deserving masses of white people coming from Europe to pursue the "American dream." While it is certainly true that Jewish Americans, Italian Americans, and Irish Americans (not to mention Greek Americans, Armenian Americans, and so on) have not always comfortably found themselves situated in the cultural category "white"—nor have they always been welcomed with open arms or open borders—a consensus developed by around the time of World War II that these "classic" immigrant groups all provided good raw material from which to make Americans.

That confidence would not be entrusted in later arrivals to the nation of newcomers. The Latino immigrants of the World War II era, most notably the Mexicans and Puerto Ricans of the bracero program and Operation Bootstrap, respectively, were constructed by the popular culture industries (as well as by legal discourse, journalistic account, and so on) as a distressing problem. The discussions that developed around these newer arrivals to the United States mainland reimagined "immigrant" as a cultural locale of fear, mistrust, and often outright hostility. In our rendering, then, "immigrant" will not denote a stable identity but rather a charged field of claims and counterclaims, an area of intense cultural activity where individual agency meets social demand in an ongoing and ever-changing dialectic. The "immigrant" discussed throughout the book has been known, too, by other names: refugee, deportee, foreigner, "illegal," criminal. Part of the historical burden of *Immigration and American Popular Culture* is to explain how these names have come into play with their own kind of cultural work to do (and see the appendix for a timeline of immigration and popular culture to supplement our main text).

Our major concerns will cut across chapters and across time. As already described, the book will circle regularly around the question of "where and when" (and how) immigrants entered the black-white dynamic that so dominates American social and cultural life: thus, our concern with the place of minstrelsy in American popular culture helps shape the questions we ask in our investigation of gangster movies and the hippie adoption of Ravi Shankar in the United States. More generally, the relationship of migrants in American cities to African Americans is central to the chapters on *West Side Story,* Shankar, and hip hop.

Technological innovation appears centrally in the chapters on gangster movies, hip hop, and cyberzines but not in other chapters. Genre functions as an important area of investigation in the chapter on gangsters and hip hop. The question of audience interpretation animates the chapters on the zoot suit riots and on gangster movies. "Deviant" youth as opposed to "model minorities" will come under discussion especially in the "Latino" chapters (2 and 3), but also in chapter 6. War, colonialism, and imperialism (cultural and economic) are central issues from chapter 2 forward. Bodily display will figure heavily in chapters 2 and 6.

And so on.

But there is no claim to completeness here: we hope that the "and" that rests at the heart of our method extends beyond the pages of the book. The best response we could hope for would be a reader who encounters something of interest here and thinks, "Yes, but also. . . ." *Immigration and American Popular Culture,* with its two authors, tries to incorporate the spirit of open-ended dialogue into its own approach.

The general questions the book intends to answer can be outlined quite simply:

- In what particular ways have immigrants consumed American popular culture? What have these new Americans done with (or done to) the films, songs, fashions, and so on that they have found in the United States? What does the world of popular culture tell immigrants about what it means to be "American"?
- How have immigrants shaped the production of popular culture? How has the influence of particular immigrant groups changed from one generation to the next? What industries or forms have been particularly congenial or hostile to new immigrants? What legislative acts and technological advances have played major roles in

the access immigrants have had to mainstream American popular
culture?
- How have immigrants been used as subject matter in American popular culture productions? Which groups have been depicted most
frequently—and in what contexts?

The answers to some of these questions will appear in each chapter.
While each case study will likely seem to tilt toward one of these three
areas (consumption, production, imagery), all will demonstrate the
complicated way that the categories shape one another. In this way, the
book will serve as a general introduction to some of the major approaches used to study popular culture; it will also move through many
different popular culture forms, from fashion to film, and from popular
music to cyberzines.

Popular culture is at once a vehicle and an object of study here. Popular culture texts take us to places that might not otherwise be accessible. In *Immigration and American Popular Culture* we proceed from the
notion that certain elements of popular culture incorporate a stunning
amount of American experience: an ethnic gangster's slang, a zoot suit,
a sitar, a Web site called bigbadchinesemama.com; all of these are
"search engines" that require us to follow their tracks through time
and space. The simultaneous leads offered by our selected moments
serve as a reminder that popular culture texts are defined by their multiplicity, simultaneity, and unfixedness.

These popular culture texts, though, are not simply convenient win-
dows onto immigration history: they are also things in themselves. A
major goal in *Immigration and American Popular Culture* is to pay close
attention to the formal and generic traditions that help define popular
culture texts. In other words, the strategy of *Immigration and American
Popular Culture* is to look not only at what lies *behind* the "mask" of the
popular culture text, but to look at the mask itself for what secrets its
very design holds and to begin to explore what work was necessary to
create and interpret that artifact.

The masks to which we have already made numerous references are
very much on our minds in the first chapter here, an investigation of
ethnic gangsters in 1930s Hollywood film. In the cinematic argot of the
time, these incredibly popular movies were "snatched" from the head-

lines of the day. The culture industries had been incorporating Jewish, Italian, and Irish American migrants to the United States for decades by the time that Hollywood took its turn. Stage performances, sheet music covers, and comic sketches in magazines (to name just a few sites) acted as a cultural Ellis Island of sorts for these European immigrants as they were "processed" again in a more diffuse social sense. But for all the laughs cajoled and tears jerked by these earlier creations, the Hollywood gangster film worked in a much more focused and persistent way to install the ethnic bad guy as an important player on the contemporary scene.

The "gangster masquerade" was an important exercise in popular culture artifice. Audiences flocked to these movies to take part in what ultimately has to be understood as a social ritual, one which, like most rituals, turned extraordinary behaviors into a seemingly organic set of practices. These "gangsters" were double agents, though: they held many secrets and told some of them. Some of the most important secrets had to do with "Jewishness"—the tough talk and urban wiles of the gangster were very much the product of a New World Yiddish—as language and culture. But audiences quickly learned to "read" the gangsters' many feints and dodges—to become expert, in fact, at decoding the genre-based conventions of speech, dress, and action that defined the gangster movie. In this chapter we introduce the idea that popular culture texts might host "secret" conversations between certain producers and consumers. In this particular case the notion rests on the fact that these Hollywood films were part of a business dominated by Jewish immigrants themselves and were reaching a large population of Jewish immigrants in American cities.

From the creation and interpretation of film gangsters we move to the zoot suit and the surprising cultural power it gained in the 1940s and beyond. As with a number of the chapters in this book, this one has a lot to do with war: the central question here has to do with how a suit of clothes (and its implied opponent—the military uniform) could come to further marginalize a group of young Mexican Americans who had ambivalent status in U.S. culture to begin with. The zoot suit has lived many lives over the past fifty years or so, but only in its first major appearance did it come to embody life-threatening possibilities.

While "actual" Mexicans were officially being welcomed into the

United States as workers during the World War II era, another Mexican, an "imagined" Mexican, was simultaneously being created by a disorganized but powerful group of Anglos who postulated the "zooter" as the degraded child of the first generation immigrants. The "riddle" of the zoot suit has been pondered for decades now, and what remains perhaps most interesting after all is that clothing could become a puzzle.

In the chapter on Puerto Ricans, important questions about what defines an "immigrant" will be raised. Here we explore fundamental issues regarding the relationship of migration, ethnicity, and race. While a later chapter (on Jamaican Americans in the South Bronx) will be concerned specifically with people categorized as "black," many of our case studies open up investigations of how centrally concerned the popular culture industries have been with "blackness": a major purpose of this book will be to chart various expressions of immigrant/ African American relatedness. In this chapter on Puerto Ricans in New York we are particularly concerned with how a group of Jewish American artists attempted, through the vehicle of *West Side Story*, to fit Puerto Ricans into a story of orderly ethnic succession. But to do so these creative artists had to erase the many ways that Puerto Ricans were "related" to African Americans in New York City. Puerto Ricans themselves were quite ambivalent about this intervention and responded in interesting ways throughout the ensuing decades to this outside attempt to define their ethnic/racial status. As with our first chapter on film gangsters, it will be of interest to notice how Jewish involvement in some of the major institutions of the popular culture industry gave certain powerful Jews the chance to project their own anxieties and hopes surrounding immigration in a safely distanced way.

The next chapter, which considers the embrace of Ravi Shankar and all things "Eastern" by the hippies of the 1960s and 1970s, also explores how the interplay between immigrants and American popular culture sometimes happens most significantly in the form of consumption that is both actual and symbolic. In the wake of a new immigration law that opened the gates to certain classes of South Asians and others, Shankar was constructed and adopted as a kind of meta-immigrant, an individual "model" minority who may have wanted to teach one lesson (about Indian classical music) but found an audience that was motivated to understand him as carrier of a different message about the "natural" mystical goodness of people from Asia. The reception of Shankar was framed not only by the new immigration law but also by the concurrent war in Vietnam and the racial strife plaguing American cities.

For obvious reasons, young Americans in the late 1960s and 1970s were struggling with the implications of the dominant culture's aggression in Asia and in the inner city. In adopting Shankar as a benign father figure of sorts, the hippies were able, at least for a time, to project a vision of globalization and cross-cultural engagement that did not have violence at its core. By counterposing Shankar's efforts with his audience's interpretations, it becomes possible to see how immigrants in American popular culture are often faced with the difficult choice of being either invisible or misunderstood. We mean to explore a seismic shift in this book, and it is one that does not only have to do with which new groups of people came to the United States from the mid-1960s on. Another major development this book attends to is the process by which immigrants to the United States began to learn how to manipulate and deploy popular culture forms to establish their place in the culture. While South Asian Indians were confronted, in the mid-1960s, with a fearsomely powerful popular culture system that very effectively cornered the market on defining the place of this new group in American culture, a decade later Jamaican immigrants to New York would be more able to hit the ground running: Jamaicans were much more familiar with American popular culture when they arrived in the United States than Indians had been, and much more able to find and define their own place.

The Jamaican Americans who helped invent hip hop in the Bronx in the 1970s found surprising ways to insert themselves in the American cultural mainstream. As we suggest in chapter 5, these "Jamericans" utilized new sound technologies and insisted on their right to name and define themselves as they came to play a major role in shaping American music in the modern era. With an approach that grew from scarcity and ended up sounding like surplus, young Jamaican Americans like Kool Herc demonstrated that it was possible for immigrants to use scraps of the dominant culture (hardware and cultural materials) to make something totally new. This Jamerican "cut and mix" strategy of making music has become a major element in postmodern art and has an interesting tale to tell about the relationship of the "powerful" and the "weak" on the global cultural scene.

The final chapter begins with a brief tour through some science fiction movies of the 1990s and then a fuller investigation of Asian American cyberzines of the 1990s and beyond. Our exploration of the science fiction movies is a shorthand way of explaining how powerful mainstream forces began to acknowledge and embrace "aliens" as representatives of innovation and promise. While the hippies of chapter 4 could very successfully project an image of Indians as carriers of an unchanging, comforting past, the Jamericans of chapter 5 make it clear that immigrants in the 1970s were beginning to insist that they, from even before they left Jamaica, were destined to be counted as among the most modern and technologically savvy of all Americans.

This final chapter of *Immigration and American Popular Culture* moves issues of globalization to center stage. Focusing on Asian American cyberzines, this chapter invites readers to revisit the most basic questions asked throughout the book (about identity, audience, and so on) in the context of globalized, virtual culture. While the creators of the zines in question form a recognizable cultural cohort, their work —existing mostly in cyberspace—forces us to think again about how "place" shapes identity and how audience expectations exert pressure on artistic creation. This investigation of cyberzines also returns to the cultural construction of gender as a major concern—as it is in the very first chapter of the book. As Gary Okihiro has pointed out, two of the dominant stereotypes of Asian Americans in the 20th century—the invading yellow peril and the docile model minority—are "gendered points on a circle" (110). The vibrant and uncompromising makers of these zines have taken all of American popular culture history as their text and are in the ongoing process of remaking it in their own image. Their playful, referential, and relentless approach to making popular culture at century's end (and century's beginning) offers a glimmer of hope—a "clear channel"—to those of us who worry about corporate control of all media.

CHAPTER 1

Hollywood, 1930

Jewish Gangster Masquerade

Toward the end of the 1935 gangster movie *Let 'Em Have It,* a brutal gangster is running from agents of the newly formed Federal Bureau of Investigation. He knows his chances of eluding the agents are getting slimmer and slimmer, so he conceives of an innovative plan for escape. The gangster and his henchmen capture a plastic surgeon and threaten to kill him unless he surgically alters the gangster's features so that he won't be recognized by the law.

The surgeon has no choice but to perform the operation. When it is over, the gangster—not so surprisingly—murders him anyway, because, of course, he knows too much. But the climactic moment occurs when the gangster is finally able to take off the bandages the surgeon has used to wrap his face. Facing a mirror, the gangster discovers that the surgeon, who had better sense than to trust a gangster and who *knew* he would be killed no matter what, has carved the gangsters' initials into his cheeks—thereby permanently identifying him for the FBI agents in pursuit of him.

Let 'Em Have It, with its shocking visuals, its ostentatiously up-to-date portrayal of the criminal justice system, and its moody, menacing gangster-characters, is a typical enough (if largely forgotten—it still

has not been released on DVD) example of the gangster genre that dominated the moviegoing experience as the United States entered the
1930s. We open with this movie—one of literally hundreds—because
it so clearly lays out the questions of masking and identity that we will
argue in this chapter make up an important part of the cultural "work"
of gangster movies during the 1930s (and beyond). (Indeed, the U.K.
release of the film used the title *False Faces*.) Just a decade after Jewish
performer Fanny Brice had her famous plastic surgery to reduce her
distinctively Jewish nose, inspiring Dorothy Parker to remark, "She cut
off her nose to spite her race," *Let 'Em Have It* challenges plastic surgery as an adequate hiding place and claims that as much as the gangster might try to hide—no matter what mask he hides behind—his
face and his name will ultimately reveal themselves.

By the time *Let 'Em Have It* played in movie theaters in 1935, American movie audiences had been well trained in the customs and pleasures of gangster flicks. The first major gangster movie was released in
1930 and was immediately followed by dozens of others: it is here we
begin our inquiry. Although the figure of the gangster became common
in pulp novels, plays, and newspaper and magazine articles as well, it
was in these genre movies that the conventions of fictional gangster-
dom were established—conventions that would remain in place, manipulated carefully not only throughout what became known as the
"classic" era of the 1930s but for the entire span of the 20th century
(and into the 21st). Perhaps even more important for our purposes, it
was in the movies of the 1930s where the gangster became recognizably
marked as "ethnic" (as opposed to earlier, less particularized representations of slum toughs).

The dubious claim is often advanced that during the 1930s—the
Great Depression, after all—people went to movies for largely escap-
ist reasons. The early generation of gangster films, though, was very
pointedly marketed as "realist." Warner Brothers, for instance, which
produced the most gangster movies of all the studios, declared dramatically that their films were "Snatched from Today's Headlines!" and
then set about to prove it (Clarens 53). This case was made in many
ways. The films showcased up-to-the-minute technology, with criminals
relying on telephones and automobiles and explosives in exciting and
fresh ways. When the main character of *The Public Enemy* (1931) is

attacked by a rival gang, for example, the studio boasted that the shots (which missed their target but fractured a wall) were fired from real machine guns, by marksmen hired by the studio.

In addition to showcasing new technologies, the gangster movies themselves made profitable use of the new sound technologies, with many critics claiming that the genre was the first place "talkies" really succeeded. Gangster movies were made using newly portable sound equipment that allowed the streets to operate as central settings, whereas in earlier films, heavy microphone equipment had limited settings to a couple of rooms. These movies employed current slang that efficiently and colorfully identified the characters as urban, as criminals, as the children of immigrants, and as hailing from working-class families. Some of this slang—"gat" (gun), "beef" (quarrel), "clip" (kill), "the joint" (prison)—found its way through the movies into the American vernacular, where it is still audible today.

The movies' aural economy conveyed a sense of immediacy, as did their urban-gritty visual punch. Interestingly, one way that filmmakers conveyed this immediacy was by calling attention to the importance of an older medium—the newspaper—to contemporary urban life. Viewers who saw a lot of gangster movies became accustomed to the newspaper figuring centrally in one way or another—sometimes through a character who is a journalist, sometimes through close-up shots of a front-page headline, sometimes through the swift and thrilling sight of papers coming off the press. Meanwhile, outside of the theater, actual journalists, whose plentiful coverage of the organized criminal world regularly included such titillating details as the amount of money spent on flowers for a gangster funeral, were busily blurring the line from their end between news reporting and the stuff of entertainment.

This blurring of the line between news and entertainment—endowing the movies and the literature of gangsters with a function that would be named some half a century later as "infotainment"—added to the impression that gangster movies were somehow "real." It is true that by spotlighting mob activity the films were depicting a current phenomenon. (Film historian Carlos Clarens has even claimed that they served a civic purpose by acquainting viewers with relevant details of current criminal law [103].) Ethnic criminal gangs were not new, as Herbert Asbury's colorful books about the historical *Gangs of New York*

(1927) and *Gangs of Chicago* (1940) showed. However, bootlegging opportunities under Prohibition (which lasted from 1919 to 1933), coupled
with expanded immigration from Europe from the 1880s to the 1920s,
did markedly "grow" both Jewish and Italian mob activity in the
1920s. The Jewish underworld flourished in ghettos such as New York's
Lower East Side, Chicago's West Side, and those in Detroit, Boston, Baltimore, and other places. During this time Jews contributed such notorious gangsters as Meyer Lansky, Dutch Schultz, Bugsy Siegel, Gyp the
Blood, and scores more of the United States' foremost bootleggers, rack-
eteers, panderers, and professional killers, culminating most famously
in the Jewish-Italian criminal syndicate dubbed "Murder, Inc." by contemporary journalists.

Jews and Italians achieved prominence in organized crime after the
so-called new immigration of the late 1890s and early 1900s. Before
1880, the majority of immigrants to New York came from England, Germany, and Ireland. After 1880, and particularly after 1900, the majority of migrants began arriving from southern and eastern Europe, and
between 1881 and 1924, 2.4 million European Jews immigrated to the
United States. After the assassination of his father Alexander II in
1881, the Russian czar Alexander III began passing anti-Semitic decrees
(the May Laws), which, along with a spate of government-sanctioned
pogroms, caused many Russian Jews to flee the country. Meanwhile, in
the Austro-Hungarian empire thousands of peasants were forced to
leave their land due to consolidation in the agriculture industry. Two
million Jews left Europe for America after 1880, three-quarters of them
Russian; a similar proportion of that total settled in New York City, and
by 1910, Russian Jews were New York's largest immigrant group. (Without getting into the complexities of European political history, it
should be noted here that "Russian" and "Jewish" are complicated categories, given the frequently shifting national boundaries of European
nations and the practice of the United States census of tracking immigrants only by country of origin, but not by nationality or religion.)
Living close together in poor ghetto neighborhoods in big cities like
New York, Chicago, and Detroit, Jewish boys joined gangs "as a matter
of course," as historian Albert Fried put it (37).

As campaigns developed to limit immigration in the first decades of
the 20th century, a spotlight was turned on crime statistics as a way

to find "proof" that immigrants and their children were dangerous to Americans. From several quarters came authoritative declarations that Jewish immigrants were contributing to the corruption of American morals through a disproportionate involvement in pimping, prostitution, robbery, and assault. A special panic developed around the idea that Jewish men were largely responsible for the business of "white slavery" (a name for enforced prostitution), for which *Scribner's* writer Edwin Grant Conklin claimed Jews were innately temperamentally suited (Ruth 13–14). Perhaps most infamously, in 1908, Theodore Bingham, police commissioner of New York, declared in a report that Jews were responsible for 50 percent of the city's crime (383–394).

The Jewish press in the United States reacted with bewilderment to increasing evidence that Jews were centrally involved in illegitimate activities: how could such a thing be reconciled with a moral code that supposedly made violent crime impossible? Jews had acquired a reputation for being peaceful and law abiding since they first began to arrive in North America in the mid-seventeenth century, and popular commentators, such as *Century* magazine, tended to single them out for praise: "Proof of the high moral standing of Hebrews is that only two murderers have sprung from their ranks in two hundred and fifty years" (quoted in Joselit 27). As Jewish gang historian Jenna Joselit has shown, not only Jews themselves, but also most Americans, seemed to believe in Jewish exceptionalism in this regard.

The presence of immigrant Jews (and their children) in all manner of criminal endeavors was real: but it also opened up social space for wide-ranging discussions about immigration, commercialization, and modernization in general. These issues were being furiously debated by a wide range of cultural critics, public officials, social workers, racial anthropologists, and educators. This chapter will explore some of the ways in which gangster movies joined this urgent conversation, at a moment when a variety of media institutions—newspapers, the Motion Picture Academy, and so on—acknowledged that these movies were a central force in American cultural life.

But despite their carefully rendered trappings of immigrant realism —and important role in providing a way to respond to the presence of immigrants in cities—the gangster movies have also been examples of what W. T. Lhamon has called a "wink and a dodge" and what Laura

Browder names "slippery characters" (in other contexts) all along, a fact about which they reminded viewers over and over again. (Lhamon discusses the subversive strategies of blackface minstrelsy, and Browder refers to ethnic impersonation by authors.) The "slippery" quality of the gangster figure is, in fact, one thing that allowed the trope of the double agent, where layered identities pile up and no one is quite who he seems to be, to flourish as it has.

Fred Gardaphe usefully uses recent scholarship of minstrelsy to "explain" the first generation of imagined Italian gangsters (6). He is taking "minstrelsy" to mean demeaning performative mimicry of one group, carried out by people outside that group: whites who put on blackface are the originators, and Gardaphe wants to make a case for how the concept can also be applied to non-Italian writers who draw wildly stereotypical Italian gangsters. It is possible to deploy here an even broader idea of "minstrelsy"—or masquerade—one that encompasses deliberate hiding, masking, and dodging on the part of those who consider themselves insiders. This wider application of the idea of masquerade can help us better understand those Jews who were most concerned with watching and creating ethnic movie gangsters. This chapter focuses on some of those Hollywood dodges. Jews were particularly well placed as a result of a decades-long process of consolidating their power in the entertainment industries to use film as a forum for articulating (and sometimes masking) group concerns with their public image. What did turning the mobster into a ritual (through the morbid but stylish conventions of what came to be called "film noir") accomplish? Why were the dodges necessary in the first place, and how did people understand them? What "secrets" did the gangster movies keep through their masquerade, and what secrets did they tell? Finally, what is the evolving meaning *of* the gangster mask for Jews and non-Jews and what is the meaning *behind* the mask?

This chapter is also intended to demonstrate the usefulness of privileging genre as an analytic category. Organizing this chapter around genre ("gangster movies") allows us to take an entire system of cultural activity into account and to notice how that system changes over time. The focus on genre demands that at least some attention be paid to those who made the movies, those who watched them, those who advertised and reviewed them, those who objected to them, those who made money from them, and so forth. This chapter intends to probe gangster movies from many positions of what Stuart Hall called encoding and decoding of meaning ("Encoding/Decoding" 130)—in short, paying close attention to arguments being constructed by those who participated in making the films and also arguments being constructed by how audiences chose to understand them. In the case of the "classic" gangster movies, the levels of meaning overlap from the start: Americans whose background included the "classic" story of immigration from Europe to the United States were found in the audience, on-screen, and in the production companies.

The Gangster Hits the Movies

The 1930s have become known, in historical cliché, as the "golden" or "classic" age of gangster movies. This is certainly true from the point of view of quantity: especially during the first three or so years of that decade, the studios kept grinding them out, hoping to repeat each box office success story. Most major male actors of the period played a gangster at some point during their careers. In 1931, roughly twenty-five gangster movies were released; in 1932, there were about forty (Clarens 60).

Hewing largely to a fairly transparent "rise and fall" formula, these gangster movies flooded the country with story after story about immigrants and their children, with the result that they presented these populations as a sort of puzzle that had to be figured out. In one realm, though, barely more than a half-decade earlier the "puzzle" had been solved already by the passage of the Immigration Restriction Act of 1924 (also known as the Johnson-Reed Act). This law severely limited the number of immigrants who could be admitted from any country (to 2 percent of the number of people from that country who were already living in the United States in 1890). The law was intended to curtail the immigration of southern and eastern Europeans, and it was successful: from 1900 to 1910, for instance, about 200,000 Italians were permitted to enter the United States every year, but after 1924, only 4,000 were permitted to enter yearly. Thus, the peak moment of gangster movies can be located as marking the *end* of the great waves of Italian and Jewish immigration—and offering commentary upon what those great waves were going to mean, now that they were a fait accompli. Gangster movies also concerned themselves with the new anxieties resulting from the mobility—or potential mobility—of immigrant families, some of whom were starting to move out of the ethnic ghettos where they had first settled.

These films, with their depictions of Italian, Irish, and Jewish gangsters who struggle to achieve class mobility through crime and violence, were capacious enough to accommodate more than one perspective on the new immigrant Americans. On one hand, as David Ruth in particular has made amply clear, the movies expressed to some viewers a xenophobic dread about what these immigrants (and their children) would do to American society. From this position, the gangsters' capacity for violence is ethnically determined, and their "outsider" status is brought about by their own cultural deficiencies.

But this interpretation cannot account for all segments of the audience; as Robert Sklar has pointed out, movie reviewers in the 1930s were frequently startled to find that audiences "took to" the gangsters (32) and that the movies attracted a "devoted following of urban ethnics" (43) who cheered them openly in the theaters. Indeed, as Michael Denning and others have acknowledged, the gangster became the "first 'ethnic' hero in American popular culture" (*Cultural Front* 254).

With the perspective brought by the distance of time, it is easy to see how particular gangster movies could invite such contradictory interpretations. The three movies that are generally considered to be the triumvirate of the "best" gangster movies (certainly the ones of the era that have continued to wield cultural power)—*Little Caesar* (1930), *The Public Enemy* (1931), and *Scarface* (1932)—illustrate, taken together and separately, an availability to bluntly divergent readings even as they all embrace the major rules and motifs of the gangster genre.

The gangster "hero" of *Little Caesar*, Rico, is Italian American. He is a minor thug who, for a short time, manages to rise on the crime ladder because he is driven to succeed in his chosen path, not because he is particularly smart or strong. What is most interesting about Rico is that his drive is not primarily to acquire wealth as such; very early in the

Figure 1.1. Edward G. Robinson in *Little Caesar* (1930): his ultimate achievement of status comes at a "society" dinner in his honor

movie, in fact, he tells an associate, "Money's all right, but it ain't
everything." What Rico lusts after is the social standing he sees more
"polished" types enjoy, and it is easy to sympathize with his desire for
inclusion. Rico does achieve this status for a while—he is never more
triumphant than when a fancy dinner is held in his honor—but in the
long run, he appears as a fish out of water: too uncouth, too rude, and
too short and dark to fit into the sleek, glamorous world he so admires.
The end of the film finds Rico lying prone under a billboard, dead and
alone—suffering the fate of virtually all film gangsters.

Released less than a year later, *The Public Enemy* is also very interested in the question of how "ethnics" will fit into cherished American
institutions. Here, the gangsters are the children of Irish immigrants
who eventually team up with a Jewish mob. Tom Powers has surveyed
the ways available to him for prospering, and landed upon crime as
the most likely prospect; as a foil for his choices, the movie includes
the character of Tom's brother, Mike, who follows the "straight" path of
night school, a modest job, and enlistment in the military. Strikingly,

although Mike speaks in a recognizably "positive" rhetoric about serving one's country when it needs you, he mostly comes across as a flunky, while Tom, through criminal enterprises that grow from petty burglary to bootlegging and racketeering, is able to leave the crowded ethnic neighborhood where both boys grew up. He moves across town into a fancy hotel, acquires a worldly blond girlfriend, and purchases fashionable new clothes and a showy car. But at the height of this material success, a fight breaks out between Tom's gang and a bootlegging rival. Tom is shot and badly wounded, and, swaddled in bandages in the hospital, is filled with regret for his choices and swears to give up crime. It's too late, though: the next day, he is kidnapped from the hospital and killed, and in a final image that remains shocking seventy years later, his dead body is dumped back into his mother's house while she sings joyfully upstairs because she's been told he's "coming home."

Scarface, which bases its plot at least somewhat on the life of real-life Chicago gangster Al Capone (who, as it happens, was sitting relatively calmly in jail for tax evasion when the movie came out), shows the same ambivalence toward the successes of its protagonist. In the movie, Tony Camonte, a low-ranking Italian hoodlum, begins to take over and consolidate the rackets after killing his own boss. He rises quickly through a combination of ruthlessness and obsessiveness (both of which crystallize in a controlling, incestuous possessiveness toward his sister), but eventually his own drive makes him a danger to everyone, including himself. Like Rico in *Little Caesar* and Tom Powers in *The Public Enemy*, Tony's final reward is not only death but disgrace: he is machine-gunned down in the street after making a cowardly and shameful dash for escape.

These widely circulating representations were important in establishing the centrality of the "white ethnic" as a key figure of American immigration and acculturation. As tales of social ascent they represented, as many critics have pointed out, perverse yet unmistakable articulations of the Horatio Alger myth. But the screen gangsters, in their inability to fit completely into "high" society no matter how much they accumulated in the way of money or goods, also provided a symbolic means for Americans to ponder, publicly and collectively, the status of immigrants that Robert Orsi and others have called "in-betweenness." It is generally accepted by now that one major story to track within the history of immigration to the United States is how it has been possible for various groups to work "toward whiteness" (Roediger, *Working toward Whiteness*). The white ethnics of the gangster movies teeter on the line. At times, it appears they will be able to "clean up" and become white—and in these movies, they are seen moving away from closeness with black people, as when, in *The Public Enemy,* the ascendant gangsters Tom and Matty airily give orders in a nightclub to the African American porter. But no matter how well they dress, the gangsters are never able to become fully respectable or occupy a stable white identity, either.

Thus, whether audiences feared or idolized (or feared *and* idolized) screen gangsters, these figures remained outside the decorum of "native" American society. The profundity of this dilemma—not accepted in the cultural and economic "mainstream," the gangster uses whatever means he can to break into it—is articulated in the 1936 movie *The Petrified Forest*. During a tense hostage scene, a benign, elderly character called Pops defends Humphrey Bogart's character, the fugitive criminal Duke Mantee, against the charge that "he's a gangster and a rat." Pops clarifies: "He ain't no gangster, he's one of them old-fashioned desperados. Gangsters is foreigners, and he's an American." Of course, Bogart's portrayal of "foreign" urban gangsters would become a standard for others to imitate.

The confidence with which Pops distinguishes between gangsters and other types of criminals also demonstrates that after a half-decade's production of these films, the gangster had already become what Fred Gardaphe calls a "necessary" figure (2): a widely circulating model of aggressive masculinity and suspect class and ethnic mobility. Necessary as he was, he was also an extremely ambivalent figure: criminal yet heroic, stylish yet tasteless, bold yet ultimately defeated. As they accorded the gangster figure his cultural meaning, immigrant Jews made the most use of just this complexity.

Hiding in the Mob

Fred Gardaphe writes that the gangster, from his earliest appearance in fictional portraits, has been mostly associated with Italians. On one level he is absolutely right: the majority of gangsters popularly depicted is Italian or Italian American. But the representation of gangsters' ethnic background in the movies has never been as simple as who the movie tells us the characters "are." Neal Gabler has claimed (in *An Empire of Their Own*) that Jews are largely absent from the screen in the early Hollywood years. Both Gardaphe and Gabler, in different contexts, are calling our attention to a conspicuous absence of Jewish representations. It is important, however, to address the meaning of this absence, and in order to do so, we must look beyond the most literal naming of Jews and Jewishness as such. Jews *were* present in the early Hollywood movies *as gangsters*. They were not identified explicitly as Jews, but they were portrayed with recognizable Jewish affect—and this affect was most frequently presented as typically "gangster." The gangster subject thus provided a sublimated way for Jewishness to be explored in the movies at a moment in film history when Jewishness is generally believed to have been kept off screen.

The Jewish masquerades that were enacted in the gangster movies must be understood as a relatively late addition to a long-standing Jewish investment in minstrelsy. By the 1910s Jews had more or less taken over the performance and production of stage blackface in the United States. For decades they had used the traditions of blackface comedy and music to establish their place at the center of the American entertainment business. Among other innovations, Jews in New York and other major cities devised ways to incorporate minstrelsy into larger vaudeville productions. Jews were so ubiquitous as blackface actors and comedians in the last decades of the 19th century and the first years of the 20th century that blackface itself became widely understood as a variety of Jewish cultural expression.

But Jews in blackface also presided over the final (culturally significant days) of the form. While important Jewish figures in the 1920s, including Al Jolson, Sophie Tucker, and Eddie Cantor, all deployed blackface as central elements of their acts, stage minstrelsy was being eclipsed by the sheer variety of other stage performances and by cinema itself. A crucial last gasp for Jews in blackface came with *The Jazz Singer,* the first full-length sound film to be released (in 1927). This was an almost exclusively Jewish affair—from script (Samson Raphaelson) to lead actor (Al Jolson) to production company (Warner Brothers). The stage version of *The Jazz Singer,* which had enjoyed great success in New York and Boston, also was presented to almost exclusively Jewish audiences. One reviewer estimated that a New York theater was filled with a crowd that was made up "almost entirely of those of the Jewish race"; a Boston audience was said to have been "predominantly of the Hebraic tradition and temperament," which explained why they could understand the "Hebrew church music" that was so important to the play (Melnick 104).

The Jazz Singer tells the story of a young Jewish man who throws off the constraints of his religious upbringing to become a blackface singer and Broadway star. The play version—geared at an in-group audience —has this young man return to the synagogue and stay "true" to his religious roots. In Jolson's movie version *The Jazz Singer* becomes a more straightforward assimilation tale (Jewish boy throws off old-world Jewishness by embracing blackness to become American) and dramatizes a both/and scenario in which it seemed possible to hang onto heritage and modern-world success.

The Jews who "invented" Hollywood (to use Neal Gabler's phrase) used blackface—especially in Jolson movies—as long as they profit-ably could. But blackface was becoming less attractive to Hollywood movie producers in the early years of the 1930s for a variety of reasons, including that for many people it was so obviously a Jewish cultural form. Furthermore, the major Hollywood movie studios discovered in the 1920s, as Henry Jenkins has explained, that they could not simply adapt Broadway productions to the movies—mostly because they were too marked with Jewish inflections (153–184). What they developed to replace blackface was a more diffuse but no less purposeful kind of masquerade, which Jews could continue to use as a way of processing major concerns surrounding their public identities. In short, just as an earlier generation of Jewish actors, comedians, and singers established blackface as a recognizably Jewish sphere of cultural activity, so too did the Hollywood industry of the early 1930s translate Jewishness into "gangster" as a recognizable performative mold.

Gangsters ethnically marked as Irish or Italian in the movies were sometimes modeled after actual Jewish gangsters whose escapades were chronicled well enough by various newspapers to be recognizable to at least some audience members. For instance, perhaps the most famous scene in *The Public Enemy,* in which Irish gangster Tom Powers shoves a grapefruit into his girlfriend's face after berating her, is loosely based on an actual episode involving Chicago Jewish mobster Earl "Hymie" Weiss. But the major way an ethnic bait-and-switch happened in the gangster movies was when Jewish actors portrayed non-Jewish gangster-characters. These Jewish actors generally felt the need to Anglicize their names for professional reasons, and clearly did not feel they were allowed to have their careers as public Jews. But Jewish audiences always kept track of which actors were actually Jews. And those who became prominent screen gangsters—in some cases, such as Edward G. Robinson (born Emmanuel Goldberg), Paul Muni (born Muni Wisenfreund), and John Garfield (born Jacob Julius Garfinkle) lastingly defining filmic mannerism through a display of identifiably Jewish affect —could sublimate their Jewishness in these roles, so that on screen, actors were frequently Jews hiding as gangsters. (A gangster plotline in the G-Man drama *Wise Guy,* running on TV in the 1980s, jokes about this legacy of Jewishness by having an Asian American character use Yiddish tough-guy slang. To get the joke is to acknowledge the hidden Jewish history of screen gangsters.)

The case of Edward G. Robinson, who acted in thirty gangster movies over the course of his career of eighty-nine films, is a strong example. Robinson's kit of actor's tools contains a variety of gestures—he talks with his hands, he shrugs his shoulders and raises his eyebrows—that would have been recognizable to contemporary audiences familiar with the "stage Jew" of vaudeville comedy. Among the early generation of "Jew comics" were Frank Bush, wearing a long fake beard and singing songs about characters with names like "Solomon Moses," and David Warfield, who would "mangle the English language with . . . what audiences took to be Judaic phrasing" (Howe 401–402). These stage Jews— with not much time on stage to perform their act and with a mixed audience with various kinds of "training"—had to establish their characters with broad strokes and "a few simple and unvarying traits" (Howe 403). With a little costuming, some hyperbolic gestures, and a few verbal cues, these performers were able quickly to declare their "Jewish" affiliations. Montague Glass's written sketches about two dialect-spewing, garment-district Jews, Potash and Perlmutter, were adapted for the stage in 1913 and became the longest-running play of that year (Howe 402–404).

Figure 1.2. Paul Muni in *Scarface* (1932): "Immigrant, but not quite Italian"

Robinson's dramatic performance is the backbone of his most famous gangster film, *Little Caesar;* of this performance film historian Carlos Clarens wrote in 1980 that it is "all gestures" (56). With breathtaking stride, Clarens then calls Robinson's performance "natural," thereby illustrating how naturalized Jewish inflection had become as criminal affect by the time Clarens was writing his book. For Robinson's contemporary audiences, his performance of Jewishness would become so seamlessly connected to screen criminality that a theatrical cartoon "starring" the character Little Audrey (1947) features Robinson's face on an egg, as a Humpty Dumpty who doesn't break. "I'm hard-boiled, see?" sneers the Egg/Robinson. Similarly, Paul Muni's performance as Tony Camonte in *Scarface* also consists of a compendium of gestures and mugging already familiar from "stage Jew" performances that had been increasing in popularity since the late 1890s; of Muni's performance, one historian was prompted to write that Muni "acted like an immigrant all right, though not quite Italian" (Clarens 87).

With characteristics recognized as "Jewish" but not named as such, Jewish filmmakers and Jewish audiences were able to use gangster characters to have a "secret" conversation about what it meant to be Jewish in the United States. It is here that the classic gangster melodrama—the choice between ethnic ghetto and rise to wealth, the pull between Old World parents and American girlfriends, the minutiae of what a man should wear—takes on Jewish specificity, at least for certain audiences. One of the sharpest examples of this specificity is a central scene in *The Public Enemy*. In this scene, Jewish gangster Samuel "Nails" Nathan (a barely fictionalized version of the Jewish Chicago mobster Samuel "Nails" Morton) plans a bootlegging venture with the owner of a brewery that has been closed by Prohibition. The owner's name—Leehman—is plastered over the brewery's gates, signaling to Jewish viewers that the owner is a German Jew (from an earlier and wealthier wave of Jewish immigration), as opposed to Nathan, who is a Russian Jew. Their conversation, full of pretension and haughtiness on Leehman's part juxtaposed to swagger and gritty honesty on Nathan's part, plays out in disguised fashion the long-standing tensions between the two groups of Jews, tensions that were culturally quite important (at least before the Holocaust completely altered the imaginative economy and reconfigured the context of what it meant to be "Jewish").

In sum, one way the gangster works in these movies is as a mask to allow Jewishness out "in public"; this was a "New World" Jewishness of body, not a stereotypical, "Old World" Jewishness of books. To this day, many of those same manifestations of Jewishness are still recognizable in fictional gangland settings, and are referred to as "hard-boiled," or "tough guy," or most suggestively, "Brooklyn."

In addition to working to code Jewishness as generically "gangster," the gangster figure worked to mask and rearticulate Jewishness through its association with the process of assimilation. In short order, gangster movies became characterized by a sense that crime was a good way for Jews to assimilate—or at the very least, to catch up. A clear example of this can be found in the opening of *A Force of Evil* (1948). This movie opens with a shot of Wall Street and a voiceover announcing that the date is July 4, the symbolic birth date of America. The protagonist-gangster is played by John Garfield, who grew up on Rivington Street in New York's Lower East Side. His character is a lawyer who works for the mob, which he refers to as "the corporation." For the duration of the movie, he tries to convince his older brother that joining the illegal numbers racket will finally rescue him from the ghetto neighborhood in which they both grew up. Significantly, the older brother has a much more pronounced Jewish accent, syntax, and manner than Garfield's character, who—because of his involvement with organized crime—is considerably more Americanized.

Robert Warshow has drawn much approving attention for his dramatic assertion in a 1948 essay that the gangster's cultural power derived from the fact that he represented the loudest "no" to the great American "yes" (130). But the idea that the gangster was, in fact, a resounding expression of that great American "yes" seems to have held more sway in the American cultural imaginary for much longer than the image of gangster outsider or outcast. Daniel Fuchs, in his gangster novels of the late 1930s, summarizes this sense of things by having his gangsters repeatedly (even ritualistically) make statements like "I worked myself up," "business is business," or just the appreciative "America!" Indeed, actual gangsters themselves sometimes publicly participated in this logic; Meyer Lansky, for instance, used to claim that he committed terrible acts of violence in order to achieve mobility in American society (quoted in Joselit 169–170). To summarize his pinnacle of organizational and financial success, he purportedly remarked, "We're bigger than U.S. Steel"—a statement as noteworthy for the mundanity of the comparison as for its grandiosity.

The vision of crime as assimilation is colorfully pictured by E. L. Doctorow in his 1989 historical gangster novel, *Billy Bathgate* (made into a movie by Warner Brothers in 1991). The title character becomes involved before he is even a teenager with New York mobster Dutch Schultz's gang. Through old-fashioned pluck, loyalty, and the ability to decipher the "true" meaning of Dutch Schultz's delirious deathbed monologue, Billy Bathgate, who has taken his gang name from the street he grew up on in the Bronx, winds up in possession of the gang's hidden fortune after Schultz's death. He uses the money to attend an Ivy League college (some of which would have had quotas on admission of Jews at the time), and is able to become lost—or rather, hidden—in the American status quo:

> I was inspired to excel at my studies as I had at marksmanship and betrayal, and so made the leap to Townsend Harris High School in Manhattan for exceptional students, whose number I was scornfully unastonished to be among, and then the even higher leap to an

Ivy League college I would be wise not to name, where I paid my own tuition in reasonably meted-out cash installments, and from which I was eventually graduated with honors and an officers' training commission as a second lieutenant in the United States Army. (320)

Clearly, the gang has been the conduit by which Bathgate Avenue (figured through Billy's nickname) stretches all the way to Harvard. Doctorow very cleverly literalizes here the function of the Jewish gangster as wearing a mask.

Satisfying the Censors

When gangster movies were hitting their stride and developing their essential ruses, the industry that was churning them out was the most controlled form of entertainment in the United States. Movies were subject to censorship from three places.

First were state and municipal censorship boards that, since movies had not yet won First Amendment protection, could deny exhibition permits to any films they disliked. The second source was from pressure groups, such as the Daughters of the American Revolution, the Catholic League of Decency, and the National Council of Jewish Women; many of these groups assigned delegates to preview films, and would then publish lists recommending or condemning new releases. The threat of boycott by these influential organizations was extremely effective in causing producers to cooperate. The third source of censorship was industrial self-regulation through a production code, which was officially adopted on March 31, 1930. The Production Code Administration (or PCA, also called the "Hays Code" after its chief, William Hays) consisted of industry-appointed censors who looked over the production of films at every stage to ensure that films conformed to the rules of its code. In setting up the PCA, filmmakers hoped to avoid censure from reform groups or the government and en-forced heavy fines against any company that released a film without the PCA's code of approval. In turn, cinema chains would refuse to show films that didn't carry the seal.

The Motion Picture Production Code of 1930 caused moviemakers to scrutinize all of their output, but the code had particular applications for gangster films, many of which were considered both immoral and overly violent. Parts of the code were clearly written with gangster movies in mind, such as the section headed "Crimes against the Law":

These shall never be presented in such a way as to throw sympathy with the crime as against law and justice or to inspire others with a desire for imitation.

1. Murder
   a. The technique of murder must be presented in a way that will not inspire imitation.
   b. Brutal killings are not to be presented in detail.
   c. Revenge in modern times shall not be justified.

2. Methods of crime should not be explicitly presented.
   a. Theft, robbery, safe-cracking, and dynamiting of trains, mines, buildings, etc., should not be detailed in method.
   b. Arson must subject to the same safeguards.
   c. The use of firearms should be restricted to the essentials.
   d. Methods of smuggling should not be presented.

3. Illegal drug traffic must never be presented.

4. The use of liquor in American life, when not required by the plot or for proper characterization, will not be shown.

As a result, a large percentage of censor cuts were from films in the gangster genre. In 1930 and 1931, for instance, half of the censor cuts in Chicago and a quarter of the censor cuts in New York were from gangster movies.

Thus, when the gangster genre was coming into its fullest expression, censorship required its own feints and dodges from the movies, with the odd result that the rather elaborately scripted nature of censorship leveled at gangster movies ended up helping to define its conventions. Most notably, the films' enforced disinclination to show truly horrific murder contributed to their perpetuation of the romantic (and, needless to say, inaccurate) notion that gangsters don't kill "civilians," only each other. Along the same lines, producers sometimes inserted "set pieces" into movies to satisfy notions of "decency" and redirect certain viewers' emotional investment away from the main characters; a particularly sharp example is a scene that was added to *Scarface* after it was essentially finished, in order to convince the PCA to permit the movie's release. In this scene, a newspaperman is confronted with a delegation of concerned citizens and politicians who accuse the print media of devoting too many headlines to criminals. The newspaperman looks straight into the camera (not at his visitors), deplores the spread of organized crime, and calls upon the government and the public to fight the problem.

But by far the most significant censor-dodge-turned-convention is the across-the-board implementation of the "rise and fall" formula, with the emphasis here on "fall." In order to avoid "inspir[ing] others with a desire for imitation," the movies, which may have been assiduously developing the charisma and appeal of the gangster for the first hour, invariably had to end with the gangster's death. The historical record, though, shows clearly that this official mandate to strip the gangster of his glamour simply didn't work.

Audience Charades

While Hollywood, with the help of Jewish actors and the added spur of the censors, was creating dodgy gangster characters, the gangster's audience had its own tricks up its sleeve as well. In the 1930s, this consisted of making heroes out of the gangsters despite pedantic instructions to the contrary. In other words, one important function of the gangster-as-symbol belonged to viewers—in particular, those who insisted on rooting for the bad guys, imbuing the gangster with layers of meaning that could accommodate changes in the political, economic, and ideological positioning of Jews in the United States.

The immigrant gangster laid out a central problematic of urban life in the Depression era: what the new immigrants would mean for "native" culture and society. David Ruth has done the most to demonstrate that "casting lawbreakers as members of minority ethnic groups remained a powerful cultural tool for exposing the perils of urban diversity" (29). Ruth rigorously investigates the "uses of crime" for observers for whom the gangster was scapegoat, bogeyman, and insurgent.

Early in the century, Jews were extremely sensitive to representations of Jewish criminality. As portrayals of Jewish criminals increased (in newspapers, police reports, and the like, as well as in the entertainment industry) many feared that the delinquencies of a few "bad" Jews would bring shame upon the entire group, and initially, it was not unusual for the Jewish press—particularly the English-language segment—to try to ignore or cover up the problem of Jewish crime. Detroit Jewish journalist Philip Slomovits acknowledges, for instance, that the Jewish community in that city was well aware of Jewish gangsters, but didn't want anything about them printed in the newspaper: " 'We panicked,' he admits. 'We worried about what the gentiles would say and submitted to our fears'" (quoted in Rockaway 58). This shame had real-politik motivations; as anti-immigration (and anti-Jewish) sentiments rose, many Jews feared that the perception of Jews as criminals would fan the flames of anti-Semitism. A writer in *American Hebrew* in 1900 argued that "the member of our faith who lives through illicit gain is not only a disgrace to us but a dangerous foe to the liberty we Jews enjoy in America. To continue liberal immigration, Jews must live pure lives" (quoted in Joselit 6). In other words, the fear was that crime by Jews (real or invented) would prevent acceptance of Jews by American society, and, by extension, assimilation into it. No doubt this has something to do with the fact that the gangsters created by the artists and businessmen of Hollywood—which Neal Gabler has pithily referred to as "An Empire of Their Own" for Jews—put their Jewishness into hiding.

But for Jews, who—as the historical story goes—had never been allowed to feel at home anywhere, there was a particular piquancy to the gangster's dauntless self-assertion rubbing so closely up against the historical reality of necessarily repressed Jewish identity. This piquancy created what Michael Denning called the "lure of the gangster" (*Cultural Front* 254) for Jewish audiences. In gangster movies (and pulp magazines), American Jews could find tough men of action who lived in the city like they did, but were free from the taint of physical "ghetto weakness" that had been associated with Jews in the Gentile mind for centuries (Gilman). "You think it's money, but it's not. It's personality," explains a brutal head man for the "Combination" in *The Big Combo* (1955), summing up the "lure of the gangster" to the cop who is dedicated to stopping him. The racketeer is describing his own rise to power, of course; but more important is the *meta-cultural* level of meaning in his claim, which articulates the attraction ethnic screen gangsters exerted on their fans. Actually, the gangster mystique included both money *and* personality: these movies positioned urban gangsters as charismatic, forceful models of consumerism at a time when, as David Ruth reminds us, the idea of "style" was being marketed by the advertising industry to an unprecedented degree—turning them ipso facto into media ideals (63–86). With this in mind, certain reviewers' expressions of surprise when audiences laughed aloud with pleasure at the gangsters' exploits (Sklar 31–32) seem falsely ingenuous.

Nor did these audiences remain idle, if admiring, receptors of these gangster portraits. Evolving from consumers of fictional gangsters to producers of them, Jewish writers manipulated the symbolic gangster for their own purposes, with movie-inspired ethnic gangsters finding their way into the novels of Daniel Fuchs, Michael Gold, Irving Shulman, Meyer Levin, Gerald Green, and many others. (Some of these writers, in turn, went to Hollywood and wrote screenplays for more gangster movies.) In other words, Jewish audiences were able to claim the gangster figure—snatching him away from the surrounding moral diatribes from non-Jews and worried Jews alike—as a way to resist both American criticisms of Jews and a way to resist what they hoped would be an outdated Jewish passivity.

Retrieving the Gangster Mask

The significant social practice of claiming the gangster as a kind of heroized model for all Jewish men has long outlasted the era of the classic gangster film even as conditions that produced the need for the "old school" gangster no longer obtained. As the 20th century moved toward its end, Jewish immigration was no longer a subject of heated discussion. The strong military reputation of the Jewish state, Israel, mostly put to rest the idea that Jewish men are all brain, no brawn. The visible Jewish presence in organized crime became minuscule at best; the end of Prohibition necessitated a restructuring of organized crime's business plan to emphasize other sources of income—not infrequently "legitimate" ones—and furthermore, following World War II, Jews in huge numbers were leaving the old urban neighborhoods that had given birth to the gangsters. By the 1950s, Jewish gangsters had disappeared from the newspaper headlines and political discussions so thoroughly that many historical works about Jewish gangsters written after 1960 open by expressing some kind of expectation that readers will find it hard to believe that there ever was such a thing as a powerful Jewish mob in the first place (Fried, Joselit, Rockaway, Kraus, Singer). Finally, Jewish actors had become more or less able to use their own names (at least within the industry's demands for glamorousness).

But with all this accomplished, the "lure of the gangsters" for Jews still has not been lost. Instead, it has taken on a historical frame, resulting in a spate of movies about Jewish gangsters from the early 1980s through the late 1990s with historical settings: *Bugsy* (1991), *Billy Bathgate* (1991), *Once Upon a Time in America* (1984), *Miller's Crossing* (1990), *Liberty Heights* (1999), *Lansky* (1999). Although these movies obviously are indebted to the gangster movies of the "golden" era, their historical approach nonetheless stands in sharp contrast to the sense of immediacy that was the central conceit of the 1930s movies. But the figure of the fictional Jewish gangster is still being used to comment on the fate of Jewishness in America—albeit in a more distant, even wistful, revisioning.

Rich Cohen's 1999 book *Tough Jews* comes at the end of this wave and can function as a kind of summary of the kind of interest in Jewish gangsters that produced this new cluster of movies. Cohen establishes himself as a deeply invested consumer of fictional gangsters; he is clearly well acquainted with the mystique of screen gangsters, and desires to stitch into this mystique the thrilling stories of elderly friends of his grandfather, whose colorful past he wants to extol and narrate.

Cohen introduces himself as someone who is bored with his safe and domestic childhood in well-off suburban Chicago (where he was born in 1968). He describes a kind of wealth and privilege that has given rise to an oppressive and tedious sameness, remarking that growing up, "[s]ometimes when I found out that some super-WASP-y family was actually Jewish, I would say, 'You're shittin' me'" (257).

In the face of what he considers to be stunting conformity, the author seeks in the Jewish gangsters a kind of cultural Viagra. For Cohen, the flinty criminals of his grandfather's generation provide a dramatic antidote to the pallidity of suburban life. Cohen deplores early on having grown up surrounded by "Jews who are indistinguishable from Americans. Jews who are Americans. Jews who go to temple with all the nonchalance of a President Clinton going to church. Jews washed clean of Odessa, the shtetl, the camps, the tenements, millionaire Jews who drive German cars, who make legit deals before breakfast that pay off just after lunch" (22).

Ironically enough, it was the gangsters' prowess that has helped subsequent generations to move out of ethnic, urban settings in the first place and into the suburbs that Cohen finds so uninspiring. A neat reversal occurs: whereas gangsters might have been furtively admired by law-abiding Jews because of their ability to escape or transcend the ghetto, the children of those escapees admire the gangsters because they allow them imaginatively to return to the city streets.

Given this paradigm, it is not surprising that Jewish filmmaker Barry Levinson followed his 1990 film *Avalon,* which pictures an ungrateful and overly assimilated second generation of Jews living in the suburbs, one year later with a film about Benjamin "Bugsy" Siegel, the Jewish gangster credited with inventing Las Vegas. The movie doesn't exactly hide Siegel's dark side—his associates called him "Bugsy" for a reason, which made him furious—but it does downplay the most unpalatable aspects of Siegel's career (such as drug smuggling), while taking pains to present a man who not only wears the classiest clothes and attracts the most beautiful women (as did the gangsters of the 1930s films), but who is possessed of genuine vision and clarity of purpose. "Sure, he had his faults, but the man had vision!" declared the headline of the *New York Times* review of the movie (Maslin).

Imaginatively speaking, for Levinson, as for Cohen, rediscovery of Jewish gangsters is a symbolic way out of the suburbs to which *Avalon*'s second-generation Jews have moved, an environment that has bequeathed the piety and smugness novelist Phillip Roth has made a career of tweaking. As David Singer and Joseph Kraus have pointed out, by 1990 the gangster was a uniquely loaded figure in the task of constructing a usable ethnic past. Cohen explains the dynamic:

> Well, to me, remembering Jewish gangsters is a good way to deal with being born after 1945, with being someone who has always had the Holocaust at his back, the distant tom-tom: *six million, six million, six million*. The gangsters, with their own wisecracking machine-gun beat, push that other noise clear from my head. And they drowned out other things, too, like the stereotype that fits the entire Jewish community into the middle class, comfortable easy-chair Jews with nothing but morality for dessert. (21)

Cohen's use of the word "wisecracking" above, of course, indicates that his sense of heroic Jewish gangsterism is based on a solid knowledge of the conventions of gangster movies, as much as any true stories his grandfather's cronies might have told him, reminding us that the connections between historical gangsters and popular representations of them are nothing if not complex.

Cohen seems rather defensive about the hinted-at charge that, by mentioning the Holocaust "too much," Jews have indulged in a culture of victimhood. Remembering the gangsters, who *made* victims instead of just *being* victims, offers him a way out. In addition, the Jewish gangsters of yore also offer him an antidote to the behavioral mandates of feminism; and rediscovered as ethnic heroes, they stand as a powerful white, middle-class "me too" retort to the general acceptance of "multiculturalism" in the American educational system. When he thinks about the gangsters, Cohen admits, he begins to find himself less bland, less passive, and less silent:

> Just the words—Jewish gangsters—seemed to bring the room to life. The air filled with bullets, curses, schemes. The hanging fern

plant looked springier. . . . My own face in the mirror looked darker, tougher. (259)

The distinctly phallic nature of Cohen's chosen image—a hanging plant that has been drooping but then springs upward—connects his admiration of the gangsters to a yearning for an ideal of masculinity he senses has been supplanted. Likewise telling is his description of his own face in the mirror, which has become not only tougher, but also less white or more "ethnic." Along the same lines—and directly connecting the valorization of Jewish gangsters as ethnic heroes to the acceptance of multiculturalism as an ideal in education—Cohen has one of his former "tough Jews" fume, "They're trying to teach my grandkid Spanish in school. . . . What the hell? If he needs to learn anything, it's Yiddish. The language of my people is dying" (15).

Mask and Masculinity

Cohen's admiration of what he sees as the gangster's irreproachable masculinity gives a new suburban, post–World War II context to an old obsession. As David Ruth has scrupulously shown, the gangster genre's creators were fixated from the start on "the meaning of masculinity in modern urban society" (88) as the social roles of both men and women were starting to change with the new complexities of corporate society. Ruth sees in the gangster's rugged vision of maleness an attempt to redefine the differences between the sexes at a time when women's suffrage and the growth of "middle management" careers seemed to threaten male independence. The criminal gang was, almost exclusively, a homosocial setting, and the gangsters' relationships to the women they did interact with were characterized by contempt, if not worse. (Reviewers of James Cagney's movies even wondered if ticket sales were hurt because of the habitual violence against women on the part of his characters.) Thus, the gangster genre developed a fantasy of male prowess that could flourish without the "civilizing" influence of the feminine. The masquerade of the gangster was one in which male muscle and courage brought power and material rewards—

including beautiful women. Picking up on the subterfuge these movies carry out in complicity with viewers, film critic Stephen Hunter referred to a 1990s gangster film as taking place "in that theme park called Testosterone Land" (3). The device of looking at the gangster movie as a "theme park" is a suggestive one; pushing Hunter's clever analogy a bit further, we can imagine that the costumed characters who come to "greet" visitors to Testosterone Land (who have come to enjoy the thrill of the "pretend") include screen gangsters—dressed up in audacity, brutality, and guts.

This fantasy of masculinity is an extremely consequential one. Furthermore, there is particular meaning here for *Jewish* masculinity, which had long been under assault. As Sander Gilman has thoroughly illustrated, a historically dominant image of Jewish men was as having a "natural" predisposition to weakness, emaciation, and effeminacy. The ways in which Jewish men have been feminized include myths of Jewish male menstruation, speculations about the effects of circumcision, and descriptions of these men as cowardly and hysterical (Gilman). Juxtaposed with this stereotype of intellectual but physically weak Jewish men, the gangsters, who are adventurous, commanding, and physically strong, have held great appeal for Jewish male audiences, with Jewish writers leading the charge: from Mike Gold in 1930 to Rich Cohen in 1999, Jewish authors have obsessively circled around the Jewish gangster as the antidote to the perceived malady of Jewish male weakness.

But just as important as the establishment of masculine codes in the movies is the fact that, time and time again, the masculinity is ultimately brought to abjection. To be sure, the gangster's downfall and death were required by censors. But if it is true that audiences insisted upon rooting for these villains, despite the producers' professed intentions to the contrary, then it is worth asking what the "payoff" for the audience is when the gangster is not only stopped (most often by his death), but deeply humiliated. Carlos Clarens invents the term "gutter endings" (101) for the ignominy that invariably comes at the close of gangster movies, and the name is apt: *The Public Enemy's* Tom Powers falls into a gushing gutter muttering, "I ain't so tough." *Little Caesar's* Rico makes a fool of himself at his first formal dinner and dies unknowing under a billboard picturing his former best friend. *Let 'Em Have*

It's Joe Keefer coerces a plastic surgeon to disguise his features—and
then sees a monster in the mirror when he removes the bandages to
find that the surgeon has carved his own initials into his face. *The Story
of Temple Drake*'s (1933) Trigger is shot with his own gun by a woman
he has raped. *Scarface*'s Tony Camonte is taunted and handcuffed, and
then shot after an embarrassingly hysterical dash of retreat. Many academic and journalistic commentators have addressed the fact that different audiences seemed to have varying investments in watching gangster movies, and came to different conclusions about what messages
they spread about the new immigration. But after nicely sketching out
these multiple positions of reception, they have tended to lump these
audiences back together when writing about the *ends* of the movies.
Gangster movie critics have tended to say that for audiences, the gangster's death saved them from the "dangerous" parts of their own fantasy, causing them to breathe a sigh of relief when he died. For those
audiences who experienced the movies as warnings about dangerous
immigrants, this was likely to be true. But for audiences who identified
with the gangsters, it seems more probable that a certain amount of
masochistic pleasure—or at least, resonance—comes with the gangster's final humiliation. Thus, if the gangster movie peddled attractive
notions of masculinity, the repeated enactment of humiliation *precisely
on those attractive, masculine terms* constantly reminded audiences of
the *disappointments* of masculinity, particularly within the American
class structure. Masculinity appears to be a meaningful privilege, one
that locates men—even if they are poor immigrants—advantageously
on the social hierarchy. But it promises more than it can deliver.

A somewhat humorous, if still dark, example of this dynamic is the
death of the gangster Samuel "Nails" Nathan in *The Public Enemy*. Nathan, the stylish Jewish gangster who teams up with the Irish mob in
the movie to secure a bootlegging monopoly, dies after being thrown
from a horse. His gang associates take revenge by shooting the horse.
The critique of macho behavior and its supposedly honorable codes is
no less sharp for the fact that it re-creates remarkably faithfully the
death of Nathan's real-life inspiration, Samuel "Nails" Morton—and
the response of his associates.

The death of "Nails" Nathan/Morton underscores an interplay between news and entertainment that is vital in sorting out the role of the

Jewish gangster in the 20th-century American imagination. There has always been a complicated and intense relationship between the gangsters themselves and those who loved to watch them, giving us a somewhat dizzying dynamic in which popular culture consumes or imitates the real gangster's style, and the gangster himself then consumes or imitates the popular culture representations of gangsters. For example, Robert Lacey, in his biography of Meyer Lansky, writes that when Jewish actor George Raft traveled to Florida to spend time with Lanksy, Ben "Bugsy" Siegel, and other gangsters he knew, Raft would study the originals upon whom his gangster roles were based. But, writes Lacey, "the reverse proved the case. It was the gangsters who spent their time studying Raft, trying to find out the name of his tailor, and who made his elegant, hand-crafted shoes" (184). Further complicating the relationship between "real" gangsters and movie gangsters, Gerald Horne has written that gangsters were actually involved in the Hollywood movie industry, particularly in trying to gain control of the fledgling trade unions there.

The gangster, in short, has indeed been a "necessary figure" for consumers and producers of popular culture. While audience desire for stylish gangsters has seemed almost insatiable since the 1930s, the uses these audiences have made of the criminals have varied over time. But for decades there was a remarkable consistency in how the gangster functioned as an articulation—or externalization—of diverse matters of American social life. In recent days, though, the dynamic of gangster creation has taken a new turn, as the American culture industries (and their audiences) have fallen in love with a new "gangster situation": the gangster in actual dialogue with a psychiatrist.

The Gangster and the Couch

Runaway admiration for Jews with muscle and passion in the face of stereotypes endorsed by Jews and non-Jews alike lasted throughout the 20th century, although the vantage point had changed dramatically. The gangsters served a real need for Jewish "action heroes"—in immigrant America, in the post-Holocaust world, in the conformist suburbs.

A look at current figurations of gangsters and Jewishness, however, seems to indicate that this need was largely gone—or at least transformed—as the 20th century drew to a close. In a remarkable but prominent new twist on the ethnic/Jewish gangster theme, America began imagining gangsters in therapy.

These offerings do not use the theme of psychiatry in order to probe into the criminal mind, as movies did during American popular culture's discovery of Freudianism. On the simplest structural level, these works are visibly indebted to Freudiana such as 1939's *Blind Alley,* which deals with a struggle for dominance between a psychiatrist and the escaped convict who takes him hostage, or 1946's *The Dark Mirror,* in which the police enlist the aid of a psychiatrist to determine which of two identical twins is a murderer. But at the turn of the 20th century, the pairings of gangsters and psychiatrists—besides providing a timely giggle at the expense of the "Prozac nation"—dispense resoundingly with the whole idea of the easily diagnosed "killer psyche" (and the meaning it might have for Jews in America) that so obsessed commentators during the early decades of the 20th century.

Indeed, in the newer cluster of representations, the idea of the gangster having a special psyche at all is part of the joke, and much of the humor derives from the rather aged idea that it is just plain funny to juxtapose an egghead with a goon. To be sure, there is a very postmodern layer of irony added to the mix; in one instance, an elderly and charmless Italian American gangster in the HBO original series *The Sopranos* says outright, with studied glibness, "It's one of them mind-body things, ya know." In case any viewers have managed to miss the point.

These gangsters go to the "head doctor" because their daily life is becoming unmanageable: they are suffering from anxiety attacks and depression. In instance after instance, though, their "jobs" are the part of their lives with which they are most comfortable. The killing they do might be brutal, but it is the gangster's family life that is driving him crazy. In *Analyze This,* a 1999 movie starring Billy Crystal and Robert DeNiro, the gangster has a psychological hang-up about his father. In *The Sopranos,* the gangster has a psychological hang-up about his mother. In 1997's *Grosse Point Blank,* starring Alan Arkin and John Cusack, it's the gangster's former girlfriend. In each case, business is going well—"I have the world by the balls," declares Tony Soprano to his therapist—but the family pressures have become severe enough to lead the gangster to seek professional help.

Notably, in these new imaginings, the gangster himself is not associated with Jewishness—not even on the "hidden" level of affect and historical referent we find in the movies of the 1930s. The ethnic exploration at the center of the story has shifted its focus. Jewishness is not absent in these dramas, but now its receptacle is the psychiatrist. In *The Sopranos,* a character—the lead gangster's manipulative mother—even refers to psychotherapy as "a racket invented by the Jews." Here the gangster figure, placed into the characteristically Jewish space of psychotherapy, has begun to operate as a commentary on the ascension of Jews: the Jew is no longer the subject of criminal investment, but rather, through the Jewish acts of asking and listening, reaches as a father figure to pull other ethnics up to the respectable, benign heights the Jew has achieved.

"We Gotta Change with the Times"

In *Analyze This,* one gangster tells another, "We gotta change with the times." To which the first gangster retorts, "Whatta we gotta, get a fucking Web site?" The joke, of course, is the ridiculousness of the picture of gangsters on the Web (although of course they must be there). The joke is that movie gangsters such as these are fashioned to operate somehow outside of real time, free of e-mail accounts and beepers and virtual reality, having been transformed into symbols. But the cultural meanings of the symbols change with the times in a remarkably adaptable manner; in fact, they are constantly in process and continually in conversation with a range of social forces. Putting the gangsters in therapy—after all a kind of laboratory for symbols and a formalized place for conversation—has been a way to show this.

In Samuel Ornitz's 1923 novel about a Jewish gangster, *Haunch Paunch and Jowl,* a Jewish psychiatrist, Lionel Crane, declares his intention to use his science to heal the Jews: "*I will take the sick ego of my people to the clinic*" (emphasis in original), he says, and the novel's callous, repulsive gangster-narrator is indeed compellingly presented by Ornitz as evidence of a sickness infecting Jews in capitalist America (200). In our own time, though, the resources of psychoanalysis are used by imagined gangsters only for a limited personal therapeutic goal, as opposed to making a larger cultural point about crime as a Jewish sickness. "I'm very serious about this process—and I know where you live," Martin Blank tells Dr. Oatman in *Grosse Point Blank.*

A work-for-hire trade paperback book that was published on the heels of *The Sopranos, Analyze This,* and other such tales, summarizes this move away from using Jewish crime as a vehicle for deep cultural and historical exploration, and toward a more ironic and performance-based orientation. The book is *Fuhgeddaboutit* by Jon Macks (2001), who parades his own Jewishness and claims, with blithe ahistoricism, that being a gangster is still "an equal opportunity job" (naming, as proof, Jewish gangsters who have been dead for decades). Through tips about gangster fashion, gangster dating, gangster vocabulary, and gangster jail time, the book—mocking the very idea of ethnic conceit as well as the validity of the "self-help" industry—promises in its very title to show "how to badda boom, badda bing, and find your inner mobster."

Of course, all along audiences were supposed to discover something about themselves through their viewing of (and reading about) gangsters; it is only worth noting that the message they were previously instructed to discover when approaching the gangster was a much more serious one about gender role, social stratification, and urban space. That Macks could convincingly turn the whole enterprise into a joke reminds us that the figure of the gangster is no longer as consequential as he once was for white ethnic audiences; the white ethnic gangster as he appears in modern popular culture is a shadow of his former self— an opportunity, really, to make jokes about the softness of modern life for white ethnics in the suburbs. Envisioning the gangster on screen once had much higher stakes: his hat and suit, his gun and his rough talk—all of these instructed audiences to notice how American city life was changing in their time. Just a decade or so after the appearance of the first film gangsters another kind of bad guy, the "zoot-suiter," would invade American consciousness—with an even more complex tale to tell about immigration, gender, and social space.

CHAPTER 2

Los Angeles, 1943

Zoot Suit Style,
Immigrant Politics

The gangster had many lessons to teach audiences in the 1930s, and among the most important were those having to do with the power of conspicuous consumption. Buying— and wearing—the right suit (as Tom Powers does in *The Public Enemy*) is a crucial part of the gangster's accession to power. The gangster's suit concealed as much as it advertised. When Tom Powers is measured for a new suit in *The Public Enemy* he ostentatiously reminds the tailor to leave "plenty of room" in here—as he stretches the waist out and looks down. Of course on the denotative level the character is reminding all in earshot that he will be carrying a gun; of course, too, he is reminding them that he is a "real" man who needs plenty of room for *all* of his equipment. The suit is meant, then, at once to hide and advertise key elements of the successful gangster's masculinity.

More important yet is how the suit helps to erase the traces of the gangster's humble beginnings in the immigrant ghetto. The suit reminds viewers that the gangster has gained enough power to remake himself in public; the suit functions as a flickering sign of underworld deviance and mainstream success. In this sense, it reminded audiences that the social self is constantly under construction and that those with the most cultural muscle could have the most input into how they

would be seen. The moment of the ethnic gangster buying a suit oper-
ates as a stand-in, of sorts, for the whole process by which Jews in Hollywood—producers, screenwriters, and actors—could "hide in plain
sight" through the circulation of gangster movies. At once recognizably
Jewish to large portions of the viewing audience, but cloaked in the
evolving gear of the all-purpose "white ethnic," the gangster hero used
his suit (among other things) to stake a claim as a central player in modern, urban America. This took place not only in the movies but in
"real" life too—"dapper" Jewish gangsters like Arnold Rothstein and
Bugsy Siegel were major style-makers in their time.

Fashion choices can, as the movie gangsters demonstrate, be a major
signal of a desire for, and achievement of, cultural mobility. But what
happens when a suit of clothes gets named as deviant? What happens
when it is proudly worn by members of an immigrant group as a badge
of nonconformity? This very different sartorial situation is what we
track in this chapter, as we attempt to explain those "style wars" of
1943 that are usually referred to as the "zoot suit riots."

In June of 1943, the New York Times opened a front-section "hard"
news story by painting an incongruously fanciful picture. The story
tells of twenty-eight young Mexican American men who had been arrested in Los Angeles. But these youths are not merely pictured lan-
guishing behind bars: the reporter, in a jolly flight of imagination, envisions the men as the object of the covetous gaze of those around
them. The story's first sentence pictures the county jail barbers "hope-
fully" eyeing the men's ducktail haircuts, mentioning that because they
have been stripped of their "garish" clothing, the men are subdued and
impotent.

The arrests so gleefully described by the Times reporter followed
the zoot suit riots, which erupted in Los Angeles in June 1943. "Zoot
suit riots" is a somewhat misleading phrase that refers to a handful of
incidents during which young Chicano, Filipino, and African American men wearing the colorful, oversized zoot suits were attacked and
beaten by white servicemen, stationed outside the city. The "riots"
went on for a week and spread across the country to other cities where
servicemen were stationed, as the Los Angeles clashes triggered a wave
of race-based attacks throughout the summer of 1943: in San Diego, in
Philadelphia, in Chicago; in Evansville, Indiana; in Beaumont, Texas; in

Detroit and in Harlem. By the time these "riots" were over, zoot suits and their wearers had been at the center of an intense public debate that involved violence, arrests, police raids, dramatic newspaper coverage, emergency city council meetings, passage of new laws, and more. The development of the so-called riot, and the reactions to it, were covered in every major national newspaper.

The racial polarization that structured the zoot suit riots was clear: white servicemen, dressed in the uniform of the United States military, faced off against young Mexican Americans, mostly the children of immigrants, dressed in the uniform of street hip. The arena for this face-off was personal style. This is made clear by the behavior of the servicemen; when they caught zoot-suiters, they not only beat them, but they stripped them of their zoot suits and sheared off the "ducktail" that characterized the zooter's haircuts. The "zoot suit riots," then, were truly a style war, in which popular culture—in this case, clothing and fashion or "expressive style"—facilitated a public conversation (albeit a dangerous one) about wartime masculinity, and about the relationship between pleasure and patriotism, assimilation and opposition. In other words, all parties in the controversy were well aware that, as Ralph Ellison would famously put it later, the zoot suit contained "profound political meaning" (381).

This chapter will consider the nature of that political meaning. How did the zoot-suiters themselves—and those most interested in looking at them, either on the streets or on the stage and screen—use fashion to explore the meaning of immigration for Mexican young people in the World War II era? And as the zoot suit remarkably continued to attract attention from various quarters all the way through the 20th century (and into the 21st), what further layers of "profound political meaning" were added to its burden? In other words, this chapter will use the zoot suit to locate and learn from a politics of consumption. It will trace the way the suit itself became a cultural icon, and the act of watching it became a cultural ritual, as its meaning evolved, shifted, and traveled across the changing American social landscape.

The Arrival of El Pachuco

The families of many of the Mexican American zoot-suiters had entered the United States as part of the enormous waves of migrants who crossed the border from Mexico during the early days of World War II. These immigrants arrived under the auspices of the United States government, which was responding to pressure from farm interests in the region to import temporary workers in order to solve the immediate shortage of farm labor. (Some of the same farm interests, such as those represented by the Grower-Shipper Vegetable Association, were among the first and most vocal to call for the internment of Japanese and Japanese Americans living in the West Coast states—many of whom were their competitors in farming.) To deal with the labor shortage, the federal government drafted in 1942 the bracero program, an emergency farm labor plan.

During its inception, the bracero program was overseen by the Farm Security Administration (FSA). But many growers considered the FSA, which had been created as part of Roosevelt's New Deal, to be too pro-union and too politically progressive for their liking. Instead, they convinced the government to transfer control of the plan to the War Food Administration, which was known as a far more conservative organization—and on whose policies agribusiness had much more influence. The bracero program was extremely and promptly successful at meeting its goal of supplying cheap labor for agribusiness: between 1942 and 1947, 219,000 Mexican agricultural workers entered the United States from Mexico (Lorey 90). Following on the heels of this success, the United States and Mexico signed another agreement in 1943 for a similar plan to provide the United States with railroad workers. This new plan allowed the United States to import 20,000 additional Mexican workers in 1943, 50,000 in 1944, and 75,000 in 1945. The bracero program continued after World War II. Congress enacted another "emergency" program with the outbreak of the Korean War, called Public Law 78. Like the bracero program, this law formalized a new arrangement with Mexico to bring temporary farm labor to the United States—one that was renewed regularly until 1964. It was during this time that the peak number of braceros was imported to California: 192,438 migrant workers in 1957.

The bracero program and its successors marked the beginning of a massive movement of Mexicans to border states in both Mexico and the United States, one that continues into the 21st century. In addition to the major population shifts that the programs brought about, the social and cultural consequences of the programs were profound. In other words, not only did these labor programs bring hundreds of thousands of Mexican people to the United States, but they established powerful narratives concerning the status and entitlement of these individuals once they entered United States society. The bracero program fostered the notion that Mexican workers were entirely dispensable, and that once they were no longer needed, they could simply be returned to Mexico. The government's notorious "Operation Wetback" is a prime example: under its auspices, two million Mexicans—and Mexican Americans who were actually U.S. citizens or legal residents—were deported back across the border between 1953 and 1955. Furthermore, the apparently inexhaustible supply of Mexican laborers allowed large agribusiness to keep wages low for non-Mexican and Mexican workers alike. Because of the vulnerability of Mexican workers, it was common for growers to refuse to pay their wages, to demand excessive hours in the field, to ignore hazardous working conditions (especially pertaining to poisoning from pesticides and herbicides), and to violate provisions for housing and transportation. In short, the braceros and their children lived in poverty, with few recourses to seek relief.

The movement of large numbers of people across the U.S.-Mexican border in both directions caused the population of the border region in both countries to swell. Rather than merely demarcating where one country ended and another began, the border started to develop its own cultural identity and particularities. Not surprisingly, this identity grew largely out of the kinds of mixing that happen when people raised with different cultural traditions are brought into close contact with each other. These new residents of the border—it is ultimately unsatisfactory to call them residents of the United States or of Mexico—had to cobble together a rather fluid identity, one that could absorb and give expression to a whole range of seeming contradictions. The migrants were in the United States as a result of government invitation, but their relative standard of living made them keenly feel their exclusion from the "American dream." Over half of all the Mexicans who entered the United States between 1942 and 1947 worked in California's agriculture business, but the war economy saw such speedy urbanization and industrialization in California that coming to terms with city life was a major challenge faced by the immigrants.

The children of the braceros created a distinctly youth-oriented culture that rejected the traditional values of parents and grandparents, but was separate (by choice and by coercion) from the youth culture embraced by their Anglo counterparts. The clothing of the zoot-suiter, through expressive style, staked out a cultural ground that encompassed, or at least voiced, the contradictions inherent in feeling not-Mexican and not-American. One result was that the clothing was generally strongly disapproved of by the young men's parents, even as it was grounds for attack by certain white men.

These defining contradictions have led cultural critic Stuart Cosgrove to emphasize what he calls the "paradox of the zoot suit." Cosgrove notes that during the "riots" of June, 1943, zoot-suiters achieved an almost mythical status for both their detractors and their defenders. Cosgrove writes, "[The zoot suit] was simultaneously the garb of the victim and the attacker, the persecutor and the persecuted, the 'sinister clown' and the grotesque dandy. But the central opposition was between the delinquent and the disinherited" (19). Viewed in this light, the zoot-suiters occupied a symbolic position reminiscent of screen gangsters, whom some viewed sympathetically while others strictly condemned them. But unlike the screen gangsters, who were seen using whatever methods were at their disposal to break into the American mainstream that sought to reject them, the zoot-suiters declared, through the affiliations loudly announced by their clothing, their own preemptive rejection of "white" American cultural values.

Before the United States transformatively discovered the "teenager" as a population with discrete cultural (and consumerist) needs in the post–World War II era, Mexican American men were carving out a brand-new space together on the borders between worlds where they didn't quite fit. A new term was coined to name them: "El pachuco." The origins of the term, used to describe a street- or gang-identified young Mexican American, are disputed, but the first definition was probably the one attempted by the Mexican writer Octavio Paz after spending two years in Los Angeles during the mid-1940s. Paz attempts to understand the pachucos in the opening chapter of his book on the Mexican mind, *The Labyrinth of Solitude,* tellingly titled "The Pachuco and Other Extremes." Although he takes the pachucos seriously enough to devote the beginning of his book to them, Paz is not able to shake his disapproval; he pictures these young people as essentially lost, trying desperately and vainly to assimilate into American culture and sacrificing Mexican identity in the process. Indeed, he asserts that "lack of a spirit" is what has given rise to "a type known as the pachuco" (13). In Paz's view, pachuco culture represents a failed answer to the immigrant's dilemma:

> The pachuco does not want to become a Mexican again; at the same time he does not want to blend into the life of North America. His whole being is sheer negative impulse, a tangle of contradictions, an enigma. (14)

Paz considers pachuco culture to be the rather tragic product of an "orphan" condition; he sees the zoot suit itself as "grotesque."

There were early attempts to account for the pachuco that take a more sympathetic view. The pachuco gangs, writes Carey McWilliams, a California lawyer and author of four important books on the race question in the United States, really took their shape because of the "iron curtain" (*North from Mexico* 238) of restrictions, refusals to admit, miscegenation laws and second-class status that plagued Mexican nationals in Los Angeles—which had, after all, been part of Mexico a century earlier and had in fact been founded by the pachucos' ancestors. McWilliams, in his essay "The Zoot Suit Riots" (1943) and in his book *North from Mexico* (1949), asserts very strongly ("dogmatically," by his own description) that the so-called pachuco gangs were merely "boys' clubs without a clubhouse." A similar argument would be made (as we will explain in chapter 3) about the so-called Puerto Rican gangs of New York in the era of *West Side Story.*

Wallace Stegner, an important writer of the American West, decried this second-class status in his book *One Nation* (1945), a collaborative effort with text by Stegner and pictures taken by various photographers from the weekly *Look* magazine as an examination of "racial and religious stresses in wartime America." Stegner's chapter on pachucos is called "The Lost Generation," recalling Octavio Paz's sense of a youth "lost between the outgrown Mexican world of their parents and the American world in which they are not accepted" (117). But Stegner's text and the accompanying photographs attempt to make clear that any difficulty integrating Mexican Americans into American society is part of "a national problem . . . of immigration and color and caste" (95).

The pachucos, according to Stegner, were actually "ordinary boys and girls" who turned to gangs for companionship, and the street for a gathering place, only after being forced to do so by a segregated, racist society. Stegner adds that those movie theaters that forced Mexicans to sit in the balcony would refuse to admit them at all if they were wearing zoot suits—revealing the way in which the style of dress had become a badge of conflict. The photographs accompanying Stegner's text are remarkable: in addition to young people spending leisure time together, there are also shots of police demanding to see pachucos' draft cards (a practice carried out only among Mexican Americans), of advertising signs for "Mexicana night" at the roller-skating rink, and of slum conditions in the "Mexican quarter."

One thing is certain: these young people were coming into adulthood, while trying to establish themselves as Americans, in a complicated ethnic arena. Three years earlier, in 1942, Roosevelt had signed into effect Executive Order 9066, which led to the internment of Japanese Americans; this greatest of American wartime "mistakes" was a grim indication of how the racial landscape was shaped by the Japanese bombing of Pearl Harbor—but certainly not the only indication. McWilliams argued that the "zoot suit riots" are evidence of the scapegoating of Mexican Americans in the same way that Japanese Americans were scapegoated through their internment; once the Japanese were removed, McWilliams argues, the Los Angeles newspapers (in particular those owned by Hearst) began to play up supposed Mexican crime as a wartime internal threat ("Zoot Suit Riots" 227). Indeed, the Japanese were even accused of stirring up the Mexicans (particularly Mexican youth) as they were being sent off to the camps (234). Meanwhile, the white navy and army men were serving in a military that was still racially segregated (and would remain so until 1948)—while supposedly defending the world against Hitler's "final solution" to the race question. Even the Red Cross blood banks that would supply these soldiers if they were to be wounded kept "black" blood and "white" blood segregated.

In this context, it is not surprising that the relationship between servicemen and pachucos would be racially fraught. The violence of the riots culminated in an evening of conflict that has become known as "the taxicab brigade." According to most accounts, about two hundred servicemen used about twenty taxis— whose drivers offered their services for free—and rode straight to the largest Mexican American barrios with the aim of destroying every zoot suit they could find. They were joined by as many as five thousand white civilians who had showed up to help. Among those beaten for wearing zoot suits were boys as young as twelve and thirteen; soon after the violence started, Mexicans not wearing zoot suits were also targeted.

Newspaper accounts of the evening used inflated language, often the language of military operations (as Mauricio Mazón points out) to promote the sailors' actions and to imply that the events were the result of a conspiracy on the part of zoot-suiters. One newspaper even printed instructions on how to "de-zoot": "Grab a zooter. Take off his pants and frock coat and tear them up or burn them. Trim the 'Argentinian ducktail' that goes with the screwy costume" (Mazón 76).

About four days after the violence began, the Los Angeles City Council passed a resolution banning the wearing of zoot suits within city limits, providing for a thirty day jail sentence for anyone wearing the suit. The resolution was adopted after hours of debate, with one council member holding out that the ban would be unconstitutional. Los Angeles was also declared off-limits for most navy servicemen. Banning the servicemen, in turn, provoked objections from area merchants and business owners, who were upset about the loss of business that was sure to result.

In addition to effects on the local economy, there were international ramifications to the attacks on zoot suit wearers. Mexico was an important American ally. The Los Angeles City Council sent a telegram to the Mexican consulate in Los Angeles expressing regret that "individual incidents of hoodlumism in Los Angeles have been interpreted as acts specifically involving nationals of either Mexico or the United States" (*New York Times,* June 11, 1945). This attempt at reassurance flew completely in the face of the copious newspaper coverage of the "riots," which consistently engaged in Mexican-bashing, and was also contradicted by the police logs, which showed that the overwhelming majority of those arrested were of Mexican descent. Despite official reassurances that the riots had nothing to do with American attitudes toward those of Mexican descent, before long the Mexican government found it necessary to appeal to all Mexican nationals to stay indoors after dark.

Sleepy Lagoon Murder Case

The lurid and hysterical news accounts of the zoot suit riots were not the first occasion for sensational media coverage of the supposed threat posed by zoot-suited pachucos in California. The year before the riots, the body of a Mexican American teenager named José Díaz was found lying in a south-central city road, near a swimming hole where there had been a scuffle the night before. The swimming hole, which would be tagged the "Sleepy Lagoon" by a Los Angeles news reporter, was a popular spot for Mexican American youths, who were prevented from using the city's segregated swimming pools. Although the cause of Díaz's death was never proved, mass arrests followed; as many as six hundred young Mexican Americans were questioned in the killing (McWilliams, "Zoot Suit Riots"). Seventeen young men were convicted of the murder in a trial that violated multiple judicial procedures. Twelve were given harsh sentences in San Quentin Prison.

During the prosecution of the seventeen youths, their hairstyles and clothing were pointed to as evidence of their guilt. The defendants were not allowed to get haircuts or change clothes during the trial: the prosecutor gave orders that packages of clean clothes be intercepted. Therefore, when the defendants entered the courtroom, they appeared unkempt and, in the eyes of some observers, unsavory. "Mainstream" publications such as those owned by the Hearst Corporation uniformly characterized the youths as delinquents and outsiders, as outlandish pollutants in American cities. The black press, on the other hand, carefully followed the Sleepy Lagoon trial from the beginning, pointing out the racial dimensions of the case and astutely observing the implications of Mexican-bashing for African Americans.

The Sleepy Lagoon case became infamous for the bizarre nature of evidence entered into the trial. In addition to noting the clothes worn by the accused, the Sheriff's Department's Lieutenant Edward Duran Ayres spoke before the grand jury about the genetic and racial characteristics that accounted for Mexican crime and made it inevitable. Ayres compared the situation to having a wild cat like a lion or tiger and a domesticated version, saying that while the two kinds of cats do have some similarities and share some traits, one has to be kept caged up forever; it is the same, Ayres maintained, with the different races of people. Ayers alluded to supposed ancient Aztec rituals that made those of Mexican descent eager to kill, while he painted violence on the part of white Americans as almost wholesome:

> The Caucasian, especially the Anglo-Saxon, when engaged in fighting, particularly among youths, resorts to fisticuffs and may at times kick one another, which is considered unsporting, but this Mexican element considers all that to be a sign of weakness, and all he knows and feels is a desire to use a knife or some lethal weapons. In other words, his desire is to kill, or at least let blood. (Ayres 131)

The young men were painted as hardened gangsters—this despite the fact that, as Carey McWilliams has pointed out, one worked in a defense plant, one was a married father who had supported his mother and two sisters since he was fifteen years old, one was a furniture worker, and so forth (McWilliams, *North from Mexico*).

Although the trial has entered the historical record as a shameful example of racially motivated miscarriage of justice, it was also striking in terms of the swift and concerted opposition it produced. The quickly formed Sleepy Lagoon Defense Committee was supported by a remarkable cross-section of organizations nation-wide. Mauricio Mazón has called the Sleepy Lagoon defense committee "one of the more enduring coalitions between Mexicans, Jews, blacks, and Anglos in American history" (23). The Defense Committee was an impressive coalition; among its members were trade unionists, members of Congress, communist organizers, Hollywood personalities, ministers, and educators. It raised enough money for an appeal in early 1944, and in October a judge overturned the convictions, citing insufficient evidence, overt bias on the part of the presiding judge, and denial of counsel to the defendants. The young men had been in jail for just over two years.

The zoot suit riots and the Sleepy Lagoon murder trial show how quickly the suit came to be seen as an evocative emblem of juvenile delinquency (acting as symbolic conversational shorthand in the same way that urban graffiti would do in the 1970s). It was defined by the powerfully political imperatives that swirled around it. In her book on the evolution of modern clothing, Anne Hollander reminds us that "fashion is . . . constantly complicated by the rhetoric that surrounds it" (13). The meaning of the zoot suit's first appearance on the national landscape was colored by a number of social and economic forces (and the rhetorics that accompanied them): the wartime mentality of conformity and vehement masculinity; the segregated nature of the city of Los Angeles; the adolescent activities of zooters; the changing structure of immigrant Mexican families; international alliances during a time of war. All of these circumstances and events must be taken into account in order to contextualize the zoot suit, and its moment, for the Mexican Americans wearing them; we might call this a "horizontal" look at the suit. What can we learn by looking "vertically"—that is, by tracking where the zoot suit itself came from?

Putting on the Style

The basic style of the zoot suit was appropriated by the pachucos from the wartime fashion of urban African Americans. Indeed, one of the more interesting lessons of the zoot is how quickly the familiar bipolar American racial obsession (of black/white) was becoming insufficient (and would remain so, as the following chapters show), especially in understanding the history and implications of style. The shared zoot suit style also illustrates the process by which groups of Americans who immigrate to the United States are evaluated as to their "whiteness" as they become Americans. In the case of zoot suits, when African American youth also were attacked in cities across the country once the violence had begun with the pachucos, a real and serious argument was being made about who was on the "safe" side of the color line, and which groups (plural) were on the other.

During the zoot suit riots, newspapers sought to clarify the origins of the clothing that was to be envisioned as such a threat to the American way. In June 1943, the *New York Times* reported that the first zoot suit was ordered in 1940 by a "bus boy" in Georgia, an African American man named Clyde Duncan (Berger 5). The *Times* claimed that Duncan's suit was inspired by one worn by Rhett Butler in the 1939 movie *Gone with the Wind,* which had opened in Georgia a few months before Duncan ordered his suit amid media hoopla that exceeded any movie premier that had gone before. Whether this theory is correct or not is much less interesting than the implications of the story the newspaper is telling; both the book and movie versions of *Gone with the Wind,* it is now widely accepted, present a dangerously racist picture of the antebellum South, particularly in their portraits of African American slaves who are happy with their situation, who fear the approach of the Union army, who are dedicated to their "masters," and who have no desire to be freed from slavery. Indeed, the National Association for the Advancement of Colored People (NAACP) protested the film on these grounds. For Duncan, a black man referred to as a "boy" by the *Times,* to adopt the style worn by the movie's white slave owner— but exaggerate it in his own quest for "style"—is a fascinating example of an important paradigm of popular culture: the ability of its consumers to subvert familiar symbols and thereby imbue them with new, altogether different, meanings. With the suit he designed, Duncan managed to enact a kind of "counter-minstrelsy": where the cultural practice of minstrelsy usually involves a member of a more powerful group taking on the alleged appearance and behavior of a marginalized group, here Duncan turns the tables.

(According to Shane White and Graham White, the zoot suit was modeled after a suit worn by the Duke of Windsor, or by George Washington [White and White]. The existence of these intriguing alternate theories of origin demonstrates the powerful impulse toward myth-building legible in the stories people were eager to tell about the suit's design; these theories also dovetail with the notion of a purposeful deformation of a style originally associated with a figure holding a huge amount of political and economic power.)

According to the *Times,* the tailor whom Duncan commissioned to make the first zoot suit thought the style was funny. He photographed Duncan in his creation, and had the photo printed in the February 1941 issue of *Men's Apparel Reporter.* "Exclusive Style Flash," the caption ran, "The newest model known in South Georgia as the Killer Diller . . . coat length 37 inches, button top two . . . 26-inch knees . . . 14-inch bottom, requiring shoehorn to get your foot through." For the white tailor trade, the "killer diller" was no more than a joke. Indeed, the tailor who made it for Duncan was anxious to make it clear that the design was not his, but that he had merely been working to specifications for a payment of $33.50.

But the suit caught on in the South, and eventually in Harlem, an important center for African American culture. The style spread despite the fact that its hugely padded shoulders and sweeping drapes brought the design into conflict with a rationing of all cloth containing wool that was part of the first rationing act, in March 1942, developed by the War Production Board. The rationing act directly forbade the manufacture of zoot suits. But a bootleg network of tailors in Los Angeles and New York readily appeared to fill the gap.

One of the most important ways in which the zoot suit style circulated was through the visibility of jazz musicians, important entertainers in the black community, who wore them on stage and screen. Perhaps the most famous zoot suit was the one worn by bandleader Cab Calloway in the movie *Stormy Weather* (1943). By refusing to allow himself to be photographed in the suit before the opening of the movie, Calloway deliberately contributed to the mystique of the zoot suit. (Calloway also maintained adamantly that he had the suit made before the cloth rationing act.) In the movie's central stage scene, Calloway appears in his startlingly white suit to sing a song called "Geechee Joe," which tells the story of an African American who finds himself in the big city: the suit itself, then, becomes a visual marker of the conflict between city and country. Furthermore, Calloway calls attention to the suit itself during the performance with movements and gestures, such as removing and replacing his hat, and standing with legs apart so that the oversized watch chain swings between his legs (see fig. 2.1).

Figure 2.1. Cab Calloway deliberately contributed to the mystique of the famous white zoot suit he wore in the 1943 film *Stormy Weather*

Calloway's performance is most interesting for the ways in which it emphasizes "Africanness." During the song, he performs a dance step that came to be called the "moon walk" when performed by pop star Michael Jackson; W. T. Lhamon traces this step as an African retention in early slave dances in the Americas (222–223). In addition, the choice of song for the big "zoot suit" number, which is set up as climax both within the movie's narrative and in the publicity that preceded the movie, about a character called "Geechee Joe," is significant. "Geechee" refers to African Americans who are the descendants of African slaves brought to the Georgia and South Carolina Sea Islands by European planters during the 18th and 19th centuries; the word "Geechee" itself is African. The number's emphasis on these African elements, set against the zoot suit, provides a shockingly new context for the coat and tails. This new context brings about what Russian structuralist critics called defamiliarization; in other words, by recontextualizing something that the audience members would recognize, Calloway's dance gives the uniform of the dominant male a new inflection, one laden with racialized meaning. (Of course, this racialized meaning seems to have been quite plain to the people who beat up the Mexican Americans in the zoot suit riots.)

Having afforded the zoot all of this racialized expressive power through Calloway's performance, the movie then pulls back as if sensing danger. The scene after Calloway's on-stage triumph is structured to undercut some of the potent "cool" in which Calloway has reveled with a parodic follow-up in which another zoot suit is being worn, this time by Calloway's helper. But here, the zoot is intended to be comic, not magical, and its wearer (who speaks an exaggerated version of bebop slang that is literally unintelligible to other characters) comes off as more ridiculous than dangerous, folded somewhat into the minstrel type of the "uppity" city African American who aims for sophistication but is instead buffoonish.

Calloway's white zoot suit might well have become the most famous zoot suit. But the suit was already part of a flourishing, hip, street-oriented culture by the time he wore it. The suits were bound up with swing music and dancing—in addition to a nightlife scene of bands and clubs—and there were a number of songs about zoot suits, such as "Zoot Suit for My Sunday Gal," "Zoot Suit Boogie," and "I Wanna Zoot Suit." Among these songs were those performed by Latin performers for Spanish-speaking audiences, but also those performed by white, "mainstream" pop musical acts like the Andrews Sisters, seeking to bring the appeal of zoot suit "cool" to their own performances and large audiences. There was also a slang vocabulary associated with the "scene"—epitomized by the "New Cab Calloway's Hepsters' Dictionary: Language of Jive" that Calloway includes in his 1976 autobiography, *Of Minnie the Moocher & Me*. This "scene" was to produce two of the most important leaders of American political movements of the 1960s: Malcolm X and César Chávez.

Politics of the Zoot Suit

The polarization of servicemen on one side, and Chicano and African American youth on the other, found its public expression around the issue of patriotism and attitude toward the war effort. The zoot suits, which made their wearers highly visible in a larger society that would choose to mark them as invisible, expressed by their very presence an increasing defiance of white supremacy. The suits were also perceived as marking hostility toward the war effort. Not only did making them violate the cloth rationing act, but the very sight of them articulated resistance to wartime unanimity. Visually, the suits stood as a clear opposition to the uniform worn by servicemen; it seemed like their wearers were announcing that instead of the one, they were wearing the other. Finally, the clothing represented an insistence on leisure and having good times: these were party clothes. With a war going on, though, insisting on partying was a motivated stance. There were rumors that Mexican Americans were not doing their part to aid the war. These rumors were flatly untrue: instead, Earl Shorris writes, "measured by the number of Medal of Honor winners who were Mexican-American and the rate at which Mexican-American suffered casualties, no other racial or ethnic group served with greater courage" (97). The president of the National Lawyers Guild pointed out that most of the zoot-suiters were themselves too young to be in the military, but that many of them had older brothers who were serving.

Nonetheless, there was an important contingent of zoot suit culture that was ambivalent about fighting what they perceived to be a white war. Robin Kelley quotes trumpeter Dizzy Gillespie's explanation of his position to his recruitment officer:

Well, look, at this time, at this stage in my life here in the United States, whose foot has been up my ass? The white man's foot has been in my ass hole buried up to his knee in my ass hole! . . . Now you're speaking of the enemy. You're telling me the German is the enemy. At this point, I can never even remember having met a German. So if you put me out there with a gun in my hand and tell me to shoot at the enemy, I'm liable to create a case of "mistaken identity" of who I might shoot. (Quoted in Kelley 171)

Newspapers began to print alarmist charges that zoot suits and swing culture weakened the United States from within, to the benefit of the Axis powers. This paranoia also prompted charges that the zoot-suiters were being used by Communists to foment social dissatisfaction (despite the fact that wartime policy of the Communist Party of the United States was to privilege unity in the struggle against the fascists over other issues). A report by the Joint Fact-Finding Committee on Un-American Activities in California, known as the Tenney Committee, stated that

> the *Pachuco* or so called zoot suit fad among Negro and Mexican youth in Los Angeles' east side was a golden opportunity for Communist racial agitation. The riots that occurred in June of 1943, together with the activities of certain communist front organizations and the vociferous charges of the Communist press, forcefully brought the situation to the attention of the Committee. (Qtd. in Mazón 98)

(In his bizarre 1978 novel *Zoot Suit Murders,* Thomas Sanchez supposes that the zoot-suiters, vulnerable because of their profound disenfranchisement, were being manipulated by both the fascists *and* the Communists.)

Of course, as many observers have pointed out, Mexicans and African Americans did not require the assistance of Communists to become aware of racial discrimination against them. There were plenty of leaders in the African American and Mexican American communities who acknowledged the radical edge implicit in the "hep cat" scene. African American writer Langston Hughes, for instance, has the protagonist of several books of short stories, Jesse B. Semple (or "Simple"), explain the connection between swing culture and black awareness of institutionalized racism by telling the narrator where the word "bebop" came from:

> "From the police beating Negroes' heads," said Simple. "Every time a cop hits a Negro with his billy club, that old club says 'Bop! Bop! . . . BeBop! . . . Mop! . . . Bop!' That Negro hollers, 'Oool-ya-koo! Ou-o-o!'
>
> "Old Cop just keeps on 'Mop! Mop! . . . BeBop! . . . Mop!' That's where BeBop came from, beaten right out of some Negro's head into them horns and saxophones and piano keys that plays it. Do you call that nonsense?" (Hughes, "Bop" 117–118)

The connection Hughes draws so efficiently here is historically resonant, for the nonconformist stance of the black "hep cat" was part of a process of self-awareness and radicalization for the generation of young

people who brought about the liberation movements of the next decades. Robin Kelley has emphasized zoot suit culture as an important
training ground for the young Malcolm X—completely reversing the
"take" of poet Amiri Baraka, who would write about Malcolm having
been "disguised" in his early years in a zoot suit (4). While Baraka's
sense is that Malcolm X participated in the "hep cat" street scene *before*
he acquired the necessary skills and consciousness for political action
—a sense that is supported by Malcolm X's own retrospective vision, in
his autobiography—Kelley understands (as did Langston Hughes) that
the zoot suit itself was an important proto-political gesture, one that
launched Malcolm X and others as future activists.

Similarly, the Sleepy Lagoon case and the zoot suit riots have come to
be seen as the beginning of Chicano identity, if not the Chicano civil
rights movement. In an interesting parallel to the story of Malcolm X,
the zoot suit scene contributed one of the most important Mexican
American activists and leaders, César Chávez, organizer of the United
Farm Workers, the union whose struggles and members would remain
at the center of Chicano politics and culture for decades. In his autobiography, Chávez finds in his zoot suit days a nascent political consciousness that preceded his move into activism, but certainly did not
contradict or counterindicate it: "We [pachucos] were a minority group
of a minority group. So, in a way, we were challenging cops by being with two or three friends and dressing sharp. But in those days, I
was prepared for any sacrifice to be able to dress the way I wanted to
dress" (82).

Observers in the black press were particularly aware of the political
underpinnings of the racialized zoot suit subculture. Calling upon African Americans to organize in support of the attacked zooters, Langston
Hughes underscored the "riots" as serving the interests of white supremacy:

> Mobs always start with the poorest and weakest people. Nobody
> cared much about the zoot-suit boys. . . . So the soldiers and sailors
> in California began tearing their clothes off.
>   But the soldiers and sailors—who were not Negro or Mexican—
> also began tearing the clothes off Negro and Mexican war workers,
> and even off of intellectuals, like one of our 20-year-old students of

aviation at the University of California. So you see, nice colored people, it would have been worth your while to begin caring about the
zoot-suiters a long time ago—before the mob starts tearing off your
clothes, too. ("Key Chains with No Keys" 27)

Reading the Zoot Suit

The zoot emerges as a complex product of social, economic, and cultural forces in wartime America, and there is much to be learned from
its careful contextualization. But it is also important to look at the design of the suit itself, for there is much to be learned by treating the
zoot as material culture, with particular meanings to be "read" in its
oversized, purposefully conspicuous design. In other words, by donning the zoot, one thing these youth accomplished was turning their
own bodies into "texts" to be "read." Cultural studies practitioners in
the last two decades or so—inspired very much by pioneers in gender
studies, African American studies and ethnic studies—have taught us
that "bodies" acquire social meaning in the moment that they are interpreted; the audience for these bodily performances can be pop music
fans, parents, or police officers. What is most important is that a recognizable exchange is taking place whereby a "producer" is being met by
a competent "consumer." The zoot suits were colorful, outsize, ostenta-
tious: the black and Mexican zooters were refusing to be invisible in a
society that preferred not to see them. (The car culture of West Coast
Latinos accomplishes the same thing, especially when you contrast the
ideal of "riding low and riding slow," so that one is noticed, to the
white California car culture that would come to be epitomized by the
music of the Beach Boys, in which the ideal is going as fast as possible.)
    Anne Hollander notes that "fashion instantly mocks sensible inven-
tions in clothing, subjecting them to unfunctional usage as soon as they
appear, so they can seem authentically desirable and never merely convenient" (15). It is easy to see how the zoot suit, with its conspicuous
(according to some, ridiculous) exaggerations makes a flag out of being
nonfunctional. The zoot takes the standard working wear of white-
collar males and makes it both playful and showy. It insists upon lei-

sure, thereby potentially mocking not only wartime military service, but also some core values of the white American mentality: work ethic, decorum, practicality. Indeed, it is for this reason that Octavio Paz finds wearing the zoot, which he correctly reads as a motivated communicative act, to be an act of aggression, for it negates its model:

> One of the principles that rules in North American fashions is that clothing must be comfortable, and the pachuco, by changing ordinary apparel into art, makes it "impractical." Hence it negates the very principles of the model that inspired it. Hence its aggressiveness. (15)

To understand the motivations of the young people who wore the zoot suits, and also the strong reactions to them on the part of Paz and other observers, we can usefully adapt what practitioners of communication studies call "speech act theory" (laid out by John Searle in 1969). Speech act theory provides a framework for understanding all acts of communication, verbal and nonverbal; it emphasizes the performative nature of language and looks for an action that is performed by an utterance. But the reverse is just as true, and we can look at zoot suit wearing as an utterance performed by an action, a "perlocutionary" act because it says something, and in doing so produces a result (intended or not) in the addressee. In this way, we can see the pachucos as "speaking" particular things by putting on the suit; and we can see those who observed them as being "spoken to" in particular ways as they decode the speech act's meaning.

One of the canniest contemporary observers to hear what zoot-suiters were "saying" through the design of their clothing was Langston Hughes, who chided his readers that they should try to understand the wearing of the zoot as a speech act. Of the zoot's exaggerated lines and enormous keychains, Hughes wrote:

> In the light of the poverty of their past, too much becomes JUST ENOUGH for them. A key chain six times too long is just long enough to hold NO keys. No keys. In California and the Southwest, you see, to Mexican and Negro boys so many doors are locked—and they do not have the keys. ("Key Chains with No Keys" 28)

By looking at zoot suits as a speech act, then, the distinguishing qualities of the zoot—its size, its color, its long chain and wide shoulders—
reveal themselves to be concrete and sophisticated commentaries on the
wearers' problematic status as American men.

Writing the Zoot Suit: Contemporary Representations (1940s–1950s)

In addition to the photographs of zoot-suiters arrested in the riots of
1943, and the much-publicized costumes of jazz musicians, the third
important way zoot suits circulated in the public imagination was
through nondocumentary depictions in the popular press. By the time
photos of those arrested would dominate the nation's front pages, using
the zoot suit to "other" young Mexican American and African American men, there had already been some discussion of the suits (and the
accompanying subculture) both from within Mexican American and
African American communities and by the surrounding, "mainstream"
culture. This section will look at some of the ways the zoot suit was
visualized by contemporary artists and writers, who thereby added
their own layers of meaning to the symbolically loaded clothing.

Because humor tends to pivot on references to the contemporary, the
zoot suit made its way very quickly into the world of comics and cartoons, both print and animated. In 1942—well before the clashes took
place in California—African American cartoonist Ollie Harrington published a series of cartoons satirizing zoot-suiters in the Harlem-based,
and Communist-influenced, *People's Voice* (on whose editorial board
Harrington himself served). These cartoons mock the priorities of those
who are more upset by the War Production Board's ban on the suits
than they are about the fight against fascism. For instance, one man
holds a sign that reads, "Hitler and Hirohito are snakes, they're killing
our drapes," while in another panel, visitors to the Smithsonian ob-
serve a display of a man in a zoot suit, sharing exhibit space with the
skeleton of a dinosaur (March 21, 1942). In addition to the cartoons that
took on zoot suit fashion as a subject, Harrington drew many cartoons
about life in Harlem that pictured men wearing the suits while not

explicitly calling attention to it. This includes his regular "strips" and also a number of tiny, but fascinating, "filler" graphics, one of which pictures Hitler in a zoot suit (August 8, 1942).

Harrington's depictions are not wholly unaffectionate, but as the riots would show the next year, black expressive style was a charged subject. An African America letter writer to the *People's Voice* promptly objected to Harrington's "jitterbug" comics as "off-base" and embarrassing, and criticized the newspaper for giving space to them (May 2, 1942). One letter writer editorialized about the zoot suits themselves as embarrassing (April 18, 1942), while another suggested that it is Harrington's cartoons that belittled African Americans, complaining that "we get enough of that from the white cartoonists" (March 21, 1942). This letter writer was perhaps more correct than she imagined; the following year, a white cartoonist, Al Capp, would focus even more prolonged attention on the zoot suit style—directly "borrowing" (to put it kindly) some of Harrington's gags but without the measure of affection that Harrington's cartoons retained.

Capp created a character called "Zoot Suit Yokum" for his "hillbilly" newspaper comic strip *Li'l Abner*. It ran between April 11, 1943, and May 23, 1943, and was reprinted in *The World of Li'l Abner* (first printed in 1952 with an introduction by the writer John Steinbeck and a foreword by Charlie Chaplin.) This collection brags that "50 million readers follow" the antics of Li'l Abner; some estimates claim that the number is much higher when both dailies and Sunday comics are taken into account.

The plot of "Zoot Suit Yokum" is a conspiracy story: clothing manufacturers have dreamed up a way to take over the United States by having a ready-made hero perform acts of charity and courage while dressed in a zoot. Because this is a dangerous job, the clothing industry seeks out the man with the lowest I.Q. in the country, turning up as candidate Capp's regular "hillbilly" character, Li'l Abner.

As Mauricio Mazón has pointed out, Capp's satirical "conspiracy" came at a time (while a war is being fought) when conspiratorial thinking was common. As noted above, the zoot suit itself was presented as a conspiracy on the part of both communists and Fifth Columnists to incite rebellion. In Capp's cartoon, the zoot suit is presented as distinctly un-American aesthetically, and when the zoot suit craze is finally ended, it is because "foreign" elements have been contained. Capp's comic strip, which like Harrington's drawings predated the zoot suit riots, indicates (and contributes to the fact) that the style was widely perceived as marking cultural difference from the American mainstream.

The wide visibility of Capp's comic strip was rivaled by the popularity of animated cartoon shorts, which were shown before movies (and later on television). These animated cartoons were saturated with images of zooters and their cultural expressions: suits, slang, and swing. Because of the uneven way these cartoons have been archived, it is still difficult to carry out a systematic study of their content. But even with a cursory overview, one finds dozens of shorts that provide contemporary commentary on the "riddle of the zoot." For the purposes of this chapter, a few emblematic examples will suffice to shed some light on how these cartoons worked.

In the year following the riots, a Warner Brothers cartoon featuring the characters Tom and Jerry illustrated how quickly the zoot suit became a complex and recognizable signifier. The cartoon, titled "Zoot Cat," depends upon recognition of already-established meanings of the zoot suit—as markedly black and urban (see fig. 2.2). The plot of the cartoon has Tom (the cat) courting a pretty female cat, who has no interest in him because of his country ways. Just when he feels like giving up, the cat hears a radio announcer talk about zoot suits as the latest thing. Tom grabs a pair of scissors and cuts himself a suit out of a striped hammock. By donning the suit, he has become hip, and the female cat is immediately interested. But he has also become "black" and urban, as evidenced by the "jive" he starts speaking, by the female cat's address of him as "Jackson," and by his immediate ability to play the piano and dance. Of course, the cat's triumph is short-lived (as it is in every cartoon): when his suit gets wet, it shrinks and pops off him, his false sophistication stripped away (in the same way that the pachucos were stripped during the zoot suit riots), leaving him to be the country bumpkin he had hoped the suit would protect him from being.

Along the same lines (and released the same year by Warner Brothers) is a cartoon by Bob Clampett called "Coal Black and De Sebben Dwarfs." This satire of Disney's "Snow White and the Seven Dwarfs"

Figure 2.2. "Zoot Cat" (1944) found humorous occasion in what it presented as the false sophistication of
swing culture. Note that the cat's "watch chain" has
been made by a drain plug.

was voiced by the mother and sister of actor Dorothy Dandridge and
boasted a swing score by Eddie Beals. In this cartoon, "Prince Chaw-
min'" is a ridiculously flashy "hep cat," who in addition to his colorful
zoot suit has dice for teeth. Many other cartoons—"Tin Pan Alley
Cats" (1943), "Goldilocks and the Three Jivin' Bears" (1944), "The
Hams That Couldn't Be Cured" (1942), to name just a few—draw on images from swing culture for comic material. ("The Hams That Couldn't

Be Cured" featured a wolf that sounded like Edward G. Robinson. See chapter 1.)

These cartoons, which often featured the talents of important African American musicians and performers, are ambiguous at best. There is a way in which these cartoons gave the new swing culture its due by quickly acknowledging and depicting its appeal and richness. But the images themselves are sometimes quite racist; for instance, in "The Boogie Woogie Man Will Get You (If You Don't Watch Out)," the zoot-suiters are "spooks"—ostensibly meaning ghosts, but the "real" racist meaning is quite plain—and the "boogie woogie man" is known by his "reet pleats."

In addition to its immediate treatment by commentators from within popular culture itself, the flashy fad suit quickly found its way into "high" art as well, generally depicted here with a much more somber tone. The African American painter Jacob Lawrence presented the wearing of the zoot suit as a deliberately performative act in his 1951 painting "Vaudeville." Against a brightly colored, abstract background of geometric shapes, two figures stand face-to-face, filling up the space of the painting, each dressed in a zoot. Both carry decorative canes. One figure gestures widely in a motion appropriate to the stage. The suits are resplendent, especially the green one, which seems to shimmer (see fig. 2.3).

But the faces of the two figures are distraught; one has tears running down his face. Lawrence has depicted the zoot-suiters as gorgeous, and by putting them on a literal stage he has raised the performativity of the wearers to the level of ritual. At the same time, the tears remind us that for black men, being the object of a desirous gaze has not been an unmixed experience. The tears even recall stories about the African American minstrel performer Bert Williams, who was said to weep whenever he applied his blackface. With the war now over, Lawrence does not want to forget the violent power struggle that was encompassed by the wearing of the zoot.

The writer Beatrice Griffith created a new form to address adequately the emotional complexity of zoot suit culture in her important 1948 book *American Me* (which Wallace Stegner suggested she write and for which she won a Houghton Mifflin Literary Fellowship Award). In order to honor the duality of the Mexican American experience—

Figure 2.3. Jacob Lawrence's 1951 painting "Vaudeville" presents the zoot suiter as tragic figure

Mexican and American, Spanish and English, delinquent and disinherited—she organizes her book so that fiction and nonfiction alternate in
pairs. A fictional segment called "In the Flow of Time" is written from
the point of view of two friends who return from a farewell hunting
trip before they join the army to find themselves in the midst of the
zoot suit riots. These youths combine a sophisticated sense of humor
about how sides get drawn—they refer to the military uniform as "that
army zootsuit"—with a tragically idealistic desire to believe that "not
all Americans is like these guys" (13).

A similarly tragicomic vision is presented by Jewish novelist Budd

Schulberg, best known for his best-selling 1941 novel *What Makes Sammy Run?* In his hard-boiled novel *The Harder They Fall* (1947), Schulberg uses the zoot suit to represent the bravado of the American male, summarizing the beauty and the swagger that are found just before he is knocked down and taught once and for all that the beauty is never a reality for very long:

> She loved them when they were full of bounce and beans, with their hard trim bodies moving gracefully in their first tailor-made full-cut double-breasted with peg-top trousers narrowing at the ankles in a modified zoot. And she loved them when the shape of their noses was gone, their ears cauliflowered, scar-tissue drawing back their eyes, when they laughed too easily and their speech faltered and they talked about the comeback that Harry Miniff or one of this thousand-and-one cousins was lining up for them. (16)

A few years later, the protagonist of Ralph Ellison's densely intertextual novel *Invisible Man* (1952) catches sight of zoot-suiters while waiting for a subway. The sight of them calls to mind for the Invisible Man the words of a former teacher: "You're like one of those African sculptures, distorted in the interest of design." He swiftly goes on to wonder, "What design, and whose?" (430). The Invisible Man's response to the zoot-suiters—a frequently quoted passage from the novel—would come to serve as the starting place for those later commentators who have tried to make historical sense of the zoot suit by asking whom it served, and how. Fascinatingly, the answer to that question would change repeatedly over time, as different groups of Americans would deploy the gesture of the zoot wearer, pressing it into service for their own agendas.

The Zoot Suit as Historical Myth: Representations in the Era of Vietnam and Cultural Nationalism (1960s–1970s)

Contemporary commentators in a range of media used the zoot suit as a container for meaning about race and masculinity during World War II and the period immediately after. Decades later, the zoot would maintain (or reexert) its extraordinary appeal as new generations of artists and audiences returned to the zoot, carefully placing it at the center of important historical myths about the origins of ethnic American identity. It is common enough that foundational myths are marshaled in support of what has come to be known as "identity politics," for they can be crucial to the construction of community and commonality. Many artists have located the zoot suit riots as the symbolic beginning of the struggle for Mexican American political and economic rights. Arguably most important among these is Luiz Valdez's 1978 play *Zoot Suit,* which was filmed as a movie (with the same name) in 1982.

Commentators have tended to view Valdez's play, which combines the stories of the Sleepy Lagoon murder and the zoot suit riots, as a corrective, as the first accurate representation of what happened in 1942–43. (In fact Valdez worked with Alice McGrath, executive secretary of the Sleepy Lagoon Defense Committee, when he was writing the play.) And indeed, compared to other accounts, Valdez's play is striking in its historicity. For instance, one year after the theatrical version of *Zoot Suit,* the movie *1941* (1979) avoids facing the most painful aspects of the "riots" by showing a zoot-suiter brawling with sailors (albeit two years early in 1941), but having the embattled zoot-suiter—and every other person in the movie, with one lone exception—be white.

But even more interesting than Valdez's very important role in setting the record straight is the way he is able to find in the zoot-suiters cultural ancestors who could both root and inspire a new generation of culturally alert and politically active Mexican Americans. Earlier, Valdez (born in 1940) had helped to found in 1965 El Teatro Campesino, a touring farm workers' theater troupe associated with the United Farm Workers, led by César Chávez (who, recall, was a zoot-suiter in his youth). El Teatro Campesino produced one-act plays, often without stage, script, or props, and staged entirely by farm workers, that dramatized the circumstances of migrant workers. This grassroots theater project kindled a national Chicano theater movement that would come to be known as *teatro chicano.* Theater groups and festivals were organized on college campuses and in community centers nationwide, and these groups indicated a commitment to ethnic pride, and to representing the experience of the average Mexican American.

Figure 2.4. Edward James Olmos in the movie version of *Zoot Suit*:
A movement in search of symbolic ancestry

Valdez wrote, directed, and produced *Zoot Suit* at the height of this
theater movement. The main character is El Pachuco (played with almost preternatural aplomb by Edward James Olmos), a mystical adviser
and alter ego to Hank Reyna, a teenaged gang leader (see fig. 2.4). El
Pachuco provides the wisdom and strength to see Hank through his
beatings, arrest, and imprisonment, telling him, "Haven't I taught you
to survive?" At the end of the play, El Pachuco and the zoot-suiters are
connected to Valdez's own generation of Mexican Americans through
a proposed ending for Reyna's family story: his children, we are told,

are activists on college campuses, who call themselves by the politically significant name "Chicanos." (Edward James Olmos would return to this notion of zoot-suiters as symbolic ancestors for politically aware Chicanos twenty years later in his directorial debut, the ultraviolent prison movie *American Me,* which takes its name from the Beatrice Griffith book discussed above. His movie opens with a flashback depiction of the zoot suit riots, during which the parents of the film's protagonist are attacked by white servicemen who strip the man and rape the woman. The protagonist comes to realize that he was conceived of this rape: the future gang member is literally a product both of mid-century pachuco "cool"—and the state-sanctioned violence against Chicanos.)

The theater movement that grew up around Valdez's El Teatro Campesino de Aztlán soon expanded to include all art forms, resulting in what is now called the Chicano Arts Movement. Artists considered their work to be an outgrowth of the Chicano civil rights movement, continuing the association of art with organized struggle that began with Valdez's involvement with the United Farm Workers Union. These artists who were members of Valdez's "brown power" generation continued to invoke the zoot-suiters in ways that were not just sympathetic, as friendly representations during the 1940s and 1950s (by Beatrice Griffith, Langston Hughes, and so forth) had been, but were outright admiring. An important example is the work of José Montoya, a California artist (born in 1932) who was a founder of the Rebel Chicano Art Front (also known as the Royal Chicano Air Force). Montoya, a multidisciplinary artist, wrote a poem called "El Louie" that is one of the first literary representations of the pachuco figure. Montoya's "Pachuco series" of ink drawings from 1977 features zoot-suiters who are not beaten down, literally or figuratively. In fact, some of the drawings are done as though looking up at the zooters from the ground, or from the perspective of a child, so that the pachuco figures appear to loom, filling the space with their confident postures (see fig. 2.5).

Montoya's text refers to pachucos and pachucas as "FREEDOM FIGHTERS AHEAD OF THEIR TIME" (137). Similarly inspired, several of Montoya's contemporaries also summoned heroic zoot suiters as artistic material: Richard Duardo in his 1978 silkscreen *Zoot Suit,* which also pictured the figures as physically audacious, and Rene Yanez's 1977

Figure 2.5. José Montoya's zoot-suiters: "Freedom fighters
ahead of their time"

hologram *Pachuco and Pachuca,* which depicts a couple dancing amid
the swirl of smoke.

But the best-known graphic representation of zoot-suiters from this
period is undoubtedly *The Great Wall of Los Angeles,* a collective mural
project spearheaded by Chicana artist Judith Baca. *The Great Wall of
Los Angeles* was begun in 1976; located in the Tujunga Wash drainage
canal at the Van Nuys/North Hollywood border, it tells a history of California from pre-Colombian times through the 1960s. During the civil
rights struggles of the 1960s, there was a renaissance of mural painting

in Mexican American Los Angeles and Southern California. Projects like *The Great Wall of Los Angeles* were considered to be important tools of organizing as well as expression. The *Great Wall*'s panel depicting the zoot suit riots is notable for the fact that no zoot suit can be seen in the mural. Refusing to aestheticize the violent events in any way, the mural instead pictures a zooter who has been stripped to his underwear and crouches on the sidewalk; the uniform boots of his attacker loom over him in the foreground of the picture (see fig. 2.6). Nearby, a discarded newspaper lying on the ground announces the clashes between servicemen and zoot-suiters.

Literary artists from this period, both Mexican American and African American, also found their way to zoot-suiters as symbolic ancestors of the new cultural nationalism. Chicano poet Patricio Paiz, writing in 1976, folded the zoot suit riots into his own growing awareness of the fact that the rate of Chicano deaths in Vietnam was, like that of African Americans, greater than the death rate for the general population, placing the two realities onto a kind of continuum of violence against Mexicans and Mexican Americans. (The Vietnam War played a big role in politicizing the Mexican American community, and Chicano opposition

Figure 2.6. The Great Wall of Los Angeles pictures the zoot suit riots—without showing an actual zoot suit

to the war culminated in the Chicano National Moratorium, a demon-stration organized in August 1970 in Los Angeles.) Trying to come to terms with the experience of the war for Mexican American men, Paiz reaches back for historical touchstones of struggle, beginning with the events of 1943:

> I remember the Zoot Suit riots,
> I remember Las Gorras Blancas de Nuevo Mexico,
> I remember Jacinto Trevino,
> I remember Pancho Villa,
> I remember Emiliano Zapata
>   Benito Juarez,
>   I will never forget. (141)

Likewise, the zoot suit was a popular motif for writers associated with the Black Arts movement, such as the poet, essayist, and anthologist Larry Neal (born in 1937), whose many invocations of the zoot include a reference to the young Malcolm X "wearing the zoot-suit of life" (9).

The zoot suit, then, was endowed with another powerful layer of symbolic meaning by Chicano and black artists of the second part of the civil rights movement, who found that it served their purposes by centering a black or Chicano aesthetic. This did not go unnoticed by certain white writers, who borrowed the myth-building power with which the zoot had been invested. For instance, Tyrone Slothrop is given a zoot suit in Thomas Pynchon's 1976 novel *Gravity's Rainbow*. It possesses mystical powers of protection. Later on, Seaman Bodine wears a zoot suit "of unbelievable proportions" that he has acquired from the Panama Canal Zone:

> It is immediately noticed everywhere it goes. At gatherings it haunts the peripheral vision, making decent small-talk impossible. It is a suit that forces you either to reflect on matters as primary as its color, or feel superficial. A subversive garment, all right. (710)

Here, the suit is imbued with special powers: to make the invisible seen, to make the superficial recede. Moreover, the zoot here insists on reconstituting America in a new global sense.

The "Zipless Cool": Beyond Myths of Origin in the 1980s and 1990s

At the tail end of the 20th century, zoot suits and zoot culture were again thoroughly mined, this time by white Americans. This new attention took place through a "swing revival" scene that returned the suits and the music to the public eye. The swing revival, which peaked in the mid-1990s, consisted of dances at clubs and other venues, dance classes using forties music and steps, and vintage clothing and retro reproductions. Dozens of white bands began recording neo-swing music, with CD covers that pictured or made reference to the fashions of the World War II era (see fig. 2.7). A few prominent bands such as North Carolina's Squirrel Nut Zippers and Oregon's Cherry Poppin' Daddies had huge hits with neo-swing songs; in particular, the Cherry Poppin'

Figure 2.7. Big Bad Voodoo Daddy: the band's publicity photographs emphasize the fashion, but not the politics, of the original zoot suit era

Daddies "Zoot Suit Riot" reached number 10 on Billboard's Modern Rock Airplay chart's Top 20 in 1998 and eventually sold more than a million copies. The song's lyrics refer obliquely to the events of June 1943, but the cultural politics are gone, and "Zoot Suit Riot" is a party song:

> Who's that whisperin' in the trees
> It's two sailors and they're on leave
> Pipes and chains and swingin' hands
> Who's your daddy? Yes I am
> Fat cat came to play
> Now he can't run fast enough
> You had best stay away
> When the pushers come to shove
> Zoot Suit Riot
> Throw back a bottle of beer
> Zoot Suit Riot
> Pull a comb through your coal black hair

The tune of "Zoot Suit Riot" shortly became available as a cell phone ring, while advertisers (such as the Gap) started to use swing originals in their commercials. Zoot suits were a visible part of the neo-swing subculture, and moved outward from there to become popular for prom nights and weddings.

Both Internet and brick-and-mortar stores continue to cater to zoot suit wearers. But by this time, the "profound political meaning" that Ralph Ellison noticed a half-century earlier is largely deliberately elided—as is the "subversive" nature of the suits claimed by Thomas Pynchon. The models wearing the zoot suits on the Web sites (for example, zootsuitstore.com) are as likely as not to be exclusively white (see fig. 2.8). (One site, Suavecito's, provides a history of the riots and the Sleepy Lagoon case.) The "hipness" has been recovered, but without the racialized meanings.

In her novel *Fear of Flying* Erica Jong coined the term "zipless fuck" in 1973 to describe an (idealized) sexual experience without any complications: not even the fastenings on clothing get in the way, let alone questions of responsibility and intimacy. Now, young men who don the

Figure 2.8. In the 1990s, zoot suits found a new popularity as wedding and prom attire

zoot suit can access the powerful sense of style and gesture with which it is laden after more than fifty years of history, but without having to undergo, or even think much about, the profound sense of exclusion and self-assertion that motivated its original wearers. Chicano performance artist Guillermo Gómez-Peña has commented on the swing revival:

> There's this great pachuco store in San Francisco and it's all Anglos buying them. The store owner is so perplexed by it. He's like, "Man, three or four years ago, I only had a handful of Chicanos in their forties and fifties coming in for custom-made pachuco suits and now hundreds of Anglos are coming in every week, wanting to look like real pachucos. And they'll come in with their Lowrider magazine in hand and they'll point to the very photograph that they want me to reproduce." It's a process of cultural gentrification where culture is reproducing the same process that happens in urban settings. (214–215)

One segment of the swing revival is strongly African American: this is hand dancing, which developed mostly in the Washington D.C. area. Fascinatingly, these dancers do not tend to dress in period garb for the dances or photographs. This speaks powerfully to the notion of masquerade as strongly important to the white participants, in a way that isn't relevant to the non-white participants.

The swing revival has not only elided the zoot suit's history, however. Because of the new popularity, much of the original music has been re-issued by archive-based record labels such as Arhoolie and Rhino. These reissues attempt simultaneously to correct and capitalize upon the swing revival's white popularity by directing the attention of participants back to the birth of swing culture. But despite such preservationist efforts, in fact sometimes aided by them, the end of the 20th century was marked by attempts to rewrite or transfer ownership of the zoot suit's ability to operate as a "speech act."

But because of what W. T. Lhamon calls "popular culture's palimpsest" (81), traces of earlier zoot suit versions have remained visible, for better or for worse. In the 1988 movie *Who Framed Roger Rabbit?*, for instance, the most evil and cowardly cartoon characters, a pair of snickering, back-stabbing weasels, are dressed in zoot suits and speak Spanish-accented English. And as such racist representations proliferate, a new generation of Chicano artists is paying its respects to World War II–era zoot suit culture. We end this chapter by briefly examining a painting by one of these artists, Vincent Valdez's *Kill the Pachuco Bastard!* from 2001. Valdez, a San Antonio artist (born in 1977, the year Luis Valdez published *Zoot Suit*) who got his start painting in collective mural projects, has created a terrifying vision of the 1943 clashes. The painting has elements of hyper-realism, but a sort of dizzy grotesquerie saturates the scene. *Kill the Pachuco Bastard!* shows the inside of a bar, with a yellow taxicab visible through the open door, invoking the taxi brigades of June 1943. In the center of the painting, a pachuco and a sailor grapple, both gory with the pachuco's spilled blood. The Virgin Mary, crying tears of blood, kneels behind them, while all around the painting's perimeter are other sailors viciously beating zooters, and what appears to be a rape in process (we just see the white sailor's dropped trousers and the high-heel-clad leg of a woman peeking out from under him). The whole scene is dark and shadowy, lending a menacing tone to what is already narratively horrifying.

But the most interesting aspect of the painting for our purposes is the number of things Valdez has placed in the composition to be read by the careful viewer: a newspaper on the table, an army recruiting poster, the tattoos worn by the sailors and the pachucos, banners reading "200 pinche gringo sailors" and "kill the pachuco bastards," tiny or translucent icons of Mexican tradition, and so forth. By forcing the viewer's attention to the act of interpreting, Valdez is reminding us that the "riddle of the zoot" has always depended upon who was doing the looking, and that while the building blocks for positive cultural expression are present, some visions can still lead to terror and phantasmagoria.

Acknowledging the reality of such horrors as the zoot suit riots has led some cultural producers to try to imagine grounds for more loving and productive intergroup meetings: the creators of *West Side Story*—inspired in part by the West Coast violence—worked hard to construct an urban space in which Anglos and Latinos could meet in peace. This effort unfolded with its own fraught racial politics.

CHAPTER 3

Broadway, 1957

West Side Story and the
Nuyorican Blues

Rioting over a suit of clothes was
one way that Americans came to process the complexities of race, immigration, and identity during the World War II era. The zoot suit riots
can be understood in many analytical frameworks, including as a labor
action, as fashion criticism, and as a crisis of white masculinity. But
perhaps the most important legacy of the zoot suit riots for students of
American immigration history has to do with how they represented a
moment when it was becoming increasingly difficult—if not impossible—to imagine that the United States could be understood in binary,
black-white racial terms. The Mexican and Filipino youths who were
the object of violent hatred during the World War II era were part of a
mass migration of "brown" people to the United States. Carmen Teresa
Whalen has written eloquently of how the post–World War II era has
often been depicted as a "hiatus" between "classic" immigration from
Europe and later immigration from Asia, the Caribbean, and Latin
America (5). But, as she explains, this era can only be seen as a "hiatus"
if "migrants are separated from immigrants and if im/migration and
labor history are treated as separated and unrelated endeavors" (5). To
understand the peopling of the United States in the years of World War
II and after, it is necessary to investigate how labor needs brought huge

numbers of Mexicans, Puerto Ricans, and, slightly later, blacks from the Caribbean to American cities.

The previous chapter documented a major West Coast branch of this new demographic reality. On the East Coast, and overlapping with this development in the 1940s, was a mass migration of Puerto Ricans from the island to New York. This new wave of neither-black-nor-white migrants (at least Puerto Ricans were not obviously, consistently, or conclusively understood to fit neatly into either category) helped to complicate even further the human landscape of the United States. Sociologists, politicians, and journalists all worked energetically to define how (and why) Puerto Ricans should be situated in American social life. Joining—and really taking over this conversation—were a group of Jewish American popular culture workers who created *West Side Story,* a fantastically popular Broadway show (1957) and an even more influential movie (1961).

West Side Story turned to Puerto Ricans as the newest "problem" group that needed to be incorporated into a national narrative of reconciliation. This musical reduced all the complexities of foreign affairs, rapidly globalizing business practices, and immigration policy into a simple story of young love between a Puerto Rican woman, Maria (played in the film by Natalie Wood, not a Puerto Rican), and an "American" boy, Tony. *West Side Story* imagines the landscape of New York City as almost free of adults (aside from a few police officers, a wizened old Jewish candy-store owner, and the token grown-up at a recreation-center dance) and completely free of African Americans (Sandoval-Sánchez, "*West Side Story*" 167). Maria and Tony could be together if only the young gang members who populate the scene—the Puerto Rican Sharks and the Anglo Jets—would let them. Avoiding the complicated geographic dynamics that brought Puerto Rican migrants into close contact with African Americans in upper Manhattan and the complicated racial dynamics that forced many Americans to come to grips with the "in-between" status of Puerto Ricans, *West Side Story* offers the comfort of two star-crossed lovers, apparently wearing exactly the same shade of light brown makeup; Pauline Kael was one of the few contemporary commentators to notice that in the movie the "Puerto Ricans are *not* Puerto Ricans and the only real difference between these two gangs . . . is that one group has faces and hair

Figure 3.1. As film critic Pauline Kael said about *West Side Story* (1961), "Puerto Ricans are *not* Puerto Ricans and the only real difference between these two gangs . . . is that one group has faces and hair darkened, and the other group has gone wild for glittering yellow hair dye"

darkened, and the other group has gone wild for glittering yellow hair dye" (Williams 133) (see fig. 3.1).

The Neo-Rican Jetliner

When they began to arrive in New York in great numbers in the late 1940s and 1950s, the "real" difference between Puerto Ricans and other New Yorkers was certainly noticed and commented upon frequently. The end of World War II coincided, as Laura Briggs has pointed out, with the dawn of relatively inexpensive air travel (166). As Puerto

Ricans began to take advantage of the cheap airline tickets, they increasingly came under discussion by the mainstream media. According to Briggs, the *New York Times* had no articles about migrant Puerto Ricans in 1946, but thirty in 1947—and all of these were about how the new arrivals from the island were a "problem" for the mainland United States (167). While it is clear to us now that Puerto Ricans became a "preferred" source of labor for American corporate and governmental interests in the late 1940s (Whalen 66), an ongoing conversation ranged across the 1950s and beyond about the fitness of Puerto Ricans to work in the United States. It was difficult to even achieve consensus on how to describe Puerto Ricans. In congressional debates in 1947 Puerto Ricans were referred to as both citizens of the United States and foreign laborers; by 1948 they were more consistently portrayed as United States citizens and their recruitment was given a patriotic aspect (Whalen 67).

But as early as 1950, the sociologists who wrote *The Puerto Rican Journey* tried to emphasize that Puerto Ricans were entering New York at a time of diminished possibilities. These sympathetic observers acknowledged that the "story of the Puerto Rican world in New York is an old story in America, a story not only of migrants from Europe, but also of America's small town and rural people entering into the life of its great cities"; after this gesture toward historical continuity, the authors then took pains to note that the Puerto Ricans were taking their journey not "in the expanding hopeful society of pre–World War I days," but in the "contracting world of a city built of migrations whose people may already have closed off the classic ways of becoming American" (Mills et al. 123–124). What C. Wright Mills and his colleagues tried to indicate in this text was, above all, that the great migration of Puerto Ricans to New York had to be understood in its political, economic, and cultural particularities. The creators of *West Side Story*, as we will see, seemed to want to stitch Puerto Rican migration into the type of grand immigrant narrative becoming so popular in this era and typified by Oscar Handlin's 1951 history, *The Uprooted*. When the makers of *West Side Story* had Anita insult Bernardo by saying, "Once an immigrant, always an immigrant," they were pretending that Puerto Ricans were no different from the Jews, Italians, Poles, and so on who had come before them—no different, in fact, from the "white ethnics" who had been so popular in the gangster movies of the 1930s.

Puerto Ricans were not, strictly speaking, immigrants—they were internal migrants, moving from one American island to another. The confusion about what relation Puerto Ricans have had to other Americans is not an accidental by-product of colonization: it is, as Laura Briggs maintains, a major component of the ideological work that has been done to support American imperialism. As Briggs writes, the lack of clarity about Puerto Ricans in the American cultural imaginary has been "produced and maintained through silences in the media, in popular culture, and in the teaching of U.S. history, which exist alongside a prominent public narrative in which the U.S. is a major anti-imperialist force in the world" (2).

What was perhaps most distinct about Puerto Ricans moving to New York at mid-century is that they came by airplane. As sociologist Clarence Senior, *Life* magazine, and many other contemporaneous observers noted, Puerto Ricans were the first ever "airborne migrants" to New York (Padilla 38; Sánchez Korrol 4). The Puerto Ricans coming to New York represented the domestic "product" of a fifty-year United States imperialist project on the island, and they were the most modern of "movers": their "transformation" in midair marked a major change in how American identities could be forged. Puerto Ricans cross no borders when they migrate; their Ellis Island is a gate at the San Juan airport. Alberto Sandoval-Sánchez has explained that this defining characteristic of Puerto Rican migration has led to a major thematic investment by Puerto Rican/Nuyorican writers in the airplane ("Puerto Rican Identity").

The "Neo-Rican Jetliner," as Jaime Carrero named it in a 1964 poem, helped give birth to a new kind of person: the Nuyorican. In this poem, Carrero's narrator boasts that he is not a "Jones Act Puerto Rican" but a "new flash": a Neo-Rican (Sandoval-Sánchez, "Puerto Rican Identity" 194). With this reference to the Jones Act—the 1917 law that imposed United States citizenship on Puerto Ricans—Carrero begins to make a claim on a new generational identity that *West Side Story* refused to consider. After some sixty years of complex United States investment in the island of Puerto Rico, the evolution of a "Nuyorican" identity represented an important moment in the ongoing "colonizer and colonized" dialectic that shaped life on the islands of Puerto Rico and New York since 1898.

Puerto Rico became a colony of the United States in 1898, as one result of the Spanish-American War. The Foraker Bill of that year denied, "for the first time in U.S. history, both territorial status and constitutional protection and citizenship to a newly acquired territory" (Oboler 37); citizenship, as already noted, would not come until the 1917 passage of the Jones Act. The political issues marked off by these two dates can only hint at the complex ways that the United States took control over Puerto Rico in these years. As Virginia Sánchez Korrol has explained, the "penetration of United States capital into the Puerto Rican economy since 1898 virtually destroyed the traditional pattern of land ownership and consolidated the dominance of large continental corporations" (25). Capital was just one part of the bigger picture, though: American "commodities, laws, and customs" were all foisted on Puerto Ricans busily being incorporated into the American empire (Duany 1). American domination was expressed in virtually every area of Puerto Rican life; officers of the United States government "pressured Puerto Rican municipal and school bands to change their calendars and their repertoires to conform with American holidays and patriotic songs," for instance (Glasser 37). Laura Briggs has neatly summed up American investment in the island with her argument that Puerto Rico is the place where the United States worked out its most important ideas about "expansionism" in general (2).

There were a number of major causes of increased Puerto Rican migration to the mainland. Curtailment of European immigration just after World War I (particularly through the Immigration Restriction Act of 1924) created more job opportunities for Puerto Ricans in New York and elsewhere in the continental United States; by 1930, at least 52,000 island Puerto Ricans had settled on the mainland (Sánchez Korrol 31; Cofer 213). A devastating hurricane in 1928, joined with the increasing control exerted by U.S. corporations over Puerto Rican agriculture, encouraged more and more Puerto Ricans to leave the island for New York (Glasser 50).

Operation Bootstrap (officially called the Industrial Incentives Act of

1947) converted what had been a steady migration of Puerto Ricans to New York into what Victor Hernández Cruz has called "one of the great exoduses of recent times" (92). Between 1940 and 1950, migration from Puerto Rico to New York increased by over 200 percent. While New York had some 45,000 Puerto Rican inhabitants in 1930, by 1950 it would have around 250,000; this number would more than double again (577,000) by 1956 (Handlin 143; Schneider 32). Operation Bootstrap represented a major economic and cultural assault on Puerto Rico; it also, on some level, reinvented New York as a cultural colony of Puerto Rico. While this program represented a business-government partnership focused on the recruitment of Puerto Ricans as laborers, it did nothing, of course, to help make sure that Puerto Ricans would be welcomed as "community members" as well (Whalen 3).

Operation Bootstrap "combined a massive industrialization program on the island based on long-term tax breaks for U.S. corporations and the export of thousands of displaced workers to the United States" (Oboler 39). The Puerto Ricans whose migration was predestined by this act of social engineering (a.k.a. the "cheap labor pool") were also prepared to serve the needs of U.S. corporate interests through a variety of educational protocols. Esmeralda Santiago has written eloquently of the Americanization propaganda that Operation Bootstrap brought to the island. Among the many baffling changes were food charts that showed up in her school to instruct students about proper nutrition: they had no "rice, no beans, no salted codfish" or any of the other staples of the Puerto Rican diet (64–66).

West Side Story, along with another 1961 movie, *The Young Savages* (at least in their more liberal, humanistic moments), wanted to show Anglo audiences that Puerto Rican youth were—or could be—just like "us." The Puerto Ricans in these movies are (more or less) white and (by and large) good kids—if, at times, good kids gone bad. These movies were part of a larger liberal attempt to build support for the idea that Puerto Ricans were assimilable; such popular culture (and journalistic and academic) attempts existed side by side with intense attacks on Puerto Ricans as representing an "invasion" and more pointed McCarthyite repression of the Puerto Rican left (Briggs 171, 173). What neither movie chose to show is that Puerto Ricans were not coming to

New York as rural innocents with "arms open"—as Anita sings in *West Side Story*'s "America." Writing just after the peak years of the Puerto Rican migration, Elena Padilla suggested, somewhat subversively, that for "those who leave the island, New York is a Puerto Rican frontier and not a foreign place" (24). In New York, Puerto Ricans improvised a new style of Puerto Ricanness that left virtually no element of their culture untouched—from language to music.

Puerto Rican music, for instance, developed rapidly on the mainland. Ruth Glasser has written convincingly of how Puerto Rican music "came into its own in the context of the migration experience." Puerto Rican music on the island was, as Glasser explains, seriously undeveloped (92, 131). Whereas musicians on the island before the great exodus were coerced to give preference to the high culture "danza"—the national dance of Puerto Rico—musical migrants to New York operated in a much freer cultural environment: the "Puerto Rican songbook" was, as Cristóbal Díaz Ayala writes, "enlarged tremendously" by the migration (7). Puerto Rican musicians used this newfound freedom to produce "lower class" forms—particularly the *plena, seis,* and *aguinaldo* associated with rural life in Puerto Rico. Nuyorican musicians made music that very often thematized migration, just as it embodied, musically, the very migration that was often being lamented (Glasser 6–7, 78, 91–92).

If Nuyorican music was itself evidence of the success that Puerto Ricans were having as cultural agents in New York, it was also evidence of the hardships faced by so many transplanted Puerto Ricans. Some songs spoke in rather veiled terms of the pain of migration: most famously, Rafael Hernández's "Lamento Borincano"—written in New York in the late 1920s—told the story of a displaced *jíbaro,* or peasant, who feels lost in the city. While not specifically about migration to New York, "Lamento Borincano" became something of an unofficial anthem for Puerto Ricans outside the island. Numerous Nuyorican songs highlighted the surprisingly harsh realities of New York, as was the case with "Yo Vuelvo a mi Bohío" by El Jíbarito de Adjuntas (1951) which put things quite starkly: "I came to New York hoping to get ahead / But if it was bad back home, here it's worse" (quoted in Manuel 28; see also *Lamento Borincano*).

Lamentation developed into a major cultural stance for Nuyoricans beginning in the 1920s. From the depression-era musical contributions of Rafael Hernández, Canario, and so many others, through the journalistic and literary works of Jesús Colón (especially his cautionary sketch "Grandma, Please Don't Come") and Pedro Juan Soto after World War II, and up through the 1970s flowering of arts revolving around the Nuyorican Poets Café, Puerto Rican artists in New York have regularly produced bitter works describing what they found in the new city. Perhaps none was as dark as Pedro Pietri's book of poems, *Puerto Rican Obituary* (1973), which develops a nightmare vision of New York as a place of death and despair. In "The Last Game of the World Series" Pietri emphasizes the pointlessness of migration:

> you will land where you
> took off from all the time
> the only thing that changes
> is the picture postcard to fool you into believing
> that you are somewhere else (83).

Supporting the notion that New York is not a foreign place but rather a "frontier" of Puerto Rico, Pietri deploys this insight in the darkest manner imaginable. But coming to New York did present Puerto Ricans with a number of major changes. Victor Hernández Cruz has written that when his family flew from Puerto Rico to New York, they "did not so much arrive to a new land as manage to shoot like in a time machine to the next age over" (6).

The seismic changes wrought by Puerto Rican migration from the 1940s through the 1960s gave rise to an ongoing, often acrimonious, set of cultural discussions about what this population shift meant for the United States. Anthropologists like Oscar Lewis strove mightily to propose that migration was a root of Puerto Rican pathology and criminality (Briggs 200). By the late 1960s Puerto Rican cultural workers—the Young Lords party, the Nuyorican Poets, union leaders, and so on—would mount a major challenge to negative academic and journalistic depictions of their community. But much harder to combat was the romanticized vision of Puerto Rican life promoted by *West Side Story*.

Abie's Spanish Rose

How did American audiences come to be so prepared to embrace *West Side Story*'s melodramatic take on the Puerto Rican migration? One answer is tautological but true: they were prepared for it because they were prepared for it. American audiences had been embracing interracial (and interethnic) romance plots avidly for hundreds of years by this time. While the last state antimiscegenation laws were struck from the books by a United States Supreme Court decision not until 1967 (*Loving v. Virginia*) inhabitants of the American continent have been obsessively telling stories about these line-crossing encounters for much longer. Over the course of the some four hundred years that this plot device has been deployed—say roughly from the time of Pocahontas and John Rolfe in the early 1600s to the 2003 teen television drama *Skin* (he's Latino/she's Jewish)—it has proven to be remarkably flexible and useful. Whether spun as national redemption, racial horror, or ethnic comedy, American purveyors and consumers of popular culture have returned again and again to the idea that major social problems can be fruitfully investigated (and perhaps even solved) through the agency of the cross-the-tracks love story; the long-running television show *Buffy the Vampire Slayer* (1997–2003) created fascinating drama for years by redeploying this "story" as a sort of interspecies romance linking vampires (Angel, and then Spike) with the least likely love interest imaginable—the Vampire Slayer herself.

These stories have appeared in virtually every form of cultural production: literary fiction, country songs, poems, Broadway musicals, and Hollywood films have all hosted the plot. To call it one "plot"—as a singular noun—is, of course, quite misleading: interracial and interethnic romances (as well as interclass and interregion ones) have been too various across time and space to reduce them to a single master narrative. The intermarriage plot, in short, has been a convenient forum for hosting multiple discussions about American identity.

One thing that is clear is that such stories seem to be especially appealing to makers and users of American popular culture at times of heightened social stress regarding major demographic changes—particularly, but not limited to, those involving wars and their attendant population shifts. Just after the Revolutionary War, American writers turned increasingly to the story of Indian-white romantic meetings as, among other things, a way of inventing a new national identity (Sollors, *Beyond Ethnicity* 102–115). Similarly, in the decades following the Civil War, Americans turned again and again to stories about Northern men marrying Southern women. This helped white Americans to process the race issues that animated the war, and allowed them to understand it as a family affair: the broken families were then put back together by the romances across region (Silber).

A related effort was made after World War II, but this time the emphasis was on reconciling America with the non-white people it had either fought against during the war, or exploited as colonies during and soon after the war. A major contribution to this culture of reconciliation in the post–World War II era was made by popular country music singers who sang songs of interracial love between white American men and various women of color from around the world. Taken together the songs reveal a new world where white American men are lovers, not fighters, and where their potential sex partners can be found everywhere (Rubin). Without ever directly admitting the specter of *real world* power relations—that is, the emergence of the United States as an imperial agent—the songs present interracial mixture as a novelty that can be easily assimilated into the national culture.

Using the form of romantic melodrama, as Alberto Sandoval-Sánchez has written, was a "strategy of power to hide and soften the racist discourse" that actually existed in *West Side Story*'s moment ("*West Side Story*" 172). The dominant grammar of the Broadway musical did not, of course, allow for much "realism": the stage is a fantasy space where all conflict is ultimately resolved in the togetherness bow of the cast after the last number. Even given these genre-defining limitations, it is worth exploring how *West Side Story* envisioned postwar New York as a haunted lovers' playground, a place where ethnic enmity could interfere with the passions of young lovers, but where Puerto Ricans—Puerto Rican women especially—appear above all as willing Anglos-in-training. This crucially important revision of *Romeo and Juliet* offered American audiences an opportunity to experience a spectacular catharsis—the tears shed over dead teenagers that also featured so prominently in the teen-oriented music of the period ("Teen Angel," "Last Kiss," and so on)—without any real reckoning of how the mass migration of Puerto Ricans in the last decade or so had changed the city. Instead, the makers of *West Side Story* domesticated this unprecedented demographic and cultural shift by stitching it into an old story—the one about how love conquers all.

When a controversy broke out in western Massachusetts in late 1999 over a planned high school production of *West Side Story*—protesters took issue with what they saw as the many negative images of Puerto Ricans in the play—defenders of the musical, including the writer of the original book for the musical, Arthur Laurents, still appealed to its alleged power to heal ethnic rifts. Laurents had no patience for opponents of the production, calling them "slightly insane" and reminding them that all along *West Side Story* had been about the "fatal consequences . . . of blind ethnic hatred" (quoted in McNamara). Likewise, one teacher at the school summarized the main position taken by defenders of the play by noting that its "very theme is that love can triumph over racial hatred" (Penniman).

But it is important to historicize and contextualize the popular culture notion that the consummation of a single romantic relationship ("One Hand, One Heart," as *West Side Story* puts it) is such a powerful cultural event that it can act as the antidote to decades of interethnic and interracial tension. It is important to notice, for instance, that the intermarriage myth has been largely—although not exclusively—shaped by Jews interested in exploring narrative solutions to age-old divisions between Jews and Gentiles. The foundational text in this respect is the play *The Melting-Pot,* written by an English Jew, Israel Zangwill, and first performed on the American stage in 1908. This play proposed, among other things, that the sorts of ancient hatreds that drove Jews en masse from Russian oppression would take no root in the United States: here young lovers would teach their elders that their own personal relationships could act as a model for group relations writ large. In her review of *West Side Story,* Pauline Kael noticed that it was imperative to have few, if any, adults on the scene: it is necessary to "get rid of the parents," as she writes with much irony, because "America is a *young* country—and who wants to be bothered by the squabbles of older people?" (Williams 130).

Reenacting this intermarriage plot so popular in novels, films, and plays, has served as a kind of comforting activity for American producers and consumers; as Joyce Flynn has written of 19th-century plays about ethnic relations, the "recurring symbols and the finite range of plot strategies" used to explore these tensions are themselves an indication that the ritualistic function of these fictions is of much larger significance than their precise content (420). But these projections are *rituals* and not *reflections:* the popularity of these romantic plots has not correlated, necessarily, with increased tolerance or support for interracial or interethnic relationships. Intermarriage between Jews and non-Jews was relatively rare in the first few decades of the 20th century, for instance, but this did not stop filmmakers from producing what David Desser has described as "a remarkable number of films which focus on intermarriage" between non-Jewish men and Jewish women—such as the 1912 movie *Becky Gets a Husband* (393–394).

This strange collective dream reached one peak in its cultural history with the 1923 Broadway play and 1928 film *Abie's Irish Rose.* In this work, Jewish Abie and Irish Rosemary come together over the objection of their parents. Parental concern over the religious upbringing of future grandchildren is answered ingeniously with the advent of twins. What is most clear about these Jewish fantasies of unity is that whatever "most" Jews actually have thought about intermarriage over time, it has been satisfying to imagine the United States as a place where love relationships could act as the solution to whatever problems of assimilation and discrimination Jews might face.

Zangwill's *Melting-Pot* effectively set this pattern, as Werner Sollors has explained. What these dramas of line-crossing affection tell audiences, in effect, is that the "consent" implied by such relationships constitutes a de facto "abolition" of the "prejudices of descent." While these dramas tell us to care about Abie and Rosemary (or Tony and Maria, in the case of *West Side Story*), what is more significant about them is that they propose that "absolute fidelity to the beloved" be honored above all other social demands—be they familial, religious, or ethnic (Sollors, *Beyond* 72). The Jewish/non-Jewish romance was also a way to tame sensationalized fears about the relationship of Jewish men to non-Jewish women: in the first few decades of the 20th century, for instance, a major cultural effort was made, on various fronts, to explain why Jewish men were so overrepresented in the "white slavery" (i.e., enforced prostitution) business and what to do about it. Novels, films, and laws (most notably the Mann Act of 1910) addressed the "white slavery menace"—usually understood as the responsibility of Jewish and Chinese Americans—as a nightmare vision of interethnic and interracial horror. The "intermarriage art" suggested a more benign narrative of how Jews and non-Jews were meeting in the modern city. *Abie's Irish Rose* was simply one major entry in this ongoing cultural discussion.

From its earliest origins it is clear that *West Side Story* was understood by its original creative team—writer Arthur Laurents, choreographer and "conceptualist" Jerome Robbins, and composer Leonard Bernstein (all Jewish, all gay or bisexual)—as a modern revision of both *Romeo and Juliet* and *Abie's Irish Rose*. In his diary, Leonard Bernstein recalls getting a call in the late 1940s from Jerome Robbins, who —according to Bernstein—had a noble idea: "a modern version of *Romeo and Juliet* set in the slums at the coincidence of Easter-Passover celebrations." At this moment of community celebration, as Jews and Christians all celebrate liberation, new life, and so on, "feelings run high" (Garebian 30).

The ethnic genealogy of *West Side Story* is fascinating: while Jerome Robbins claimed late in his life that the idea for an updated *Romeo and Juliet* came to him when he was helping a friend prepare a reading of Shakespeare's play for an audition, Russ Tamblyn, who played Riff, suggests that earlier on Robbins had admitted that film actor Montgomery Clift had first given him the idea during a party on Fire Island (*West Side Story* DVD, disk 2; Greg Lawrence 125). (The sexual identities of Clift, Robbins, Bernstein, Laurents, and lyricist Stephen Sondheim—all gay, if not always admittedly so—raises interesting questions about how gay men in particular might have been attracted to the intermarriage plot as one way to process concerns about prohibited love relationships. Many gay and lesbian American creative artists in the 20th century—from Gertrude Stein in her 1909 book *Three Lives* to Todd Haynes with his ironic 2002 movie *Far from Heaven*—have promoted "interracial" as a stand-in for, or parallel to, "same-sex").

The creators of *West Side Story* began with a religious idea revolving around Jewish-Catholic relations: Robbins and Bernstein at first tried to keep the "two houses" story close to home and translate it into a more contemporary vernacular. Arthur Laurents was clear, as soon as he was

brought on board to write the "book" for the musical, that the concept
—being discussed with the title *East Side Story*—was tired: it reminded him, as he recounts in his memoir, of *Abie's Irish Rose* (Laurents 330). At bottom, the idea for *East Side Story* lacked the potential
for creative tension onstage: Broadway historian Ethan Mordden has
argued cogently that the problem with *East Side Story* was that "there
was no story there, for the Jewish East Side of memory had vanished
long before—and where today, in New York, was there a Jewish-Catholic hostility?" (239).

According to Laurents, the Jewish/Catholic idea died in the pool of
the Beverly Hills Hotel, where he and Bernstein were completing "tax-
paying projects." Writing in the *New York Herald* in 1957, Laurents
suggests that it was the ongoing tension in Los Angeles between Anglos and Mexicans that encouraged him to remap the action of the play
—to move it, in effect, from the Jewish Lower East Side to the Latino
Upper West Side (http://www.westsidestory.com/site/level2/archives/
bibliography/herald1.html). In other words, somewhere deep under-
neath the creation of *West Side Story* we can find the traces of the zoot
suit riots. As Laurents tells it, he pushed his colleagues to consider
mapping the *Romeo and Juliet* story on the "blacks and Puerto Ricans
in New York because this was the time of the appearance of teenage
gangs, and the problem of juvenile delinquency was very much in the
news" (in Sandoval-Sánchez, "*West Side Story*" 169).

West Side Story, onstage and in the movies, tells the simple story
of Maria and Tony, two young lovers kept apart by tribalism: she is
Puerto Rican and he is white and they will not be allowed by their
respective tribes to come together. As Doc, the grizzled Jewish owner
of the musical's candy store, tells the assembled gang members, "You
make this world lousy." Maria was brought to Manhattan, presumably,
to marry Chino; Chino is played by one of the few actual Puerto Ricans
in the cast and comes off as something of a sad sack. Maria is not interested in Chino and instead falls for Tony—a former Jet who is trying to
go straight by working in Doc's candy store. Tony's obvious interest in
Maria leads Maria's brother Bernardo, leader of the Sharks, to challenge
the Jets to a rumble. Confused violence ensues and ends with Riff, Bernardo, and Tony all dead. The Jets and Sharks seem to unite over the
bodies of their fallen comrades, but it is too late for Maria and Tony—

he is dead and Maria's identity has been spoiled. She now is filled, as she says, with enough hate to kill too.

The Lasting Significance of *West Side Story*

Ultimately *West Side Story* is a not very novel update on the *Romeo and Juliet* legend. What remains very interesting about the musical is how it cornered the market on representing the huge migration of Puerto Ricans from the island to the continent in the years surrounding World War II, displacing virtually all other representations, and how it worked, in particular, to create a distinct *ethnic* identity for Puerto Ricans. Playwright Arthur Laurents may have wanted to turn *East Side Story* into a meditation on Puerto Rican and African American youths in New York, but somewhere along the line African Americans were dropped from the picture: their erasure is, perhaps, the single most important and lasting fact about *West Side Story*. Raquel Rivera has written that to ignore areas of "cultural overlap among African Americans, Puerto Ricans and other Caribbean people in New York City is to distort history, which results in the marginalization of some of the richest forms of contemporary urban creative expression (x). The hip-hop music that Rivera is interested in (and that will be discussed in chapter 5) is one major product of that "overlap."

It is not as if the makers of *West Side Story* were especially well situated to write about Puerto Ricans: lyricist Stephen Sondheim could have been speaking for all his collaborators when he said of his role in the production, "I've never been that poor and I've never *known* a Puerto Rican" (quoted in Garebian 37). But of course personal biography is not predictive of creative imagination. What is telling about the creators of *West Side Story* is how careful they were to sidestep the realities of Puerto Rican migration to New York City: above all, their play worked to erase the web of relations that connected Puerto Ricans, Euro-Americans, and African Americans in New York and offered instead a simple and more familiar "white and ethnic" equation. In doing so they kept *West Side Story* within the boundaries of the familiar interethnic/interracial romantic melodrama, thereby making at least an

implicit argument that Puerto Ricans should be understood as no different from the earlier immigrant groups (Jews above all) that the creators of the show were most familiar with. There is much evidence to
suggest that the liberal creators of *West Side Story* understood their
efforts as a "gift" they were giving to Puerto Ricans *as* Jews. (That
West Side Story could function in a particularly "Jewish" way is borne
out by the fact that when Jerome Robbins was searching for a way to
get his original Broadway cast to "feel" their roles more deeply, he separated them into "Jews" and "Nazis" to help them work up the proper
feelings of hatred. Which only begs the question of whether the Jets or
the Sharks got to be the "Jews" [Laurents 358]).

   West Side Story continues to matter because of what it says about
Puerto Rican migration to the continental United States and for what
it does not say. Ramón Grosfoguel has argued that the film version of
West Side Story is emblematic of a moment when Puerto Ricans were
coming into high visibility in American culture as a distinctly racialized Other, "no longer to be confused with blacks or Chicanos" (164–
165). This was, by and large, a negative public identity: joined now
with the Chicano "greasers" of the zoot suit era were the Puerto Rican
"spics" of the East Coast (Bender xiv, 9).

   West Side Story made Puerto Ricans *available* to other Americans as
an ethnic "type"—not strictly as Latin spitfires (women) or Latin lovers (men) or *bandidos* anymore (Rodríguez)—but as a kind of doomed,
tragicomic presence haunting the "assumed coherent and monolithic
identity of the Anglo-American subject" (Sandoval-Sánchez, "*West
Side Story*"167). Puerto Rican writer Judith Ortiz Cofer recalls being
in graduate school at Oxford University and getting on a bus with a
young man who gets down on his knees and "with both hands over his
heart" breaks into "an Irish tenor's rendition" of the song "Maria"
from *West Side Story*. This reminds Cofer that "you can leave the Island, master the English language, and travel as far as you can, but if
you are a Latina, especially one . . . who so obviously belongs to Rita
Moreno's gene pool, the Island travels with you" (Cofer 148). Scholar
Albert Sandoval-Sánchez recalls similarly that he has frequently been
serenaded with versions of "Maria" that go "Alberto, I've just met a
guy named Alberto" ("*West Side Story*"164). Absurd and sophomoric
on the face of it, these narratives remind us that *West Side Story*—espe-

cially the film version—has exerted a considerable amount of influence on how Euro-Americans think about Puerto Ricans. More specifically, such performances remind Puerto Ricans that they exist for many white Americans mostly as bits of mildly stimulating, if ultimately irrelevant, ethnic fantasies. The powerful cultural agents who created *West Side Story* took young Puerto Ricans—perceived in their time as a fairly serious threat to the proper functioning of American culture—and incorporated them into a familiar story of ethnic succession.

This was, to many observers in its initial moment, an optimistic cultural vision. Few observers in the years of the musical and the movie of *West Side Story* found much to object about it. To many people it seemed like a fairly radical attempt to promote the important idea that Puerto Ricans have feelings, too. Supreme Court Justice Felix Frankfurter, for one, was supposedly so taken with the "brotherhood" message of the ending that he told composer Leonard Bernstein that the "history of America is now changed" (Garebian 123); at least one Puerto Rican newspaper, *El Mundo,* praised the musical for the "positive representations of Puerto Rican immigrants in New York City" (Sandoval-Sánchez, *José* 77). In its first heyday (1957–60), *West Side Story* seems to have sparked only one mini-controversy and that was over one line in the song "America" that referred to Puerto Rico as an island of "tropical diseases." The Puerto Rican newspaper *La Prensa* threatened to picket the show when it reached New York after its out-of-town tryouts if that phrase were not removed. Three days later, a doctor named Howard A. Rusk published an article in the *New York Times* that noted that in the previous month there had been in Puerto Rico "no cases of cholera, dengue, fiariasis, typhus, or yellow fever, and only one new case of leprosy." Dr. Rusk goes on to note that "Puerto Rico is a healthy island" and suggests that it would be great if New York City "could find as effective measures to control our social blight of juvenile delinquency as Puerto Rico, island of tropical breezes, has found in controlling its 'tropical diseases'" (Garebian 122, 138).

While Rusk raises the specter of *real* juvenile delinquency only to score an analogy point against the *alleged* tropical diseases of Puerto Rico, *West Side Story* makes no such effort to erect a barrier between "Puerto Rico" and "blight." What the musical play and movie do, in effect, is to reinterpret Puerto Rican migration to New York as a youth invasion: Alberto Sandoval-Sánchez has written that the film depicts the way that Puerto Ricans were seen to have upset the "spatial order" held dear by Anglo-Americans in New York City—the "turf" so fiercely protected by the Jets (*"West Side Story"*167). It seems important to clarify Sandoval-Sánchez's important insight by adding that it is *young* Puerto Ricans who have launched this "attack" on the neighborhoods of New York: while Anglo-American authority at least gets *some* representation through a few adult characters, *West Side Story* does not allow a single Puerto Rican "grown-up" to appear onscreen. What *West Side Story* accomplished, above all, was to install "Puerto Rican" in the American cultural imaginary as a synonym for "dangerous youth." *West Side Story* emerges as a split image: while its romantic plot promises that Puerto Ricans will take a comfortable place in the culture, the gang story hints at a more troubling possibility—that Puerto Rican migration represented an assault on the "Americans" of New York City.

"A Spic Tried to Jap Us"

The two gangs of New York in *West Side Story* have surface similarities but it is their differences that ultimately tell the major story. It is the mixed-white Jets who serenade a police officer with a song that includes the line "I'm depraved on account I'm deprived," but it is the Puerto Rican youth who, as the song puts it, appear "sociologically sick." The Jets, by and large, seem unthreatening. With the major exception of their attempted rape of Anita in Doc's candy store, more often the Jets seem like the kind of lovably misbehaving teens that Paul Lynde sang about ("what's the matter with kids, today?") in the 1960 musical *Bye, Bye Birdie*. While the "Jet Song," performed early on in the musical, at least allows audiences to indulge in the fantasy that the white gang functions something like a family, the Sharks get no similar number. Flashing switchblades, looking ominously sexual in their bright, richly-colored clothes, the Sharks operate as a marker of unrestrained youth in the modern city.

The musical's interest in "deviant" Puerto Ricans was overdetermined, to say the least. To begin, the Puerto Rican migration to New York City, which reached its peak in the early 1950s, coincided with a large national project having to do with "juvenile delinquency" (Pérez 148). From social science tracts to Senate hearings on the evils of comic books and numerous movies about "wild" youth (*Blackboard Jungle, Rebel without a Cause, The Wild One,* and so on), a generalized sentiment had developed in United States culture that fighting World War II overseas had left a mess on the homefront. The rioting teenagers of *Blackboard Jungle* and the apron-wearing father of *Rebel without a Cause* (both from 1955) were two sides of the same coin: sending American men off to fight the war and encouraging American women to work outside the home had, many commentators believed, distorted American gender roles and undercut parental authority.

Early sociological works on Puerto Rican migration to New York—as with sociological writing about virtually *every* immigrant group to the United States—claimed these culturewide problems were exacerbated by the pressures of acculturation. Writing in a 1950 sociological study of Puerto Ricans in New York, C. Wright Mills and his coauthors described how Puerto Rican children who learned English now held a "whip hand over the parents who speak only Spanish, or speak English brokenly" (98). A little over a decade later, Nathan Glazer and Daniel Moynihan surveyed the same landscape and charged, in an ideologically complex statement, that migrant parents in New York City often claimed to have been told that "the government prevents disciplining of children." Rather than accept what these Puerto Rican subjects explained, Glazer and Moynihan instead argued that this was likely a "rationalization" to explain their own parental shortcomings in the face of the challenges of acculturation (124). The key figure between Mills, on the one hand, and Glazer and Moynihan, on the other, is, indisputably, Oscar Lewis: Lewis did incredible damage in his many works on the "culture of poverty," in which he "sympathetically" portrayed the "plight" of Puerto Ricans in New York.

The Puerto Rican migrant population in New York City *was* remarkably young: in 1950 the median age of Puerto Ricans in New York was twenty-five, as compared to thirty-five for all other New Yorkers (Pérez 145). But it was not a foregone conclusion that non–Puerto Ricans would interpret the Puerto Rican migration as a youth "problem." In fact, in one of the first instances of extended media coverage of the migration, a *Life* magazine photo-essay of 1947 (titled "Puerto Rican Migrants Jam New York"), the dominant image was of a large, extended family together in a small space with a caption that told of a father who "makes a home for wife, seven children and mother-in-law" (Kozol 138).

But as the 1950s unfolded—and particularly toward the latter end of the decade—the interest in Puerto Ricans took a decidedly "pathological" turn. Richie Pérez and others have documented how the "failings" of Puerto Ricans became a common sociological topic in the 1950s (146–147). This mainstream interest in Puerto Ricans climaxed midway between the Broadway (1957) and film (1961) versions of *West Side Story* in 1959 with the infamous "Capeman" murders. (The Capeman would later get his own musical in 1998 thanks to another Jewish composer, Paul Simon.) In short, Puerto Ricans moved into American popular culture as delinquents.

The "Capeman" murders represented a "West Side Story" even more brutal than that choreographed by Jerome Robbins. In August 1959, Salvador Agrón—a sixteen-year-old who had been in a home for troubled youth by age ten—was arrested for the murder of two white youths in a West Side park. Agrón wore a cape while committing the murders (in *West Side Story*'s neighborhood, at 45th and 46th Streets between 9th and 10th Avenues) and showed no remorse for the crimes: he famously allowed himself to be quoted as saying "I don't care if I burn" (http://www.thesmokinggun.com/capeman/capeman.html).

Agrón, who seems to have been of diminished intellectual capabilities, was a member of the Vampires, a well-known Puerto Rican gang in New York. The Vampires were imaged by the press and in popular gossip as "deviant" in a number of ways: these "Spanish" boys were, according to most accounts, ruthless, out of control, and perhaps gay (Schneider 7). In their name alone, as Eric Schneider has pointed out, the Vampires appeared as "alien" and "predatory"; journalists covering the case could assume that their audience was more or less prepared (by *West Side Story,* above all), to understand Puerto Ricans as less than desirable migrants in New York (Schneider 8). As with the media coverage of the zoot-suiters just over ten years earlier, a general consensus developed that these juvenile delinquents were somehow more dangerous than the native-born white kind. After many official attempts to "rehabilitate" him through the network of social service agencies in New York failed, Agrón's mother briefly sent him back to Puerto Rico to live with her sister. Originally sentenced to death, Agrón had his sentence commuted by New York governor Nelson Rockefeller.

For many observers the Capeman murders represented clear evidence that Puerto Rican migration was best understood as a dangerous youth invasion. In response, some politicians called for at least a temporary cessation of Puerto Rican migration. What is particularly poignant about the timing of Agrón's crime is that it came during a major movement that saw many Puerto Rican "fighting" gangs going "social." Going "social" was a crucial process whereby a group of marginal teenagers, who previously had established themselves through physical turf battles, tried to reconstruct their collective and individual identity in a more positive, peaceful, and ultimately more powerful way. Earlier generations of young Irish, Italian, and Jewish Americans had converted fighting gangs into adult "gangs": these adult gangs often played an important role in solidifying the urban political power of the group in question (Wakefield 128). By 1959 Puerto Rican youth gangs had only begun to explore how "going social" might improve their standing in the city at large.

Studying Puerto Rican life in New York in the 1950s, journalist Dan Wakefield discovered that some teenage gangs were attempting to go legitimate. Wakefield was amazed to discover that one of these gangs, living "in a world of poverty and violence" had "given up fighting and 'gone social'": these young men called themselves the Conservatives (117). The Conservatives established stringent rules for group inclusion: members either had to be in school or working regularly, for instance. Among other activities, the Conservatives sponsored a singing group of their own, called the Persuaders. From their origins in a feared fighting gang called the Enchanters, the Conservatives became an important progressive force in the Puerto Rican community in New York—the kind of grassroots organization that a decade later would lead many young people into civil rights activity (Wakefield 124–125, 134, 139). A year before Wakefield published his book on Puerto Rican life in New York, Elena Padilla published a more strictly ethnographic study of Puerto Ricans in New York titled *Up from Puerto Rico*. In this work Padilla made clear that "gang" was a broad rubric that for years had been applied to a wide variety of social institutions; "social" gangs were an important community institution with, as Padilla put it, "ramifications and membership all over the city" (226). It is Padilla's work that makes it more possible to understand how these gang members would, commonly, transform themselves into revolutionary Puerto Rican activists (Schneider 222–223).

But the stage and screen versions of *West Side Story* proved much more powerful than any competing popular contributions to the conversation. Journalistic and academic work such as that published by Dan Wakefield and Elena Padilla could not shake a developing consensus that Puerto Ricans represented a threat to municipal order in New York City. The Capeman murders confirmed what *West Side Story* had already proposed: that Puerto Rican youth were out of control, knife-wielding outlaws. The critical and commercial success of *West Side Story* (it won the Best Picture Academy Award for 1961) made it impossible, for instance, for another 1961 movie about Puerto Rican youth in New York, *The Young Savages,* to make much of an impact. Based on a fascinating 1959 novel by Evan Hunter (author of *The Blackboard Jungle* who later reinvented himself as popular crime novelist Ed McBain), *The Young Savages* strove for social realism where *West Side Story* chose romantic melodrama.

The Young Savages took the Capeman murders and flipped the script: here the murders are committed by three white youths, one of whom has diminished intellectual capabilities, wears a cape, and calls himself "Batman." The three white boys kill Roberto Escalante, a blind, harmonica-playing Puerto Rican youth who lives in Spanish Harlem. Two gangs, the white Thunderbirds and the Puerto Rican Horsemen, have been battling over turf for some time, but it is clear that the white gang is the aggressor: drawing from an actual race riot that took place in Detroit in 1943, *The Young Savages* depicts a moment of extreme cruelty committed by the Thunderbirds that has its origins in the unwitting desegregation of a swimming pool (see fig. 3.2).

What is perhaps most important about *The Young Savages* is that it represents Puerto Ricans as family-oriented people with actual inner lives. Zorro, the leader of the Horsemen, loves Picasso's art and feels a "Spanish" kinship with the artist; this insistence on "Spanishness," of course, again neatly erases the "blackness" of (some) Puerto Ricans.

Figure 3.2. *The Young Savages* tried to correct the romantic melodrama of *West Side Story* with a grittier realism

When prosecuting attorney Hank Bell visits Zorro's family, the layout of the family home seems to be modeled on the *Life* magazine spread of 1947. These Puerto Rican youth have families, speak Spanish regularly, and analyze their place on the American racial landscape with insight and passion.

Much of the movie, however, is taken up with the personal and professional turmoil of Hank Bell, who grew up in East Harlem himself and whose family used to have a longer Italian last name. The movie never takes sides exactly but makes it clear that the "city" is ruining the young people and not vice versa. This, in itself, represents a more or less "progressive" stance on Puerto Rican migrants in New York.

The white youth, on the contrary, seem much less dimensional. They claim self-defense as a motive (in the book version, one claims that "a spic tried to jap us" [Hunter 54]) and prove that Roberto Escalante was a pimp and major player in the Horsemen, but overall the white Thunderbirds lack the kind of complexity that Zorro embodies. Both

The Young Savages and the originary book argue in favor of the proposition that youth violence is merely a symptom of a "sick" society:
the district attorney in Hunter's book calls Puerto Ricans "the new
scapegoats, the new whipping posts for a neurotic society" (32). The
feeling here is not that youth, per se, are out of control, but that the
larger culture has lost its moorings—mostly because parents have become unable or unwilling to control their children. Even attorney Bell
knows nothing about his own adolescent daughter and is amazed to
discover, among other things, that she has begun dating and wearing
a bra.

West Side Story and *The Young Savages* reach some opposing conclusions about the "problem" of Puerto Rican youth in New York. Where
West Side Story traffics familiar stereotypes of hot-tempered and par-
entless Puerto Rican youth, *The Young Savages* at least opens up the
possibility that deviance had been, one way or another, imposed on
Puerto Ricans in New York. But ultimately both films support Dan
Wakefield's contemporaneous assertion that New York itself is somehow
to blame for any Puerto Rican "problem"; based on anecdotal evidence,
the journalist suggested that in Puerto Rico the "high school boy hangs
around after school to hear poetry readings. In New York City, the
Puerto Rican high school boy . . . is more likely to be found hanging
out with a gang in a candy store" (169). What neither film could manage to convey was that their Puerto Rican subjects—soon to be known
as Nuyoricans and Neoricans—were in New York for a reason; Puerto
Rican migration to New York was one fruit of a decades-long process of
social and political engineering overseen by the United States government and military, and American corporate interests. Both *West Side
Story* and *The Young Savages* present these new migrants to New York
as a "given"—fixtures on the scene. In doing so both films hid how
intensely they were invested in "naturalizing" the unprecedented population shift that had only just recently changed the culture and demography of New York.

The Young Savages and *West Side Story* drop viewers down into the
middle of a zero-sum game: constant new arrivals to the city have
turned New York into a walled-in, claustrophobic place in which geographic gains for one group must represent an absolute loss of ground

for some other group. The turf battles that structure the plotting of both *West Side Story* and *The Young Savages* hint at how Puerto Rican migration shaped post–World War II New York. *West Side Story* tells us that the Jets hang on to what little they have (Tony's relatively good job at Doc's candy store, the right to delimit which streets belong to them) primarily because their own immigrant parents—"tinhorn immigrant scum" in the words of Lieutenant Schrank –have proven so disappointing. But the Puerto Ricans are even "worse" to Schrank: calling them "cockroaches," Schrank denies them even the shred of humanity he allows the "boys" of the Jets to hang on to. *West Side Story* establishes this feeling with a long tracking shot that opens the film. Starting at the narrow southern end of the island and moving slowly north, the camera finds no open space. Before *West Side Story* introduces a single character the filmmakers have already established that the movie is about space—or the lack of it. The aerial view is rarely returned to in the movie: bizarrely, in an age when multistory housing projects were offered up as one "solution" to the problem of space in New York City and elsewhere, *West Side Story* shields our eyes from the "vertical." This horizontal bias makes it all the more striking when Action (a Jet gang member) finishes the song-and-dance number "Cool" by looking straight up and pretending to shoot a gun at the camera: the power dynamic implied by his upward glance (is he shooting at police, parents, viewers?) is one of the few moments when *West Side Story* allows meaningful social hierarchies to enter the picture.

The Young Savages alludes to the modern competition for space in a more oblique way. With an early shot of a wrecking ball destroying a decrepit apartment building, director John Frankenheimer offers up a visual reference to "urban renewal"—the complex process of city engineering and suburb-building that so altered New York and other major American cities in the 1950s and 1960s. The northward migration of African Americans and Puerto Ricans in the World War II era had already, as Eric Schneider notes, "set up a bitter contest for residential space, jobs, and resources" (28). Urban renewal intensified feelings of competition by shaking African Americans and Puerto Ricans out of their homes and into white, working-class neighborhoods where they were not usually welcomed with open arms (45).

"Nigger-Reecan Blues"

Perhaps the biggest change faced by Puerto Ricans coming to New York had to do with race: while *West Side Story* and *The Young Savages* tried to pretend that African American people did not exist, Puerto Ricans in New York quickly discovered that their own lives would now be tightly bound with those of black people—from street level realities (settlement patterns, political organizing) to rhetorical inventions. In fact, those two 1961 movies signal an important "last" moment in American popular culture history. It was no longer possible, by the middle of the 1960s or so, to pretend that Puerto Ricans were simply the newest "white ethnic" group to arrive in New York City. Their in-between racial status would become the occasion for much cultural discussion and the founding principle of much creative work. The central axis around which this conversation would resolve was the intersection of Puerto Ricans and African Americans: as Juan Flores has rightly explained, since at least the 1960s Puerto Rican life in New York "has been entwined with the social and cultural experiences of African Americans and with the problematics of Blackness" (163).

Nuyorican poet Willie Perdomo has made clear that the question of the "blackness" of Puerto Ricans has remained relevant well up through the 1990s. Writing in "Nigger-Reecan Blues" (1996), Perdomo's narrator (named also "Willie") laments:

I'm a Spic!
I'm a Nigger!
Spic! Spic! No different than a Nigger!
Neglected, rejected, oppressed and depressed
From banana boats to tenements
Street gangs to regiments . . .
Spic! Spic! I ain't nooooo different than a Nigger. (19–21)

Both *West Side Story* and *The Young Savages* construct a firm barrier between Puerto Ricans and African Americans (and of course between Puerto Ricans and Anglos), mostly by pretending that African Americans did not exist in New York. While *The Young Savages* has the nerve at least to situate itself in Harlem—with at least a few hints that black folks might be nearby—*West Side Story*'s fantasy of reunification requires that African Americans be "disappeared" from the screen. Avoiding East Harlem as a setting was one easy way for the musical to retain at least a modest amount of "realism."

But the acculturation of Puerto Ricans in New York has, from at least the time of the initial U.S. colonization of the island, been largely defined by their own sense of "racialness" as well as by the "common-sense" concepts of race foisted upon them. World War I was a particularly complicated time for the Puerto Rican race question. Among other "problems," Puerto Rican soldiers often refused to "designate themselves as black or white in ways familiar to those from the United States" (Briggs 61). American debates over the political status of the island, as Laura Briggs argues cogently, have usually pivoted on the question of whether Puerto Ricans are mostly Spanish (and thus racially prepared for independence) or mostly black (and thus in need of U.S. intervention).

It is important to note that the case of Puerto Ricans in New York demonstrates in a number of clear ways that whiteness pays many wages (Roediger, *Wages*). Writing during the peak years of the migration (the 1950s), C. Wright Mills and his coauthors noted that those "Puerto Ricans who can prove they are pure white often make a point of doing so" (7). A decade later, Elena Padilla confirmed that "whiteness continues to be regarded as an important social attribute"; Padilla speculated further that it was more recent migrants who feared most "being associated with Negroes" (81).

Puerto Ricans coming to New York were confusing to the host culture. As Joseph Montserrat explains, Puerto Ricans landing in New York were already an "integrated" group and it was not clear how they would choose—or be allowed—to affiliate racially (in Wagenheim and Jiménez de Wagenheim 318). As sociologists observed early on, many Puerto Ricans attempted to establish themselves as white people. But for those too "dark to pass" (as one of the Jets jokingly says of Rita Moreno's Anita as she attempts to walk by) it could become attractive to maintain an aspect of "foreignness"—primarily through speaking Spanish—as a way of marking off the boundary between Puerto Ricans and African Americans. Aware that they were moving into a world in which African Americans had numerous restrictions placed upon them, many Puerto Ricans worked to construct "Spanish" as their primary category of identity (Mills et al. 87; Schneider 41). At least one sociological report suggested that "some American Negroes in Harlem are attempting to learn Spanish" as a way of improving their own status (Mills et al. 133).

The processes of identification and disidentification that locked Puerto Ricans and African Americans into a complicated dance worked in myriad and unpredictable ways. Among the first of the Puerto Rican migrants to establish themselves as a visible (and audible) presence in New York City were island-based musicians drafted to serve in World War I army regiments who then settled permanently in New York. For these musicians, often brass and reed players in jazz bands and veterans of the army, living as black men in New York offered them a "new and potent identity," one that often resulted in increased work opportunities (Glasser 53). Certainly the invention and elaboration of Afro-Latin jazz in the post–World War II era was rooted in a widely shared idea that African Americans, Cubans, and Puerto Ricans shared some kind of Afro-diasporic commonality.

But the question of racial identity in the labor context could cut both ways. Jesús Colón, in his collection of sketches *A Puerto Rican in New York,* recounts applying for a job as a translator for the text cards for silent movies to be shown in Latin America. After a promising written correspondence, Colón is met at his job interview by a man with "a cold and impersonal attitude" who curtly explains to Colón why he cannot have the job even though the sample translation he did was flawless: "I thought you were white" (49–50). Decades later, when writer Piri Thomas tried to argue with a bus driver in the South that he was Puerto Rican and not "colored," the driver tells him "I don't care what kinda nigger you are. . . . Get your ass in the back or get off this damned bus" (in Torres and Velázquez 275).

From at least the time of World War I up to the present moment, Puerto Ricans have been forced to navigate the treacherous waters of race—and racial indeterminacy—in the United States. Puerto Ricans on the island may well have been living in a context that allowed for more flexible definitions of "race" than would be true of the mainland culture they were joining in such large numbers. In New York, often living on the margins of African American ghettos, or being pushed by "urban renewal" *with* African Americans into the same white, work-ing-class neighborhoods, Puerto Ricans have confronted again and again a requirement that they choose racial sides (Schneider 40, 45). Numerous memoirs and other accounts make it clear that information about how to make that choice was very often complex. Writing about her family's post–Operation Bootstrap move to New York City, Esmer-alda Santiago describes walking down the halls of her New York City high school between the Italian Americans and African Americans— looking like a "combination of both" but not fitting in with either group (230). Santiago's mother had already armed her with a formula for understanding race and ethnicity in New York that basically boiled down to throwing in with Italian Americans because African Ameri-cans hated Puerto Ricans on the grounds of labor competition (225).

Many other commentators have suggested ways that Puerto Ricans and African Americans came to be mutually defining, in a social sense. Judith Ortiz Cofer, for one, remembers that "the hierarchy for popular-ity" in her high school years in the 1950s went "pretty white girl, pretty Jewish girl, pretty Puerto Rican girl, pretty black girl." Ronnie Spector, born Veronica Bennett, child of one black parent and one white one, was also coming of age during the years of the great Puerto Rican migration; she would go on to be leader of the popular girl group, the Ronettes. Spector remembers that Puerto Rican girls set the fashion standard that the Ronettes would ultimately try to emulate: "If we copied anything, it was the look of the girls we'd see on the streets of Spanish Harlem" (Cofer 143; Spector 43).

West Side Story and *The Young Savages* offer compelling evidence of how the culture industries articulated the separation of Puerto Ricans from African Americans. The career of Rita Moreno herself in the 1950s offers another bit of testimony on this front. Even before *West Side Story* Moreno had found a niche in Hollywood (in eighteen movies) as a sort of all-purpose "of color, but not Black" player. Moreno appeared in these years as a Filipina, a Cajun, an Asian princess, an Arab, and at least three different Native Americans (Suntree 44–45, 47, 56; *West Side Story* DVD, disk 2). One story told by Moreno's casting from the early 1950s on is that a Puerto Rican woman could "look like" or "be-come" many people on screen—as long as none of them was black.

By the 1970s Moreno herself had become aware—and quite critical

—of how she had been used as a visual and aural shorthand for all things "ethnic": she laments having always been cast as the "Indian maiden" who "knew where the gold was hidden" and said things like "Ju no love Ula no more?" (Williams 158). Moreno later felt able to gain revenge for having had her in-between racial status exploited in this manner by creating a caricature of this "type"—a character named Googie Gomez, for Terence McNally's 1975 Broadway play *The Ritz* (later a film): according to Moreno, by "playing Googie, I'm thumbing my nose at all those Hollywood writers responsible for lines like 'Yankee peeg, you rape my seester, I keel you!'" (Suntree 81–82).

The popular music of the mid-1950s up through the 1960s provides a fascinating forum for examining how fully Puerto Rican and African American cultures interpenetrated each other. No matter how hard *West Side Story* tried to pretend that firm boundaries separated African Americans from Puerto Ricans, the musical culture of the 1950s and 1960s demonstrates that such attempts were doomed—wonderfully and productively doomed. If an index were created, for instance, to track the actual meetings (and the less concrete meetings in the realm of "influence") of Puerto Ricans and African Americans in vocal group music in these years, the number of cross-references would be staggering. Perhaps most famously, Frankie Lymon's group, the Teenagers, brought together African Americans and Puerto Ricans who met in upper Manhattan to create a music that "crossed over" to find a large audience among white teenagers; the utopian possibilities of this racial crossover should not, of course, obscure the fact that rock and roll disc jockey and promoter Alan Freed had his weekly television show canceled in the mid-1950s after a camera found Lymon dancing with a white girl (Warner 242).

Just as censorship could not, ultimately, tame the stark ethnic dramas told by the gangsters, neither could it stem the tide of African American–Puerto Rican crossover in what later came to be known as "doo-wop" music. The Crests, based on the Lower East Side of Manhattan (now a major area of Puerto Rican settlement), brought together African Americans, Puerto Ricans, and Italian Americans. Their first minor hit, "My Juanita," served to call attention, in a limited way at least, to their Latino membership. From here the Crests became a straight-ahead "teen dream" vocal group: their biggest hit came in 1958 with

"Sixteen Candles"—a teen-oriented rewrite of a song originally titled "21 Candles" (Warner 128–130). The Eternals, another mixed group, also utilized "Latin" stylings in their few releases; in this case they drew more from the Cuban mambo craze of the 1950s than any particularly Puerto Rican sources (http://www.electricearl.com/dws/eternals.html).

Even more significant than any direct Puerto Rican influence in the youth music of the era is the fact that so much early rock and roll was infused with what John Storm Roberts—after Jelly Roll Morton—has called "the Latin tinge"; the black vocal group, the Gladiolas, for instance, had a strong "Latin" sound in their 1957 song "Little Darlin'," which would turn out to be a huge hit for a white group, the Diamonds (Runowicz). Jewish songwriters and producers Jerry Leiber and Mike Stoller quite regularly incorporated "Latin sounds" into their work with the Drifters; Stoller himself claims to have joined a pachuco social club during his teen years in Los Angeles. When Ben E. King left the Drifters, it was Leiber who cowrote his first hit "Spanish Harlem"— about a beautiful Latina with eyes "dark as coal."

Another less well-noted moment of "crossover" in the world of popular music came with the late 1950s marriage of white Texan rocker Buddy Holly to Maria Elena Santiago, a Puerto Rican woman who worked at Peer-Southern, his music publishing company. Contrary to Holly's widely circulated image as a simple country boy in the city, Santiago has recalled that the Texan was something of a bohemian, who especially wanted to settle in Greenwich Village and who went with her frequently to jazz clubs such as the Village Gate to hear cutting-edge African American musicians. Living in New York at just the moment that *West Side Story* set its tale of doomed "crossover," Holly and Santiago seem to have managed quite well and do not seem to have faced much social ostracism (except for some reservations on the part of his mother). The lessons that American fans might have taken from Holly's cosmopolitanism were lost, however, in the melodramatic moment of his death: Holly died soon after marrying, in a plane crash near Clear Lake, Iowa (Amburn 149, 154, 202, 206).

The relationship of Holly and Santiago is just one small indication of how Puerto Ricans were moving into the mainstream of New York culture—a mainstream that was in the process of being redefined by African Americans *and* Puerto Ricans in the late 1950s and 1960s. In opposition to the Broadway/Hollywood vision of racial/ethnic segregation promoted in those years, the cultural spheres of music and dance told a different story—one about healthy hybridity. Perhaps the best evidence of the unofficial and usually unspoken black–Puerto Rican alliance came with the rise of "boogaloo"—a dance *and* a style of music —that rose to popularity in the middle of the 1960s. Taking its name from a novelty hit of that name by Tom and Jerrio, an African American duo, "boogaloo" was, as Juan Flores has so ably described, the first "Nuyorican" music (82; Kempton 385). Sandwiched between the popularity of Cuban mambo in the 1950s and the salsa boom of the later 1960s and early 1970s, boogaloo (sometimes called Latin bugalú) captured a large audience in New York from around 1966 to 1968 (Flores 80).

Flores explains that the sounds of boogaloo "attest to the guiding, exemplary role of African American culture and politics for that generation of Puerto Ricans growing up in New York" (82). Boogaloo, in short, is the meeting of Puerto Ricans and African Americans that *West Side Story* and *The Young Savages* could not suppress: as ethnomusicologist John Storm Roberts describes it, boogaloo did not "simply imitate black music, but incorporated it into a sound that fused Latin rhythms and piano montunos with rhythm-and-blues and even jazz" (167). Many of the central players in boogaloo's creation had come up in the vocal group music of the 1950s (Flores 88) and the novelty-song edge of that genre shows: the music had a "slightly zany, good humored . . . sound with as much Cuban as black gospel flavor" (Roberts 167).

What is particularly fascinating about boogaloo is that as much as it was shaped by African American popular music stylings it, in turn, exerted a major influence on later African American productions. Once popularized by Puerto Rican musicians such as Joe Bataan, Joe Cuba, and Johnny Colon, the "boogaloo" found its way into the center of African American popular music. Joe Bataan himself was not Puerto Rican: as he explained, "My father was Filipino and my mother was African American, and my culture was Puerto Rican" (Rivera 35).

In 1967, an African American soul singer known as "the Fantastic Johnny C" combined two dances—the boogaloo and the "funky Broadway"—and came out with a major hit, "Boogaloo Down Broadway"; one year later James Brown included the boogaloo in a roll call of dances he listed in "There Was a Time" (Kempton 386). Among other things, Puerto Ricans were, in this moment, helping to reframe the concept of "crossover" altogether: it was becoming more and more difficult to separate out strands of popular culture to identify them by race or national origin. Journalist Tom Smucker has traced out the implications of this cultural shift in an article on a singer named India, a Puerto Rican woman who grew up in the South Bronx listening to "English" music, who later "crossed over" to make salsa music. As Smucker concludes, there are no "sides" to India's career: just a long walk down "Main Street" in Manhattan.

Puerto Rican–African American connections were hardly limited to popular music. As James Smethurst has recently demonstrated, many of the Puerto Rican writers who would come to define the "Nuyorican" literature of the 1970s were "closely associated" with members of the Black Arts movement—a loose band of African American cultural and political activists—in New York City. Victor Hernández Cruz and Miguel Algarín, among others, were heavily influenced by ideas about nationalism, language, and music that were first developed by Black Arts essayists and poets (Smethurst). The self-described "Nuyoricans" would consistently and powerfully insist that their identities were intricately tied up with vanguard African Americans.

What is perhaps most exhilarating to notice about this Nuyorican linkage of Puerto Ricans and African Americans is how powerfully it countered the generation of social scientists, popular culture figures, and politicians who had insisted that the major link between the two New York City groups was as marginalized denizens of a "culture of poverty." From Oscar Handlin's insistence on the deviant families of African Americans and Puerto Ricans, to Oscar Lewis's extrapolation of Puerto Rican life based largely on the testimony of prostitutes, a consensus was developing around the putative "pathology" of African American and Puerto Rican families (Briggs 163, 175). The Young Lords party, the Nuyorican poets, and the stars of boogaloo music had a different tale to tell about what connections should be made between Puerto Ricans and African Americans in New York.

This connection is underlined wonderfully in Aretha Franklin's 1971 hit cover of Ben E. King's 1961 song, "Spanish Harlem." King's original was released on his first solo album after leaving the Drifters, which was full of "Spanish" songs from "Besame Mucho" to "Perfidia." King's "Spanish Harlem"—written by Jerry Leiber with Phil Spector—came out the same year as the film version of *West Side Story*. It has a light "Latin" sound to it—you can almost hear the castanets in the background, but not quite—and aims for the authenticity *West Side Story* repudiated by situating itself in an actual Latino neighborhood. But in all other respects, "Spanish Harlem" belongs to a tradition of exoticizing "cross-the-tracks" narratives discussed at the beginning of this chapter: the love object here is another dark-eyed beauty who will be plucked from her homeplace and replanted in a new "garden." (Spector himself had married Veronica Bennett in 1968 and, according to many reports, abusively controlled her inside their Southern California home.) The narrative clarity, such as it is, gets lost in Aretha Franklin's version. What Franklin's cover emphasizes instead is a set of backup singers rejoicing in a lyrical change: "A rose in black *and* Spanish Harlem." While the denotative meaning never comes completely clear, Franklin's version of "Spanish Harlem" offers, on the level of musical and lyrical affect, the unambiguous message that African Americans and Puerto Ricans are joined in New York by the beauty of their creations.

From the Nuyorican moment on, it would no longer be possible to conceive of New York as neatly divided by geography, race, or ethnicity. African Americans and Puerto Ricans had, by now, redrawn the map of New York. While still shamefully underrepresented on the musical stage, they had taken over New York's Main Street with their "Boogaloo Down Broadway."

Coda: Wild or Innocent?

From the late 1950s through the 1970s, Puerto Ricans very successfully chipped away at cultural norms described and prescribed by *West Side Story* and other creative works, urban sociologies, and so on. Writers, poets, musicians, political activists (especially those associated with the Young Lords Party), and the graffiti artists leaving their mark all over New York City—another important African American/Puerto Rican nexus—were insisting that the days of *West Side Story*'s dominion had come to an end. No longer would white fantasies about Puerto Rican life be allowed to proliferate without challenge—as the Broadway musical and film of *West Side Story* had. A flowering of Puerto Rican arts and politics that ranged from youth political organizing to Piri Thomas's memoir *Down These Mean Streets* (with its in-depth consideration of the blackness of Puerto Ricans) through the rise of salsa music in New York challenged the power of *West Side Story* and related representations.

This does not mean that white people (and white ethnics) would stop making artistic arguments about the Puerto Rican migration to New York City; the range of those representations are efficiently indexed in two works of popular art of 1973. The movie *Badge 373*, directed by Howard Koch and scripted by New York journalist Pete Hamill, and Bruce Springsteen's second record, *The Wild, the Innocent, and the E Street Shuffle*, seem particularly revealing in this context. *Badge 373* and *The Wild, the Innocent, and the E Street Shuffle* are obsessed with Puerto Ricans in New York, but whereas *Badge 373* offers up a nightmare vision of bad (white) cops and worse (black and Puerto Rican) criminals, the Springsteen album offers up a vibrant ode to the Afro–Puerto Rican "makeover" of New York City.

Badge 373 is a dark and ugly movie, the creation of a strange combination of Hollywood and New York Irish, Italian, and Jewish Americans. The film stars Robert Duvall and includes a cameo appearance by Felipe Luciano, a member of the Puerto Rican Young Lords Party who had been heavily involved with Black Arts projects in New York. Duvall plays Eddie Egan, a rogue cop in New York who had already been the subject of another Hollywood feature, *The French Connection* (1971). As Richie Pérez has noted, *Badge 373* "criminalizes" the Puerto Rican political movement in New York (157), but that is only in the process of criminalizing all Puerto Ricans in New York—from police officers on down.

The movie, at bottom, wants to depict New York as a city ruined by African Americans and Puerto Ricans. It begins in an "innocent" looking, multiracial salsa club, where Egan has gone undercover "as" a Puerto Rican (wearing a wig and mustache). The club turns out to be a den of iniquity: Egan chases a suspect out after the planned bust goes wrong and corners him on a rooftop. After taunting the Puerto Rican man, Chico, by suggesting that he was probably raped by a "spade" while in prison the last time, Egan then pushes him off the roof to his death. This dark fantasy of another kind of Afro-Puerto Rican connection (the alleged sexual attack) is emblematic of *Badge 373:* the movie imagines a wrecked New York, a place where African Americans lounge idiotically in stairwells, while Puerto Ricans commit all manner of mayhem. Its "white cop ruined by the modern city" would become a staple of crime television shows and movies, such as *Fort Apache, The Bronx* (1981). The ultimate villain in the movie, "Sweet William," explains that he is one of the few Puerto Ricans from the island to go to Harvard (and notes that the first was one of the Puerto Rican nationalists who tried to assassinate President Truman in 1950). This speech, coming late in the movie, joins the argument made earlier by Egan that Americans had taken Puerto Ricans out of "banana trees," given them social and economic support, and all they have gotten in return is a new criminal class in New York.

The curse that *Badge 373* puts on New York is lifted in the grooves of Springsteen's *The Wild, the Innocent, and the E Street Shuffle.* Springsteen approaches New York from the point of view of the "bridge and tunnel" brigade—he was raised in and around the beach towns of southern New Jersey. Springsteen's biographer, Dave Marsh, has written that the New Jersey–bred musician has a romantic outsider's vision of New York: "As with any outsider, his belief in the City is stronger than a native could ever afford" (66).

Springsteen's later career as purveyor of broad-scoped anthems has led academic critics, too often, to treat him as a sort of deracinated meta-American, following mostly in the political and artistic footsteps of Walt Whitman and Woody Guthrie (Garman). First generation rock journalists—Marsh, Robert Christgau, Jon Landau, and Ariel Swartley among them—correctly heard "the Latin tinge" in Springsteen's early music and connected this record to *West Side Story.* Making a slight error about the percussion, Robert Christgau called Springsteen's second album "Latin music out in the street with zero conga drums" (*Any Old Way* 367); similarly, in a concert review originally printed in Boston's alternative *Real Paper,* Jon Landau called Springsteen a "Latin street poet" (22). Ariel Swartley and Dave Marsh make the *West Side Story* connection plain. In describing the album's opening song, "The E Street Shuffle" (sort of a Jersey Shore version of "Boogaloo Down Broadway"), Swartley suggested that in trying to organize a dance *about* teenagers, Springsteen was at least unconsciously imitating Leonard Bernstein who "put the corner kids on the stage, wrapped them up in literary allusions, and orchestrated the thing" (51). For his part, Marsh suggests that the characters populating this record "bring the teen exploitation era up-to-date": Marsh postulates a continuum that runs from Leonard Bernstein to the "real" Latin New York and insists that Springsteen is much closer to the latter than the former (67). It would perhaps be more apt to suggest that Springsteen was more influenced by the "Latin" stylings of late 1950s and early 1960s popular music than by any "real" Latino life in New York (Onkey).

Briefly put, *The Wild, the Innocent, and the E Street Shuffle* tells the story of a young man from the provinces (Asbury Park, New Jersey, to be exact) leaving for the big city. Originally released as a long-playing album, with two distinct sides, Springsteen's characters spend most of the first side on the beach: after the opening dance number ("The E Street Shuffle") sets the scene, the record's "narrator" concludes early on that "this boardwalk life for me is through" ("4th of July, Asbury Park [Sandy]"). The hero then begins examining other options—including joining the circus ("Wild Billy's Circus Story"). But the lure of the city is too great, and by the time the record is flipped over, we are no longer at the beach, but right on 57th Street in New York, the approximate site of *West Side Story*.

On the second side of *The Wild, the Innocent, and the E Street Shuffle* this white, ethnic New Jersey boy (Springsteen's lineage is Italian and Dutch) sends a valentine to the Afro–Puerto Rican city. Thematically, this album side begins with an update of *West Side Story* ("Incident on 57th Street"), only this time all the characters are Puerto Rican (namely "Spanish Johnny" and "Puerto Rican Jane") and the real division comes along the lines of gender, not ethnicity. Working with allusion rather than linear narration, "Incident on 57th Street" tells of a "cool Romeo" and "late Juliet" who struggle to maintain their relationship in the face of all the pressures of the city. Springsteen's Puerto

Rican characters operate in a complex, thriving multiracial city. The African American presence in their life is noted, at least in passing: Ariel Swartley notes quite rightly that the line "Let the Black boys in to light the soul flame" no doubt is Springsteen's metaphor for turning on the radio to listen to some black music (56).

Springsteen's *West Side Story* continues in "Rosalita (Come Out To-night)" which also manages to act as a hilarious rewrite of the old "white man/ethnic woman" tradition. Springsteen's own access to this cluster of images is likely to have come from Jay Black and the Americans' 1964 hit "Come a Little Bit Closer"—which takes place "just the other side of the border." Springsteen's presumably white narrator (he, like his creator, is a young rock and roller) spends the whole song begging his ideal lover to go out with him. And unlike the story told by *West Side Story* and so many other romantic melodramas, Springsteen's interethnic romance is not doomed: while Marty Robbins's narrator in the country song "El Paso" dies trying to be with the young Latina he first sees in "Rosa's cantina" and Tony dies trying to be with Maria, the young man beseeching "Rosalita" merely has his tires slashed and almost crashes in the swamps of New Jersey. If this couple is doomed, they are going to die laughing.

What is so lyrically compelling about "Rosalita" is that it undercuts the melodramatic tradition (upheld so faithfully by *West Side Story*) with unrelenting humor. It is a shaggy dog story that Springsteen tells here, which revises *West Side Story*'s portentous fantasy "Somewhere" ("Somewhere a place for us / . . . Someday a time for us") with the simpler "Some day we'll look back on this / And it will all seem funny." If Springsteen is able here to drive a stake into the heart of *West Side Story*'s pretensions, it took the African American rock and roller Little Richard to kill them, with finality, in 1996 when he sang his own gleeful version of Maria's "I Feel Pretty."

The story might start at the Jersey Shore where Springsteen's narrator has been stuck for too long, but it is clear by the end of the song that he is destined to be a big-city boy. No one is getting hurt in this song and the two main characters are equals; if anything, the white narrator has to convince the Latina Rosalita that *he* is worthy of her. In the song's climax this would-be Romeo acknowledges that Rosalita's mother doesn't like him (because he plays "in a rock and roll band") and then chants along with the band, in fine, boogaloo fashion, "your papa says he knows that I don't have any money." But he has a trick up his sleeve: the record company just gave him a big advance!

"Rosalita"—like "The E Street Shuffle" on the first side of the record—actually *sounds* like boogaloo. With "crazy" sounding vocal chants ("Everybody form a line" in "The E Street Shuffle"), careening saxophone, and an overall looseness in song structure, Springsteen's compositions use rhythm and blues conventions as the basis for community-building affirmations. After releasing this record, Springsteen actually took out a classified advertisement in the *Village Voice* announcing that he was searching for new musicians for his band, including a trumpeter who played "Latin" and jazz (Guterman 80).

If the boogaloo connection is not clear enough in these two songs, it is made explicit in the album's final song, "New York City Serenade." Here Springsteen gets pretentious. Opening with the strings of a piano being strummed, followed by a mock-classical piano piece (some hear Chopin, others Grieg), Springsteen goes for a big "city" statement here, along the lines of George Gershwin's "American in Paris" (1928) or Bernstein's overture to *West Side Story*. But once the vocal starts, Springsteen brings his characters (here called Billy and Diamond Jackie) right back to the street: after completing the (illicit?) job they're on, Billy and Jackie are "gonna Boogaloo down Broadway / And come back home with the loot."

Badge 373 found African Americans and Puerto Ricans in New York to be a shock and an affront to white ethnics. *The Wild, the Innocent, and the E Street Shuffle* takes the demographic and cultural shifts augured by the great black and Puerto Rican northward migrations of the World War II era as a given and as an inspiration. New York's lure, for Springsteen, is inseparable from the black music that underpins so much of his own on this record and inseparable from the Puerto Rican characters that populate the songs. Overly romantic, no doubt, still Springsteen manages to avoid the melodramatic pitfalls of *West Side Story* and the racist ones of *Badge 373*. While white artists continue, of course, to mine the vein of *Abie's Irish Rose,* Springsteen helped promote a more progressive vision with which white people could approach such interethnic contact. Never much of a hippie himself, Springsteen was still, no doubt, influenced by the way that his generational cohort of young white people had invested in the promise of intercultural exchange. As the next chapter will demonstrate, this engagement was expressed in a particularly full manner as young Americans embraced the cultures and religions of South and East Asia.

Monterey, 1967

The Hippies Meet Ravi Shankar

> I suspect that more rubbish has been
> thought, spoken, and written about
> India than any country in the world.
> —Louis Bromfield

Hey, Hey, It's Ravi Shankar

From *West Side Story* in 1957 to Bruce Springsteen's early 1970s work (and others beyond), it is clear that there were plenty of sympathetic white observers of the Puerto Rican migration who wanted to use popular culture forms to make their arguments about the proper place of Puerto Ricans in mainstream United States culture. It is also clear that these dominant culture interventions were regularly and effectively challenged by Puerto Ricans themselves who were using music, literature, graffiti, and other visual arts to carve out their own space in America. Beginning after the Puerto Rican migration, but ultimately running parallel to it on the cultural scene, was the migration of South Asians (from India, Pakistan, and Bangladesh in particular) to the United States after 1965 as a result of the Hart-Cellar Act. This 1965 law (technically amendments to the 1952 McCarran-Walter Act) changed the math surrounding immigration quotas and established new professional preferences that made it possible for large numbers of people from Asia, the Caribbean, and Latin America to immigrate legally to the United States for the first time.

Unlike the Puerto Ricans before them, or the Jamaicans who started coming around the same time, these South Asian immigrants faced a popular culture landscape that gave them few openings for their own expression. As Sandhya Shukla has written so persuasively, it is "not that India did not exist in U.S. popular culture, but that Indians were yet to be recognized within the complex of an awareness of Indian things" (57). This chapter is concerned with how Indians were incorporated—mostly as the "Indian things" that Shukla describes—into American cultural life in the 1960s and 1970s. It begins with a moment when the Indian sitar master Ravi Shankar was embraced by American hippies, then offers a broader evaluation of a cultural habit that stretched to at least the 1840s, but took on special urgency in a moment when the United States was wracked by its involvement in an Asian war and reconsidering its policies about immigration from Asia at the same time. Shukla and many other anthropologists, historians, and religion scholars have noticed that there was a meaningful disconnect in the 1960s between a deep American investment in a "somewhat exoticized perception of national Indian culture" and "actual developing Indian communities" in the United States (55–57).

The stakes involved in this broad cultural appreciation and adoption of Shankar and "Indian things" were quite high. What was developing here was a sense of Indians as an example set for other immigrants—a "model minority." Indians themselves were not "numerous or organized enough to exert influence over this process" in the 1960s, and (unlike Puerto Ricans) they were not much worried over by government officials or social critics. These conditions, along with a generally favorable stance adopted by white people toward them, "ultimately enabled a kind of mobility" that Indian immigrants did not have in other countries, and that other immigrants (and members of other minority groups) did not enjoy in the United States (Shukla 56–57).

This chapter, then, focuses on mainstream incorporation of "Indian things" as one of the major ways to understand the first years of mass South Asian migration to the United States. The guiding assumptions that shaped the reception of actual Indian immigrants after 1965, in other words, came through popular icons, styles, and religious adaptations and not through the social realities produced by large numbers of Indians themselves.

Figure 4.1. Indian classical sitarist Ravi Shankar was greeted by the hippies at the Monterey Pop festival with a reverence bordering on religious awe. Courtesy © Elaine Mayes

The Monterey Pop Festival of 1967 offers a rich opportunity to examine this process. According to the *Monterey Pop* film (and journalistic accounts), the audience at the festival adored Shankar. This rock concert, held in June 1967, kicked off what came to be known as the "Summer of Love," and if the evidence of D. A. Pennebaker's film of the event is to be trusted, no other performers—not the Who, nor the Mamas and the Papas (whose John Phillips was a main organizer), nor Jimi Hendrix —were received with anything like the rapturous appreciation that greeted Shankar. The film *Monterey Pop* is organized to climax with Shankar's performance. Up until this moment Pennebaker has shown very few crowd shots. During Shankar's set, however, the camera finds a number of musicians, including Jimi Hendrix and Mama Cass (of the Mamas and the Papas), seriously grooving to the music: the rock festival was a new cultural form at the time of Monterey Pop, and the performers involved had not yet frozen into the role of uninterested celebrities.

As Shankar's eighteen-minute performance in the film ends, the camera finds Mickey Dolenz of the Monkees, a prefabricated group whose television show debuted in September 1966. Pennebaker offers a tight shot of Dolenz, dressed in full Indian (as in Native American) garb, smiling beatifically and leaping out of his chair to lead a standing ovation for this other kind of Indian. In a documentary made about Shankar in the early 1970s we get to see a different shot, this time of Dolenz in his Indian headdress and moccasins, trailing closely behind Shankar as the Indian musician makes his way through the crowd at the front of the Monterey stage (*Raga*). Many white hippies used costume and other forms of masquerade, somewhat paradoxically, as an expression of their larger cultural Declaration of Independence. At Monterey, then, Dolenz personified the often focused and politically serious, sometimes absurd, quest for authentic experience that marked hippie life in the late 1960s (Braunstein and Doyle 251). The visual confusion in this moment—it freezes Christopher Columbus's navigational error in one efficient shot—opens up fascinating avenues for exploring how Shankar embodied what Arjun Appadurai has called an "ethno-scape": the "tourists, immigrants, refugees, exiles, guest workers and other moving groups and individuals" who "constitute the shifting world in which we live" (33). The white hippies surrounding Dolenz (not just at Monterey but all through the peak years of the counterculture) found—and constructed—in Native American Indians and South Asian Indians models of how to live a fuller and spiritually rich life in America (see fig. 4.2).

The aim of this chapter is to explore why so many young (mostly white) Americans discovered Ravi Shankar as someone to "follow"; this exploration will open up questions about what it meant for these young people to "turn East" just as so many actual Asian Indians, encouraged by the Hart-Cellar Act, were turning West. A look at Shankar's career in the late 1960s and early 1970s offers a convenient way of tracking the relationship among diplomatic concerns, immigration policy, and popular culture: in his actual person and his "star image" Ravi Shankar provided Americans with an occasion to talk about Vietnam, race relations in the United States, religion, drugs, and the meaning of consciousness. He also found himself incorporated into a new approach to marketing in the 1960s that cultural historian Thomas Frank has named "the conquest of cool."

Shankar certainly had little in common with the thousands of South Asians simultaneously reaching the United States, and this difference

Figure 4.2. Mickey Dolenz wears an "Indian" costume while watching Indian sitar master Ravi Shankar at Monterey. Courtesy © Elaine Mayes

was in itself important. Embracing Shankar was a way for at least *some* Americans to process the South Asian migration to the United States, without actively engaging with communities of new immigrants. What is at work here is a kind of sublimation, whereby young white hippies acknowledged their deep concerns about Asia and Asians, but largely through a flamboyant engagement with certain "Eastern" styles. Richard Seager has written wisely that the "big" stories in immigration history do not always involve a "mass phenomenon with dramatic consequences"; sometimes the important moments in history must be understood as having to do with "a handful of newcomers" exerting their power over "a limited number of individuals" (44). Shankar was one of that "handful of newcomers" for young white Americans in the 1960s.

Ravi Shankar's own sense of himself was not as a popular musician. He plays the sitar—a notoriously difficult instrument to master—and, with a few exceptions, has usually limited his repertoire to a carefully delineated body of traditional Indian works. On the face of it, Shankar seems an unlikely cultural hero for Americans, particularly young Americans. But for a brief period, stretching from the Monterey International

Pop Festival of 1967 through the Bangladesh fundraising concert of 1971, Shankar became a star—a "superimmigrant" of sorts—an idealized version of the new "brown" immigrants who were coming to the United States in the wake of the Immigration and Nationality Act of 1965.

The sociological term for *groups* of immigrants who operate as a putative example for how all immigrants should act is *model minority*. But Shankar's presence on the American scene transcended the rather tame behavioral slot described by this term.

The appearance of Shankar in the second half of the 1960s—his very ubiquity in the youth culture of the time—places him in a different category altogether: celebrity. His hypervisibility was synergistic with this mass migration *and* with the ongoing spiritual seeking of young (mostly white) Americans. Shankar had first been embraced by the Beatles, and became especially important as a musical and spiritual mentor to George Harrison (see fig. 4.3). But his influence spread far beyond the Beatles, and by the time he landed at Monterey he reached an audience, largely made up of what the American public had only recently come to call "hippies," who were prepared to welcome him as an avatar, a living manifestation of spiritual principles. Ravi Shankar became an occasion and an opportunity for a wide variety of Americans to consider major social questions having to do with race, religion, and immigration.

When President Lyndon Johnson signed the Immigration and Nationality Act he essentially did away with the national-origins provisions that had dominated American immigration law ever since the United States had immigration laws. Because the Hart-Cellar Act came into play at around the same time as the Voting Rights Act and the Civil Rights Act, it has come to be popularly understood as part of this revolutionary time of democratic change (Ngai 227). Along with the material changes wrought by the act, the "symbolism" of it was, as Sandhya Shukla explains, "even further-reaching than its immediately perceptible policy or demographic changes. During this year, the United States was deeply involved in Vietnam, had only recently emerged from two other wars in Asia, and was at the same time crafting an image of itself as the leader of the 'free' world" (55). The Hart-Cellar reforms did have revolutionary—if unintended—consequences, especially given that much of American immigration law from 1882 (the Chinese Exclusion Act) up until 1924 (the Oriental Exclusion Act) had been explicitly con-

Figure 4.3. The hippie embrace of Ravi Shankar was prefigured by the Beatles' embrace of Indian religion and music

cerned with limiting the numbers of Chinese and other Asians who
would be allowed into the United States and with limiting the rights of
those accepted into the nation as laborers.

With the exception of a small group of migrants from the Indian
state of Punjab to California in the early 20th century, very few South
Asians had come to the United States before 1965 (Leonard; Song 81–
82). Those South Asians who had made it to the United States in the
pre-1965 era were generally classified along with Chinese, Japanese,
and other Asian immigrants as non-white and were not eligible for naturalization. Indians in America, regardless of their religion, were called
"Hindus" (or "Hindoos"), notwithstanding the fact that this first small
wave of Indian migrants to California were actually Sikh. (In fact, in a
1911 "Dictionary of Races" published by the United States Immigration
Commission, "Hindu" referred not only to Indians, but to Filipinos as
well [Song 81–82]). While immigration law left some gray area when it
came to official control over the movement of Indians into and inside of
the United States, common practice (as validated by the U.S. Supreme

Court) made it clear that Indians were, by and large, not welcome as equal players on the American scene. The first Congress of the United States had established in 1790 that only white people could become naturalized citizens. But who should be defined as "white" (or "Caucasian" as the relevant category was sometimes called) was an argument Americans had been having for over a hundred years by the time that Indians first made their presence felt in the United States (Jacobson).

In the years leading up to World War I, as historian Joan Jensen has explained, the Supreme Court of the United States would often settle the issue on an ad hoc basis: that is, they would look at a particular Syrian, or Armenian, or Indian, and rule on whether that individual should be understood and treated as a white person (Jensen 250–254). So, in 1923, when the case of Bhagat Singh Thind, a U.S. army veteran, reached the Court, this body declared that it was "a matter of familiar observation and knowledge that the physical group characteristics of the Hindus render them readily distinguishable from the various groups of persons in this country commonly recognized as white." While the Court denied its interest in placing any social value on these "readily distinguishable" characteristics, the language it used made it clear that visible difference needed to be understood as stigma: "The children of English, French, German, Italian, Scandinavian, and other European parentage, quickly merge into the mass of our population and lose the distinctive hallmarks of their European origin. On the other hand, it cannot be doubted that the children born in this country of Hindu parents would retain indefinitely the clear evidence of their ancestry" (www.multiracial.com/government/thind.html).

But immigration law—and high court adjudication of the ambiguities in those laws—is only one way to track how native-born Americans have understood South Asian Indians. Frank Chin and Jeffery Paul Chan wrote in 1972 about two processes of social control by white people that they term "racist hate" and "racist love." Racist hate is the system of law and social practice whose aim is to control those marginalized figures who seem most unacceptable to powerful white Americans: slavery, lynching, restrictive immigration law, and inflammatory speech would all fall under this rubric. But "racist hate" does not operate in a vacuum and its work of social control is often supported by what Chin and Chan call "racist love"—the process by which outsiders are "domesticated" through a web of representations (stereotypes, in short) that render them trustworthy, pliant, and aesthetically pleasing to the dominant culture. Weaving in and out of the narrative of "racist hate" that is articulated most fully by anti-Asian immigration law, then, is a related story of "racist love" that for some 150 years now has depicted South Asian Indians as more spiritual and less materialistic than mainstream white Americans (Chin and Chan). That episodic history of white American investment in South Asian people, religion, and imagery became more central to the mainstream culture in the 1960s than it had ever been before; this investment continues to pay dividends in the early years of the new century.

The Woodstock-era career of Ravi Shankar stands as a compact example of how the complicated currents of American minstrelsy, global politics, and new patterns of consumption could position young white Americans to fall in love with a certain type of brown immigrant. "Falling in love" with Ravi Shankar was (among other things for the hippies) a kind of racial masquerade. As we discussed in the introduction, the United States culture industries have relied heavily, since at least the 1830s, on the notion that it is somehow fun, useful, and/or necessary for white people to "act" black. Beginning with stage minstrelsy in the first few decades of the 19th century, white Americans have demonstrated what seems to be an insatiable appetite for "black" cultural stuff—whether produced by actual African Americans or by white imitators, adapters, interpreters, and so on. Scholars of minstrelsy have found in the cultural practice countless motivations and effects: longstanding debates continue to rage over the racial politics being worked out in and through minstrelsy. This is no place to rehearse the debates that have followed in the wake of these cultural impersonations, but it is important to note that the practice of racial masquerade has been employed by Americans for a long, long time to articulate major social concerns and enact "solutions" to those problems.

Since its inception, blackface minstrelsy has been much more than a simple white/black affair. At the beginning it was dominated by Irish immigrant and Irish American performers; in later years (and in early film productions utilizing blackface), Jewish Americans were particularly significant players (see chapter 1). The adaptation of black style has been a major forum for native-born white Americans to explain to themselves and to others what their "whiteness" means and how it functions. In related fashion, immigrants to the United States and their children have used blackface to figure out what access they have to whiteness and how they will deploy whiteness in the context of their own hyphenated identities.

Donning blackface makeup, "acting" black—and later "sounding" black on musical recordings or "dressing" black—have been crucial tools used by white Americans as they confront major social changes or cultural challenges. Immigration has itself been a primary flashpoint for all manner of minstrelized performances since the 1840s or so: the world of popular culture—from the minstrel stage of the 1840s to early sound recordings and Hollywood film in the 1910s and 1920s—has hosted an ongoing discussion, *through* racial impersonation, about the proper shape and content of American identity.

Racial impersonation has evolved over time and has many faces and places of articulation. "Acting" black has been joined by "playing Indian," for instance: white American boys and men have for centuries imitated Native Americans, as historian Philip Deloria explains, as a way of dramatizing their own complicated relationship to the exploited indigenous peoples of the continent. Such "acting" (whether onstage or in the Boy Scouts) demonstrates both a felt need on the part of participants to do or say *something* about the social relations of white people and non-white Others, and a certain pleasure taken in the occasion. By the 1960s racial masquerade was a reliable vehicle for white Americans to ride their anxieties and aspirations on. As the creators of *West Side Story* demonstrated, racial impersonation (and/or "ventriloquism") could take many forms and could be prosecuted with numerous complex motives.

Members of the American counterculture did not invent Ravi Shankar, nor did they have much to do with the shape of his career in the Woodstock era. But they did *use* him as an important medium for their own explorations of race, identity, and world politics. Even if these young white Americans did not invent a new way of "playing Indian" —turning East now as well as to the Native American Indians (that had been an American habit since the 1840s or so)—they did "play" (South Asian) Indian with an unprecedented energy and motivation.

In their embrace of Shankar along with Eastern religions, fashions, and visual arts, the hippies seized an opportunity to develop a non-racist, anti-imperialist relationship to the darker people of the world. This moment of the hippie turn East reminds us that the politics of racial masquerade and Orientalism are unpredictable and often cleft by contradictory expressive acts. But what the hippie's fond embrace of Shankar at Monterey and beyond meant, above all, is that this rising generation of American culture makers was finding a new way to welcome "brown" people into the center of life in the United States. This inclusion came with a steep price: the hippies required of Shankar and the other new immigrants that they relinquish at least some measure of control over their cultural stuff. The incorporation of South Asians, in particular, was accompanied by a demand that young white Americans be allowed to borrow their clothes, their religions, and their music.

The legal reforms of the Hart-Cellar Act led to a large influx of "new" brown immigrants—especially from Asia, Latin America, and the Caribbean. In this period Ravi Shankar came to represent a sort of immigration best-cas(t)e scenario: unlike the brown youth held responsible for the social unrest that crested in the zoot suit riots of 1943, the next generation of Mexicans and Mexican Americans who would agitate for expanded rights as members of the growing farmworkers movement, the "Capeman," or the Young Lords, Shankar seemed unthreatening above all.

But of course Americans had been "turning East" for more than a century by the time Shankar delighted the hippies in Monterey. To understand some of the ways the hippies had been prepared for his arrival, we will first need to take a brief tour through American versions of the "mystic East."

Turning East/Moving West

Writing in 1941, an Indian immigrant to the United States named Krishnalal Shridharani wrote, with tongue in cheek, about Columbus's "discovery" of America: "We Hindus take a pardonable pride in the fact that had it not been for us 'undiscovered' Indians, America would not have been the same America from 1492 on. It was Columbus's eagerness to find out what we were doing and how much money we were making that gave him the idea of sailing the seas in the first place" (499). What Shridharani makes explicitly clear in this mock boast is that India has been a major object of fantasy for Europeans, and later, Americans, for centuries. It was not the "real" India that Columbus (or his hippie descendants) was after; as religious historian Harvey Cox has explained, insofar as India (as part of the "Orient") has existed in the cultural imaginary of Westerners, it is as "a myth that resides" in their heads. This India, Cox suggested at the height of the hippie embrace of the "mystic East," functions as a convenient screen on which the West projects reverse images of its own deficiencies" (149).

Insofar as India has been important to Americans' ideas about themselves and their place in the world, it has been as part of a larger mythical entity known alternately as "the Orient" or "the East." Critic Edward Said, along with many others in his wake, has explained how economic imperialism (that is, the actual exploiting of people and resources) has been joined by the cultural colonization of the Middle East, South Asia, and East Asia—a process that Europeans and Americans have carried out in literature, film, visual arts, and so on. For Americans, there has been a continual shifting of imperialist and neoimperialist allegiances, as it were, with cultural investments being made variously in India (in the 1840s, 1890s, and 1960s, for instance), the Middle East (especially in visual arts and film culture of the late 19th and early 20th century), and Tibet (in the 1990s and early 2000s) (Said, Schell, Hansen, Edwards).

Particularity has never been a central component of the American "turn East." Ashis Nandy rightly notes that all "interpretations of India are ultimately autobiographical" and it is important to notice that when Americans "turn East" it is just as fruitful to ask why they are "turning" at all as it is to focus on the object of their attention (in Taylor 147). Even so, it is plausible to suggest that since the 1840s or so, Americans have had a special place in their hearts and minds for "India"— even as they refused to make a special place for actual Indians until 1965 (and even then not necessarily consciously).

The 1840s is a reasonable time to begin this investigation because it marks the moment when American intellectual and mercantile interests in India dovetailed; Harvey Cox implies that the ideology of manifest destiny, in fact, augured both of these aspects of the turn East (154). As Joan Jensen has explained, this period found American merchants working in a focused way to deepen their investments in India (trips that Salem merchants had been making since the late 1790s) just as Boston aristocrats were thrilling to India-themed performances such as *The Rajah's Daughter* and *Cataract of the Ganges* (14). The intellectual and cultural pursuit of "India" had few practical applications; unlike the hippies of the 1960s and 1970s, few Boston "Brahmins" (a name that grew out of this India-interest, of course [Jensen 15]) made changes in their own devotional practices. As Harvey Cox has wickedly said of Emerson, there is no evidence that the sage of Concord "ever sat in a full lotus" (9). Even so, Joan Jensen is quite right to note that by the time Walt Whitman wrote his poem "Passage to India" in 1868, "the idea that the wisdom and art of India could act as a mirror for Americans was strong" (15). Even so, India has been a major "site of spirituality for Americans" since the middle of the 1800s and continues to be so "unabated to this day" (Shukla 33).

The beginnings of a second major wave of American interest in India, Indians, and "Indianness" (mostly in the form of the Hindu religion) can be dated quite precisely to a visit to the United States by Swami Vivekananda in 1893. Swami Vivekananda came to Chicago in that year to deliver a speech at the World Parliament of Religions, an adjunct to the World's Fair being held in Chicago at the same time (Prashad, *Karma* 32). (The fair's Columbian Exposition was planned as a celebration of the 400th anniversary of Columbus's journey.) Swami Vivekananda's presence in Chicago, and the Vedanta Society he founded (1894), set off an intense decades-long conversation among white Americans about the meanings of Hinduism, Indianness, and Asian immigration to the United States. Vivekananda's visit to the World Parliament of Religions came in the middle of a period, as Holly Edwards explains, when Orientalism was having a heyday in the "form of paintings, prints, decorative arts, advertisements, photographs" and later "films, fashion, and a variety of performing arts." Due in part to "increased travel opportunities" enjoyed by Americans and other Westerners, this burgeoning Orientalism was also a sign "of the efflorescence of mass media and the development of a department store culture" (16–17). While Swami Vivekananda was himself warmly welcomed, the growing strength of his Vedanta Society and the interest it sparked—especially among elite American white women—became the focus of quite a powerful backlash. His success led to quite a bit of hand-wringing over the perceived vulnerability of these women to Hindu wiles.

Fears of the Hindu "menace" represented by Swami Vivekananda and his disciples were joined with a growing sense that Indian immigrants to the Pacific Northwest were offering themselves up as a cheap labor alternative to native-born workers. The last few years of the 19th century and the first few decades of the 20th century saw an unprecedented attack on Indians in the United States. As early as 1897, Mark Twain wrote of Swamis in India as being mostly interested in money and sex (Prothero). This line would be elaborated—in pamphlets, books, and even lawsuits—by a number of elite Americans who found these religious leaders a threat to their own cultural position. The general idea was that hypnotically powerful fake-Swamis were seducing white women into giving up their money and perhaps their "virtue." Such thinking came to a head in a 1911 lawsuit filed by the daughter of Sara Bull who, according to Stephen Prothero, was a "high-society woman whose Cambridge salon had attracted authors such as Julia Ward Howe, Irving Babbitt, and Gertrude Stein." Bull had become a follower of Swami Vivekananda in the late 1890s and left a large part of her fortune to the Vedantists in her will. According to her daughter, though, her mother had been "duped by her swamis"; this argument, according to Prothero, "carried the day and the bequest was nullified" (Prothero).

The fear that American women were giving themselves over to "filthy" Indians came to a head with the publication of, and response to, Katherine Mayo's 1927 book *Mother India*. Coming on the heels of a decade's worth of magazine articles and pamphlets denouncing the new power of Hindusim in America, Mayo's screed attacked Hindu religious leaders for being sex crazed and power mad; Mayo worried that the various Yogis enjoying a bit of a vogue in the United States in the 1920s represented a true threat to the dominant religious and cultural practices of Americans (Sinha 4, 13). Mayo was racist and anti-Hindu to the core; even so, she did notice that a new social paradigm had been evolving (and would continue to grow into the 21st century) that held up Eastern spirituality as a corrective to Western materialism. (This, of course, was the same point being made by Gandhi as part of the Indian case against British colonialism at just the same time.) One of the "menacing" Yogis in Mayo's purview, Paramahansa Yogananda, who came to the United States in 1920, himself suggested that his own journey to America was predicted by his teacher's teacher, who said that "India has much to learn from the West in material development; in return, India can teach the universal methods by which the West will be able to base its religious beliefs on the unshakable foundations of yogic science" (Yogananda 389).

Mayo's alarmist book developed, according to Mrinalini Sinha, out of her distaste for all the Women's Clubs then entertaining "notions about Eastern spiritual superiority" (14). But, as Sinha also notes, it is impossible to isolate Mayo's purple anti-Hindu rhetoric (with all of its emphasis on deflowered virgins and oversexed yogis) from its function as an anti-immigration tract. From the first few years of the 20th century, Indians in the United States had been attacked as usurpers—not usually in the sexual and religious contexts delineated by Mayo, but in the world of organized labor. These Indians, mostly in northern California, Oregon, and Washington State, were Punjabi Sikh men, not Hindus at all. Most were agricultural workers and many, as Karen Leonard has explained, skirted existing antimiscegenation laws by marrying other "brown" people—in this case, Mexican and Mexican American women.

Their small numbers and social marginality (as well as the marginality of India to U.S. diplomatic concerns—Great Britain having sewed up that concern long before) helped these immigrants stay off of the xenophobia radar for some time. Joan Jensen explains that no laws in the early 1900s were explicitly aimed at banning Indians from coming into the United States, but very few came anyway: 20 in 1903, 258 in 1904 (15). Foreign policy was a major engine of immigration policy in this era, as at most times in United States history, and Japan was the major focus of American-Asian relations in these years (Jensen 83–85). The situation had changed by 1907, when a major anti-"Hindu" riot erupted in Bellingham, Washington—followed by other nativist actions in California. Aimed at expelling "cheap labor" from mills and other industrial sites, these racist actions also helped put Indians on the map for the Asiatic Exclusion League, which previously had satisfied itself by attacking Chinese and Japanese immigrants as being unfair competition for Euro-American workers (Jensen 42–51; http://www.lib.berkeley.edu/SSEAL/echoes/chapter4/chapter4.html; Prothero). This attention, in turn, helped mobilize congressional support for the Immigration Act of 1917, which placed India in a "barred zone" of Asia—a zone that was set by latitude and longitude (Maira, *Desis* 6). The 1917 act, along with the Thind decision of 1923 and the 1924 law, thoroughly confused race (in the Thind case) with nationality (in the immigration acts): whatever internal contradictions may have obtained in the complex of legislation and judicial ruling, the clear outcome is that Indian immigration to the United States would not gain much steam again until 1965, and Indians already in the United States would be denied citizenship. But denying Indians a stable identity niche over time served U.S. interests: welcome laborers now, a Hindu menace then (when their labor was not so desired)—Indians were used to fill a variety of material and rhetorical needs over time.

The publication of Mayo's book represented a last gasp of sorts for India-interest in the United States, up until the revolutionary changes of the 1960s. Mayo's book can be understood, at least in part, as a response to Senator Royal Copeland's Hindu Citizenship Bill of that year, a fairly modest proposal to reclassify Indian immigrants already in the United States as white people. The act would allow these Indian Americans social and economic rights (having to do with land ownership, marriage, and so on) but would not change the new immigration math at all (Sinha 15). According to Mrinalini Sinha, Mayo's scandalous book was the catalyst for a "mini-industry" of more than fifty books and pamphlets (2). One of the most interesting responses came in 1928 with Dhan Ghopal Mukherji's *A Son of Mother India Answers;* here Mukherji suggested that Mayo write a companion volume about the United States, a book that should include chapters on lynching, industrial life, and child labor (Prothero). The "Mayo wave" crested within a few years: when Mersense Sloan published *The Indian Menace* in 1929, it was interesting not for its repetition of the usual charge that Indian Swamis were seducing American women, but for how it stitched that charge into a broader-based analysis of the place of Indians and Indian-ness in American culture. Sloan noted in *The Indian Menace* that Americans were witnessing "a considerable craze for eastern things, even to the point of cherishing oriental fabrics, colors, musics and entertainments. With strange inconsistency this country excludes poor, ignorant laborers from the Far East, but admits a thousand-fold worse element— teachers of Hinduism who push corrupting propaganda too vile for full description" (Tweed and Prothero 212, 214). The 1965 law would make room for Swamis and "laborers"—that is, if you can call doctors and engineers "laborers"!

Between 1927 and 1965, the major Indian figure to appear on the U.S. cultural map was Mohandas Gandhi. Leader of the Indian nationalist movement and proponent of nonviolent resistance, Gandhi was, of course, a major inspiration to American peace activists and civil rights leaders. As Jeffrey Paine writes, "nearly every black political figure of note before" Martin Luther King, Jr., "puzzled over applications of Gandhian techniques." The African American press was, according to Paine, "filled" with stories about Gandhi "for decades" (248). African American intellectual and civil rights leader W. E. B. Du Bois had made contact with Gandhi as early as 1929 (Prashad, "PropaGandhi"). For his part, King liked that Gandhi himself was so influenced by the American Henry David Thoreau and that Thoreau, in turn, had appropriated Indian source material such as the Bhagavad Gita and the Upanishads (Paine 247). King spent a month in India in 1960 "hoping to return with a new vision for America" (Paine 2). After King's assassination, Bill Mauldin depicted the slain civil rights leader in a cartoon, meeting Gandhi in the afterlife (Paine 254). Of course Gandhi operated for Americans as much more than an anticolonial political figure: what his rhetoric, political activity, and perhaps above all his *image* communicated to Americans was that they might find in the "East" an antidote to the crushing materialism and social narrowness of life in the United States. While Gandhi's own focus was, for obvious reasons, on England, his following in the United States acted as a kind of dress rehearsal for the full-blown "turn East" of the 1960s.

But if Gandhi's nationalism was a significant inspiration to Du Bois and others (as evidence of the coming end of white supremacy), many other articulations of India (or "India") were equally powerful for Americans in the middle decades of the 20th century. As Krishnalal

Shridharani made clear in his fascinating 1941 book *My India, My America,* a variety of Indian "figures"—stereotypes, really—had a major hold on the American imagination by this time. Shridharani came to the United States himself in 1934 as a student, but argued that finances and prohibitive immigration laws kept many others from coming (69). In *My India, My America*—which is part sociology, part autobiography, part brief for Gandhi's nationalism—Shridharani acutely notes the few roles available to Indian immigrants in America: "either a fortune-teller, a snake charmer, a magician, or a freak" (106). Taken up by a number of "those strange American women who go 'Hindu'—wearing India prints, quoting the swamis and putting kohl on their eyelashes," Shridharani found himself expected to do magic tricks and meditate on demand (53, 93, 95–96). Realizing the superficiality of these Americans "going Hindu" (and recognizing it as a kind of aristocratic sport with obvious European antecedents), Shridharani was an amazingly sharp—and early—observer of how Indian religious practices could become part of the American consumer menu. At his most perplexed, Shridharani recounts meeting a "Swami Sulaiman" (a bizarre convergence of Hindu title with Muslim surname) at a society function. Only in America, Shridharani thinks, and then wonders: can Pope Bernstein be far behind? (95, 97).

In 1941 Shridharani was aware that a sort of bait-and-switch was operating within the American embrace of "mystic" India. While Americans between the world wars (and then again after World War II) made a collective cultural argument that India was superior to the United States with regard to spiritual matters, lurking in this "compliment" was the implicit suggestion that the "land of mystery" was too tied up with cultish beliefs and practices to be an independent nation (179). The American cultural domestication of "India" over the course of the 20th century had political work to do, Shridharani makes clear, even (or perhaps especially) when it seemed to be operating in a completely apolitical fashion. The multiple acts of erasure embodied in the very terminology of "East" and "Orient" (representing, as Shridharani saw in his time, the people and cultures of China, India, and the Arab world [166]) functioned as a denial of historical subjectivity—in other words, as a way to claim that certain people lived outside of history and did not require full access to the activity of the political world. The "turn

East," then, must be seen as part of a broader impulse in the first half of the century by which Americans at once paid lip service to national self-determination while also finding ways to indicate that certain non-white peoples (Indians, Filipinos, Haitians, and Puerto Ricans—to name just a few) were not quite ready for full independence.

In tracking the history of America's turn East it is important not to reduce these complex social processes to either an expression of nonconformity or an elaborate (if masked) defense of the status quo. There is certainly plenty of evidence for the position that the turn East (whether to India/Hinduism or Japan/Zen Buddhism) grew out of a revolt against the horrors of Hiroshima and the excessive consumerism of post–World War II American culture. The major American purveyors of the turn East in the 1940s and 1950s were renegade artists such as the gay British novelist Christopher Isherwood, who followed Swami Prabhavananda in Southern California, and the Beat writers Gary Snyder (who spent years in Japan) and Jack Kerouac, whose novel *The Dharma Bums* (1958) has been described as the "first handy compendium of all the Zen catch phrases" that would become so important to the hippies (Roszak 131; Ellwood 44; Isherwood).

The "turn East" made a decided "turn West" in these years: California became its center of gravity. From Isherwood and his circle in the Los Angeles area (with a Swami who loved the movies—especially Greta Garbo [Isherwood 132]) to the burgeoning Bay Area scene, California replaced Boston as the hub of this particular universe. Helen Swick Perry has hypothesized that the "high caliber of Asian scholarship in the Bay area generally and the [then] new collection of Asian art objects in the De Young Museum in Golden Gate Park" helped establish San Francisco and Berkeley as important centers for "Eastern" endeavors (Perry 83). Also significant was Zen teacher Shunryu Suzuki's move to the Bay Area in 1959 and the ensuing founding of the San Francisco Zen Center (Downing). Many of the Beat writers (Snyder, Kerouac, and Allen Ginsberg in particular) combined a selective appropriation of Eastern religious practices with elements of African American culture as a strategy of resistance opposed to the crass commercialization of mainstream United States culture. But when their hippie children borrowed the strategy, they forgot (or rejected) the antimaterialist message in favor of a much more marketplace-oriented approach.

Turning East was not a painless process for all California enthusiasts in the years following World War II. Jeffrey Moussaieff Masson's Los Angeles memoir of his parents' religious quest and their embrace of a shady "guru" named Paul Brunton in these years is shot through with self-doubt, feelings of marginalization, and ultimately disillusionment: as Masson summarizes early in his account, it "was not easy to have a guru in urban Los Angeles in 1946" (27). The "phantom India" that Brunton concocted for his disciples led, in Masson's case, to further disillusionment: when the young man finally went to India in the mid-1950s he felt completely unprepared "for the poverty and human suffering" glimpsed from "the window of the taxicab" (162, 112).

Mostly, though, Masson's family adopted Brunton's eclectic teachings as a way out of their own conflicted Jewish identity. Brunton's own nose job, meant to blunt the most visible sign of the guru's Jewishness, spoke loudly to this family of outsiders about how far they had to travel to escape their own ethnic identity. In just one more generation, Jew-Bus (Jewish Buddhists) and other East-turning Jews would find no contradiction in developing hybrid identities: they would publicly "perform" these new roles in much the same way that actors created "Jewish" gangsters in the 1930s (Appel; Kamenetz; Cox 95).

Have Sitar, Will Travel

For white Americans figuring out their relationship to India and the rest of the "East" there were, of course, other challenges. The changes wrought by the new immigration law of 1965 required Americans to update—or at least shore up—their sense of how Indians and others from the East fit into the modern American landscape. The 1965 law, as Vijay Prashad has explained, "reconfigured the demography of South Asian America" (*Karma* 4). The sheer numerical transformation is astounding: where before 1965 there were about 50,000 Indian Americans, one generation later there would be over 800,000 (Maira, *Desis* 7). Additionally, where the relatively small numbers of Indians who had come to America before 1965 had worked in agriculture and heavy industry, the "special skills" provision of the 1965 law assured that the new wave of immigration would feature a different type of immigrant: from 1966 to 1977 for instance, of the Indians who migrated to the United States, 83 percent were professional or technical workers. Most of these immigrants came, as Rajiv Shankar has noted, of their "own volition," and with "a high level of skill or education that has often allowed them to become affluent in the first generation" (Prashad, *Karma* 75; Rajiv Shankar xii). It is no surprise that young white Americans turned to a figure from the world of music (from classical music, as previously noted) to stand as a representative of all things Indian: all of the Indian radiologists and civil engineers hitting the American scene were not likely to make much of an impact on young seekers in the audience at Monterey, Woodstock, and so on.

Shankar, it seems, quite consciously took on the role of a meta-immigrant, a highly visible public figure who would allow mainstream white Americans an opportunity to process the meanings of the new immigration. Shankar was more than willing (and able) to interpret "Eastern" music (and religion) to a mass audience: in one of his two autobiographies Shankar describes a meeting with an Indian diplomat in Belgium who challenged the musician to bring Indian music to the West (*Raga Mala* 130). Shankar feels confident that he can do it: "At that time there were no quality performing artists who could speak fluent English and were capable of articulating the nature of our music to a foreign audience" (*Raga Mala* 130). Shankar was an ethnic entrepreneur of sorts: a variety of cultural changes (in generational politics, migration patterns, and so on) had opened up "Indianness" to new interpretation. Ravi Shankar offered up an attractive package of "Eastern" goods that included music, fashion, religion, and more.

The hippies happily adopted Ravi Shankar. They were, of course, following the example set by the Beatles (and especially guitarist—and alleged sitarist—George Harrison), who had already been to India to meet with the Maharishi Mahesh Yogi. Harrison had quickly entered into a student-teacher relationship with Shankar, who has always reported feeling quite surprised by the attention bestowed on him by pop musicians: "Even if it is not pop music," Shankar said, "I am happy my music has become a popular music" (Santelli 49).

In picking up on Harrison's example, and promoting a particular image of Shankar as a benign father figure/spiritual guide, the hippies made one fairly clear statement about how and where Indians might function in American culture. Shankar, as the hippies "used" him, personified an important myth about Asia and Asians that Lisa Lowe has described as a belief that all Asian immigrants to the United States came from cultures that were "stable," "traditional," and "continuous" (16). As Lowe explains, a major social function of this myth was to mute the reality that most of these new immigrants came from places that had already been "disrupted by colonialism and distorted by the upheavals of neocolonial capitalism and war" (16).

Shankar was perfectly suited to his role at Monterey and beyond— beaming, spiritual, unthreatening—not because he actually was a simple and pure Indian religious man, but because he understood how to play the role. He was, by any token, a much "safer" exemplar of the new culture of the West Cost than were the rioters in the Watts section of Los Angeles, who, as Stuart Hall has explained, had enacted through their violence a "potential imaginative liberation from the cultural imperialism of white racist and white fellow-traveler alike." With African Americans no longer completely "available" (as Hall put it) for use by hippies, Ravi Shankar stepped in as a promising replacement (*The Hippies* 7). Sandhya Shukla has written with good insight that Indians coming to the United States in the middle 1960s came "to a social world deeply stratified by race and a biracial formation . . . in which there was no clear place for the racial identity of non-African Americans who were not white" (56). Shankar helped "place" South Asians, at least for young white countercultural types.

By the time he got to Monterey, Shankar already had decades of experience in show business in the West, having started his career as part of his brother's touring dance troupe in the 1930s. Shankar spent a great deal of time in Paris in that decade, but especially loved the hurly-burly popular culture of New York City: "I was completely intoxicated by Broadway and all the lights and nonstop cinema. I spent all my days at Loew's, the Rivoli, and the Paramount, reluctant to miss one cartoon, newsreel, or vaudeville act. In New York, we heard jazz played live for the first time; there were Duke Ellington and Louis Armstrong, so young and spirited" (*My Music* 69; *Raga Mala* 47).

Even in this first incarnation as an "exotic" Indian in the West, Shankar understood the value of being marketed to Americans as a delightful relic. When newspaper photographers came to take pictures of the Shankar troupe, the Indians "were all dressed like maharajahs, in very formal attire. . . . It was the idea of Solomon Hurok that we should all be dressed like that. He was our impresario, and the greatest of all time" (*Raga Mala* 50). Shankar was more than willing to have himself presented to the public as some kind of secular king or spiritual guru —from the 1930s through the 1970s—and even participated quite avidly in the marketing efforts. When it came to playing at Monterey, for instance, Shankar insisted on being given a Sunday afternoon slot with no rock acts immediately preceding or following him. Creating a "sacred" space of sorts for his music, Shankar made it clear that he did not want his music tainted by the theatrical effects of rock performers or the behaviors of rock audiences (*Raga Mala* 198).

Shankar had no problem, though, with living like a rock star. By his own admission he had affairs around the globe; one, with concert booker Sue Jones, resulted in the birth of daughter Norah Jones (*Raga Mala* 57). While Shankar alluded to the presence of an unclaimed daughter in his autobiographies, the information was only widely disseminated in 2003 when Jones won eight Grammy awards. More relevant than Shankar's sexual escapades is the fact that from his first visit to American shores he has acted like the focused small-scale entrepreneur that successful popular artists have needed to be in the modern era. Aware of his function as a musical and cultural "ambassador," Shankar carefully nurtured an image that meshed with the expectations of his audience: covering the Monterey festival as a young rock critic, Robert Christgau credited Shankar's success there with his ability to operate as a "preconceived symbol" for the "love crowd."

As Christgau reported on the festival, Shankar was able, along with Jimi Hendrix (the "spade" in Christgau's formulation) and the Mamas and the Papas (the "supergroup"), to adopt a performance stance that was immediately pleasing—and confirming—to his listeners (Christgau, *Any Old Way* 23). The beatific smiles on the audience members' faces in *Monterey Pop* suggest that Shankar and "India" could be marketed quite effectively to young Americans. The purveyors of this Eastern chic were very often approximate contemporaries of the target audience: using a kind of "insider" knowledge about hippie consumer taste, these purveyors of what Gita Mehta would later call "Karma

Cola" found in Shankar a perfect embodiment of their marketing plan. A complicated dynamic was being worked out here through which a skilled and willing cultural purveyor (Shankar) offered up his goods to an audience that was poised to deploy those goods in ways neither imagined nor desired by the producer.

Shankar was not the only guru to go on the "hippie tour" in the wake of the 1965 law. A. C. Swami Bhaktivedanta Prabhupada arrived in New York in late 1965 and began chanting first on the Lower East Side of New York and then in San Francisco—garnering a huge amount of coverage in the alternative press. In January 1967 he went to the Avalon Ballroom in San Francisco and led thousands of young people in the Hare Krishna chant; that same year the Maharishi Mahesh Yogi (the Beatles' one-time guru) also toured the States (Ellwood 143−144). In 1966 Swami Satchidananda came to the United States at the request of two American followers, the filmmaker Conrad Rooks, and the artist Peter Max. Three years later he would be featured giving the opening invocation at the Woodstock festival (Tweed and Prothero 253). *Life* magazine was so impressed by this newly energized interest in the "East" that it called 1968 "the Year of the Guru" (Tweed and Prothero 399). While Americans had been turning East since at least the 1840s, never before had such an effort been made, on so many fronts, to sell "India"—as religion, music, fashion, and visual art—to the masses. The hippie embrace of the East was overdetermined to say the least: immigration law changes, the war in Vietnam, the Beat Generation investment in Eastern religion, innovations in psychedelic drug production, and so on, all conspired to bring young Americans to a whole new place (at least in their minds).

Thank U India

The ecstatic audience response to Ravi Shankar at Monterey marks one significant moment in the modern American India boom. But to get a truer sense of how a set of subcultural activities (that mostly involved bohemians, hippies, and far-out academics) turned into a major social movement, it will be necessary to look not only at the world of music but also to other popular arts and fashion. Only then will it be possible to understand how this "sell"—of Indian "spirituality"—was promoted. It might help to start with Johnny Carson and his Nehru jacket.

The dapper talk show host wore a Nehru jacket one night on television in 1968, a jacket that was designed by Oleg Cassini (who had previously crossed the American radar as the favorite designer of Jacqueline Kennedy). The jacket—most notable for its lack of lapels or collar —was based on the favorite style of Indian prime minister Jawaharlal Nehru. Cassini explains that he had seen one on the maharajah and had also admired "the more conservative ones" he had seen "Nehru himself wear at the White House": in pure fashion terms, Cassini recounts, he "liked the clean, uncluttered simplicity of it." As a perfectly superficial value-add of sorts, Cassini also notes that "then too, my mind was on India during that period" (370).

Whatever Cassini's motivation, the momentousness of Johnny Carson wearing the jacket must be emphasized: although Carson was the consummate showbiz insider and beamed *The Tonight Show* out from Southern California, a large part of his appeal was as an "aw-shucks" Midwesterner, slightly bemused by the glitz of his surroundings. Historian Thomas Frank explains that Carson's donning of the Nehru jacket led to "an overnight mania for the garment": "The changes that followed constitute one of those highly visible and instant mass shiftings that are so often pointed to as distinguishing one historical era from another." According to Frank, "square middle America became hip almost overnight" (191). What Frank really means is that once again the popular culture industries had successfully incorporated a marginal or avant-garde, or racially "suspect" form into its mainstream offerings, as is so common in 20th-century marketing. Frank himself notes that for all the popular history that insists we understand the 1960s as a time of revolt and change, it was "also the high watermark of American prosperity and a time of fantastic ferment in managerial thought and corporate practice" (6). A major focus of these "thoughts" and "practices" in the 1960s was on how to bring the unconventional (for most Americans) styles, sounds, and religious practices of India into the marketplace. This, in turn, was part of the more general effort made by which "business dogged the counterculture with a fake counterculture" (Frank 7).

The promotion of the Nehru jacket—while rooted in the very so-
ber personage of the Indian prime minister—communicated something
about the desire of American men to break away from the rigid stan-
dards of white American masculinity. As has often been the case with
the adoption of Indian "stuff," the message was political, spiritual, and
sexual. On the one hand, the Nehru jacket's original connection with
one of the leaders of the Indian nationalist movement signaled a kind of
serious political purpose and Third World consciousness that so many
Americans were searching to communicate in the 1960s. On the other
hand, it marked its wearer as a "swinger"—a nonconformist, at least
on the sartorial level.

Soon the Nehru jacket was everywhere—and not just for men. Simplicity pattern 8102 (1969) included a design for a women's Nehru
jacket: of the three models pictured on the front, one wears the jacket
made with a paisley pattern (also, originally, an Indian design), and
one has accessorized her simple white Nehru jacket with some love
beads (see fig. 4.4). A year earlier, Mattel had joined the marketing
frenzy with Barbie's boyfriend New Good Lookin' Ken, who wears a
red Nehru jacket and says, "Let's go to the big game," among other
things (http://www.manbehindthedoll.com). Writer Mark Salzman, in
his memoir *Lost in Place: Growing Up Absurd in Suburbia,* remembers
how this fashion became a visible emblem of his oppositional pose.
Salzman remembers feeling pleased when his girlfriend went "to a fab-
ric store . . . bought a few yards of Indian-print cloth and a pattern
called 'Nehrudelic' [Nehru + psychedelic] and sewed" a garment that
looked like something Siddhartha would have worn "before he gave up
the comfortable life" (144–145).

Before too long, not surprisingly, the Nehru jacket itself came to
function as a sign of "selling out" (or "buying in"). Actor Peter Coyote
recalls going between his Diggers (a radical Bay Area activist group)
and some Los Angeles music producers to discuss organizing a music
festival to benefit the Diggers. Noticing that the L.A. businessmen are
all wearing white to indicate "refinement and spiritual evolution," Coyote acidly notes that he and his group do not want to be co-opted by a
"bunch of Nehru-shirted aesthetes whose monthly tab for weed and
cocaine equaled any of our annual incomes" (98–99).

Nehru jackets were one important item on the textile front. Numer-

Figure 4.4. This Simplicity pattern for a women's
Nehru-style top demonstrates how completely the
Indian garment had become a mainstream fashion by
the late 1960s

ous other Indian and Indian-inspired fashions also reached Americans
in the 1960s. While madras and paisley were the most obvious "Eastern" influences earlier in the decade, the second half of the 1960s saw a
turn to loose flowing robes, beads, and India prints (Ettinger 85; Piña
6). At the Human Be-In held in Golden Gate Park in 1967, for example, poet and youth leader Allen Ginsberg shared the stage with Zen
teacher Suzuki, and dressed himself in "wild naive India white cotton
and beads" (Law 54). The United States was inundated with "Indian"

products in the late 1960s, as Gita Mehta puts it, "the great Western marketing machine disgorged peasant skirts with hand-printed mantras, vegetable dyes, and lentil soup" (7).

With few exceptions, this multifaceted marketing effort was kindled and carried out by white American individuals and corporations. Krishnalal Shridharani noticed a couple of decades earlier that Americans, "with their native understanding of business and advertising . . . make better Swamis and Yogis than Indians" (97).

The material and visual culture of the United States of the late 1960s and early 1970s was full of Indian and Indian-inspired goods. Historian Robert Ellwood, reflecting on his younger days in California, remembers the "sacred spice of incense" in the air, "wafting in cloudlets past magic posters giving on eternity, bright cloth-of-India hangings, Tibetan *tankas,* meditating buddhas, and many-armed escapees from the Hindu pantheon" (2). Harvey Cox evaluated the same moment more critically, bemoaning the fact that the "smiling Buddha himself and the worldly-wise Krishna can be transformed by the new gluttony into collectors' trinkets" (134).

The collection of Eastern visual signs and symbols was, of course, part of a larger social, spiritual, and political rebellion. Writing about the counterculture from its heyday (1969), Theodore Roszak was taken with how the alternative press (*San Francisco Oracle, Berkeley Barb,* and so on) combined elements of direct political protest with more diffuse spiritual offerings; Roszak noted that the *Berkeley Barb* might have a page 1 attack on political policies emanating from Washington, D.C. and then devote its center spread to "a crazy mandala for the local yogis" (141). Perhaps no individual working in the visual arts cashed in on the India boom so successfully as the popular artist Peter Max. As a child, Max escaped from Hitler's Germany with his family and actually settled in Tibet for a brief time. When Mao Tse-tung's army approached, Max's family went first to Shanghai and then on a boat to the newly created state of Israel (with a forty-eight-day stop in India). Before emigrating to the United States in 1953, Max made a brief stay in Paris where he went to art school. After more schooling in America and a career as a graphic artist, Max found his calling when he met the Swami Satchidananda (http://www.aejv.com/max-bio.htm). Combining —vaguely—elements of Eastern iconography with the swirling colors and patterns of West Coast psychedelic printmakers, Max forged his own version of "Nehrudelic." His prints would become a staple of interior decorating in college dorm rooms and beyond. Later, Max would illustrate Swami Satchidananda's collection of wisdom, *Beyond Words* (1977).

What makes it so difficult to get a handle on the turn East of the late 1960s is that the players came to the table with such a wide variety of resources, motivations, and skills. If the turn East could represent sincere spiritual seeking, musical adventurousness, and political protest, so too could it (and did it) offer unprecedented opportunities for commercial exploitation. In September 1968, *MAD* magazine, itself the product of a brokering between alternative and mainstream cultures, began to take notice of the marketplace absurdities wrought by the turn East. This issue featured cover boy Alfred E. Newman in full freak garb and being held aloft by the Beatles and the Maharishi; it included a parody of a countercultural magazine called *Hippie*. Among the classified ads in *Hippie* was one for a "Turned-On Gift Guide" that came with a tattoo kit showing all the "meditation mountains" of Tibet. "THROW AWAY THAT TRUSS!" shouted another fake advertisement: there was now a better (if unspecified) "new cure for hernias resulting from Yoga Lotus Position" (*MAD about the Sixties*).

The purpose here is not to question the sincerity of any individual American who sought in Eastern religion, visual, or musical culture a personal route to salvation, peace, aesthetic pleasure, or comfort. Historian Judith Smith suggests that the "warm and busy" psychedelic style of Peter Max and others functioned as an exciting option for those young people who were rejecting the starkness of high modernism on the one hand, and the overstuffed mediocrity of suburban middle-class life, on the other (Smith, personal communication). But if "collective representations" must, as Arjun Appadurai has explained, be taken as "social facts," then it becomes necessary to come to terms with the idea that developed in the late 1960s that the cultures and religions of India could be carved up, packaged, and sold in parcels of varying shapes and sizes (5). The most devastating "fact"—or really an argument—that materialized here had to do with the relative social power of Indians in America at play in this set of marketing ventures. It set up a subject-object relationship, as Harvey Cox noted, within which Americans could at once flood the "East with American products," all while Americans began "to dress in their costumes and help ourselves to their religions—conveniently packaged for Western consumption" (155). In addition, the marketing of "India" to white Americans in the 1960s helped enact a social erasure of the actual Indians coming to the United States in these years.

The amazing social sleight-of-hand at work here should not be missed. In this mercantile process, white Americans performed a kind of minstrelsy: they "played" (or worked) at being Indians and did so effectively enough that they quickly established a new math by which student became "teacher" (or "guru") and consumer became producer (Deloria). Allowing, as Vijay Prashad has outlined, that Indians are "intensely spiritual" but "apolitical" and "knowledgeable but not cosmopolitan," the marketing efforts that accompanied the modern "turn East" had a built-in justification for exploiting marginalized "others" (*Karma* 68): for centuries this sort of logic had been applied to everything from music (as in the case of white musicians developing the "raw" materials of African Americans) to land (Native Americans don't improve their land so *we* might as well take it). Critic Sunaina Maira has more recently railed against this white American tendency to rationalize the capitalization of Indian "stuff": "We are not unmaterialistic by choice. It isn't something Indian in nature. People [in India] always valued commodities and hoarded cans of sausages; brand names were important" (Bhudos 93). Compare this with the American tourist overheard on a beach in India in 1993: "The people in India are so happy. Even the poor people; they all look so content" (Bhudos 90). In many ways the marketing of Shankar and "Indianness" made it hard for white Americans to imagine that Indian people had needs and desires of their own.

The implicit cultural logic of this consumers' turn East was even more disturbing in a "having your cake and eating it too" way. The breathtaking innovation of the cultural imaginary that was in development at this time is that it presented cultural and racial masquerade as a kind of ennobling activity that conferred spiritual superiority on the major practitioners. Much of the rhetoric of turning East, as already described, had to do with the spiritual superiority of the East as opposed to the material achievements of the West. But in the modern era

of turning East—from the 1960s right up through the New Age cornu-
copia of the early 2000s—it became possible to imagine (and fashion a
life around the idea) that the consumption of Eastern goods was itself a
spiritual practice—or at least a valid part of spiritual seeking. Decades
ago, T. J. Jackson Lears noticed that the marketing of consumer goods
very often relied on an explicit appeal to the "therapeutic" appeal of
purchasing. All of the India-print wall hangings, beads, incense, Herman Hesse books, and so on, became the signs of allegiance to the East;
the owners of said goods enacted, then, a kind of material/spiritual
transubstantiation whereby they became, in their own self-presenta-
tion, avatars of a new consciousness. In our own time the rolled-up
yoga mat is probably the single most powerful signifier of this move.

One of the sharpest critiques of this type of cultural masquerade
came in a song by Steely Dan, a 1970s band that, early in its career,
looked like hippies but made a number of moves to distance themselves
from their long-haired contemporaries. Their second record, *Countdown
to Ecstasy* (1973)—the title itself a joke about attempts to rationalize a
spiritual state—began with a song called "Bodhisattva," a reference to
those Hindus who have achieved spiritual perfection but remain in the
material world to act as helpers to other people. A number of the India
references in the song seem to have been lifted directly from Herman
Hesse's novel *Siddhartha,* originally published in the 1920s but available, and wildly popular, in new English translations in the mid-1960s
and turned into a movie by Swami Satchidananda follower Conrad Rooks
in 1972 (Ellwood 136). But Steely Dan's "Bodhisattva" is all about how
buying and selling can lead to redemption. The song pivots on a dumb
joke: its protagonist asks the Bodhisattva to take him by the hand and
show him the "shine of your Japan / the sparkle of your china." Purposefully confusing the name of the country (China) with the plates
and cups, the song also conflates Japan, China, and India (in the titular
reference to Hinduism). The twist in the song comes when the narrator
pledges to sell his "house in town" so that he will be able to move East
and "shine in your Japan / . . . sparkle in your China." First attracted
by the "sparkle" of Eastern religion and material goods, this character
has figured out a way to sell his own goods—his home—and incorporate himself into the East. Songwriter Donald Fagen (who joked in a
later song, "Aja," about how "Chinese music always sets me free" [1977;

www.purelyrics.com]) has himself summarized the point of the song: "Lure of East. Hubris of hippies. Quick fix" (http://home.earthlink.net/~oleander1/countdo.htm).

The Sitar Spoke to Me

For all of that, it is worth mentioning that "Do It Again," the very first song on the very first Steely Dan album (*Can't Buy A Thrill*, 1972), featured an extended electric sitar solo. Ravi Shankar's sitar was at the heart of the hippie-era turn East. The sound of the sitar became an aural identification tag for the counterculture, not only in songs by the Beatles, the Byrds, the Box Tops (!), and the Rolling Stones, but on television and movie soundtracks as well. The electric sitar played on "Do It Again" had come on the market, only briefly, at the end of 1967. It was designed by session guitarist Vincent Bell, sold by Danelectro, and stayed on the market only until the company folded the following year. But the influence of this "short-cut" instrument (play the sitar and amplify it without having to really learn to play the sitar) continued to be felt for decades, particularly in soul records coming out of Philadelphia and Detroit in the 1970s and hip-hop records associated with the "underground" of the 1990s (http://www.guitargonauts.com/pick-46.html).

Shankar's own classical ragas—or to put it more accurately, the very sound of the sitar—became a major carrier of meaning in the late 1960s. The meanings produced by the sitar were varied: the sitar's major signifying function, of course, was to denote "difference." Anytime a sitar cuts through the ambient noise in an American movie or television show of the late 1960s or early 1970s, you can be sure that something freaky is about to happen—whether in the realm of spirituality, drugs, or sex. Shankar's ascension as a culture hero was accompanied by the embrace of the sitar as a vehicle of the countercultural gestalt. The counterculture's embrace of the sitar was based on a variety of misunderstandings about its original uses in Indian classical music; these misapprehensions were—in a classic pattern in the history of American popular music—then organized to represent "authenticity" (in this case of Indians, or the East, or Hinduism).

The key to the Western adoption of the sitar was the notion that playing it was somehow a mystical experience. Its main function in Indian music, as Shankar himself struggled to make clear, was as an improvisatory vehicle, the mastery of which took years of training with a teacher and years of individual practice: the very fact of popular musicians taking up the sitar always struck Shankar as "strange" at best (*Raga*). For some time early in his career, it seemed that Shankar would find a much different sort of home in Western music: he had found supporters among American classical musicians (most notably Yehudi Menuhin, with whom he occasionally collaborated) and jazz musicians, with saxophonist John Coltrane standing as his most important fan. Coltrane and Shankar met in the 1960s, and Shankar gave him a brief lesson in the architecture of ragas (Shankar, *Raga Mala* 177–178). Shankar was also taken up by British folk revivalists in the first half of the 1960s (*Raga Mala* 180). But ultimately Shankar—with a little help from his friends the Beatles—cast his lot with the hippies.

The hippie rush to the sitar was prefigured by the Beatles' turn East, and George Harrison's relationship with Shankar and Indian music. Harrison studied for six weeks with Shankar but, according to most reliable critical sources, never turned into much of a sitar player. Shankar, who came to consider Harrison his "son," thought that Harrison's sitar work as first recorded (on "Norwegian Wood") sounded "terrible" (*Fresh Air*). Harrison used sitar on a number of later Beatles songs, including "Baby, You're a Rich Man" and "Within You, Without You" (Poirer).

On the American scene a group called the Folkswingers released an album called *Raga Rock* in 1966 that had some sitar on it (Gracyk 93). Much more important for the burgeoning hippie scene on the West Coast was the release that year of the song "East-West," on the album of the same name, by the Paul Butterfield Blues Band. "East-West" featured guitarist Mike Bloomfield experimenting with a number of different non-Western modes. Bloomfield, according to one source, wrote the song while on LSD and listening to Ravi Shankar (DeRogatis 54). For the "West" half of the title, the band played "on the one" and included a brief reference to "Joy to the World" toward the end of the number (www.bluesaccess.com/No_25/butter.html). Originally titled "The Raga," as the band was rehearsing it into "shape" (if there is any shape to this long improvisational piece that could sometimes stretch on for as long as an hour in concert), it influenced a number of musicians in the Bay Area who heard it in 1966 during a three-night stand that the Butterfield band played in San Francisco (http://www.bluesaccess.com/No_25/butter.html). A number of white artists previously dedicated, in a narrow way, to playing blues music (Steve Miller is one) began incorporating ragas into their repertoire (Hoskyns 141).

At least as influential that year was the release of the Byrds' "Eight Miles High," a song inspired by Shankar and Coltrane. Band member David Crosby had long thought Shankar and Coltrane to be the most important musicians alive, and he was one of the major influences on George Harrison's turn East (DeRogatis 50). Roger McGuinn's twelve-string guitar was used on this song to evoke the sitar effect; joining these sounds with the title invocation of drug use, the Byrds helped forge the growing association of Indian culture with psychedelic consciousness. Shankar was distressed by the tendency of countercultural artists to associate sitar playing with both drug use and free sexuality and objected to how the "twang" of the sitar came to be heard whenever movies show "orgy" scenes (*Fresh Air*).

The mystification of the sitar was noted by all manner of friendly and unfriendly commentators in the 1960s. In its *Hippie* magazine parody, *MAD* ran a classified ad for a "raga rock" group seeking a fourth member, whose job it would be to "explain the melodies" to us (*MAD about the Sixties*). Joan Didion, in "Slouching toward Bethlehem," her classic essay on the new youth culture, tangentially noted how the sitar had become the soundtrack for drug experimentation. During a description of an acid trip that three young people embark on, Didion wrote that except "for the sitar music on the stereo there was no other sound or movement until seven-thirty, when Max said 'Wow'" (106). Bhagavan Das, the American hippie who later acted as tour guide in India for the countercultural leader Ram Dass (born Richard Alpert), emphasizes this drugs + sitar = higher consciousness equation, too. Leaving the United States in the early sixties, Bhagavan Das initially went to London, where he smoked marijuana for the first time: "Stoned, I swayed with the Indian music that was playing. I really connected with it. I knew that I had to go to India. The consciousness of the sitar was pulling me there" (14). After years on the hippie trail, searching for enlightenment in India, Nepal, and elsewhere, the American finally has his own personal musical epiphany: "One day, the sitar spoke to me, and told me to pick it up" (156).

The idea that you could just "pick up" the sitar and play it was anathema to Shankar. As early as the writing of his first autobiography in 1968, Shankar describes being frustrated by the misunderstanding of his music by American hippies: "I started my own rebellion against these rebellious youths. I had to put down my sitar and explain what the music stands for and what it means to me and my *guru,* and what it meant to his *guru,* and all the generations of musicians who have handed down these sacred traditions to us" (*My Music* 96). Again and again Shankar complained about the "terrible distortion" that young Americans were inflicting on Indian culture (*Raga*). But these protestations reach us now as almost ritualistic attempts by Shankar to maintain a public image (and perhaps an inner sense) of his own uncommercialized purity. One of the ironies built into Shankar's success was that he needed to promote himself, continually, as operating apart from the din of the Western musical marketplace that he had become a player in.

By the early 1970s, it appears that Shankar had grown somewhat more sanguine about how young Americans were receiving and using his music. At the Concert for Bangladesh, the audience applauded wildly after Shankar and his supporting musicians tuned up. The Indian master responded, famously, by saying, "If you appreciate the tuning so much, I hope you like the playing more."

The young Americans drawn to Shankar's music were only erratically—and only on their own terms—drawn to the "sacred traditions" animating his playing; the political dimensions of their turn East are similarly hard to track in any linear way. A central question facing historians of the 1960s and early 1970s in general has to do with the comparative force of the intertwined political and spiritual revolutions of the era (Ellwood 7). A number of players inside of the countercultural scene have launched a defense of the musical turn East as itself a political activity: perhaps thinking of the Butterfield Band's "East-West," producer Joe Boyd has suggested that in the 1960s it "was a political statement to get stoned and listen to somebody improvise on an Indian modal scale for twenty minutes with an electric group playing around him" (Puterbaugh and Henke 51). Likewise, Bob Dylan's road manager has suggested that the Monterey International Pop Festival was "a very political event in which nobody got on a soapbox to say the obvious" (Law 70).

But in the period bracketed by the concert at Monterey and the concert for Bangladesh, it became increasingly common for young (and not so young) Americans to turn to the East as a method of turning "away" from the more pressing social and political concerns of the day. Eric Utne, later an alternative magazine publisher, was certainly not alone in discovering that his "participation in political protests came to a quick end in '69, when he discovered Oriental philosophy" (Mungo vi). This detachment from protest politics had a coming-out party of sorts with the Human Be-In of 1967 in Golden Gate Park; its name was a conscious play on the civil rights sit-ins of the 1950s and early 1960s. Beat poet and Be-In participant Allen Ginsberg—who had turned East over a decade earlier in his own poetry and spiritual practice—says that the "purpose was just to be there. That was the whole point. This was after the sit-ins, and the idea was more Buddhist-influenced . . . simply be there, not having to do anything particular except to enjoy the phenomenon of being together outside the realm of the state" (Puterbaugh and Henke 33; Braunstein 250). (Posters for the Be-In featured both kinds of Indians, and the ceremony was "hosted" by a familiar Bay Area figure named "Buddha" [Puterbaugh and Henke 125; Hoskyns 131]). Of course the sit-ins themselves had their own Indian connection: they had been inspired by Martin Luther King, Jr.'s engagement with Gandhi's ideas about nonviolent resistance in India.

My Karma Ran over Your Dogma

"My karma ran over your dogma." It is just a silly bumper sticker but it captures nicely the process by which white Americans domesticated Indian culture and religion and incorporated it into a "spiritual revolution" that many historians see as more significant than the political change that dominated the headlines of the times (Ellwood 7). With typical intertextual bumper-sticker efficiency, "my karma ran over your dogma" at once makes reference to *other* bumper stickers ("Missing your cat? Look under my wheels") and makes a claim about the real world: the American version of "karma" (a.k.a. "shit happens") has frequently been joined by—if not made possible by—a detachment from the nitty-gritty of political activity. American devotees of Eastern religions have very often been attracted by this very feature: picking and choosing the parts of Hinduism (or Buddhism) that work for them, (mainly) white Americans have been favorably disposed to the possibility that they could use their adopted religious practice as a justification for "nonattachment" to "Maya"—the "illusory" material world.

Cultural critic Gita Mehta, writing in her book *Karma Cola* in 1977, was understandably incensed by the American cheapening of the important Hindu concept of karma: "America has taken our most complicated philosophical concepts as part of its everyday slang" (99). Noting that "karma" had come to mean "a sort of vibration," Mehta argues that in the late 1960s "karma" became a cultural keyword—a word that got brandished as a sign of countercultural resistance and nonconformity. "Karma" could get radically perverted too, as it did in the philosophy of mass murderer/cult leader Charles Manson, who, according to one source, would frequently tell his followers that "the karma is turning" (Sanders 132). With respect to the American adaptation of "karma," Mehta went on to joke that it "is fortunate that the elaborate Hindu pantheon . . . does not culminate in a Zeus or a Jehovah waiting to let you have it with a lightning rod for the crime of blasphemy; because if ever the karma was right for the gods to warn Here comes the Judge, it would seem to be now" (100). The sarcasm here should not obscure Mehta's important point: while many white Americans turned East in a dramatic way (moving to India, or to an American commune or ashram), it could be a fairly low-stakes venture that mostly had to do with fashion and vocabulary. Harvey Cox noted this (also in 1977), recounting that during a visit to the Naropa Institute in Colorado (an important node of turning-East activity) phrases like " 'bad karma' and 'more evolved person' swirled like incense smoke screens over meals and conversations" (61).

What were these "smoke screens" obscuring? Cox himself thought that a major motivation for the American turn East was a collective "bad conscience" about Asia—especially the murderous attacks on Hiroshima and Vietnam (155; Perry 82). Bob Dylan's road manager, Victor Maymudes, tried to make this connection explicit during the Monterey Pop Festival by carrying around a "mandala of burnt plastic babies" (Law 70). In the film *Monterey Pop,* director D. A. Pennebaker also hints at the connection: before letting the camera reach Ravi Shankar at the beginning of his performance, Pennebaker first has it linger on a poster that clearly features the word "Hiroshima." While there may have been something loosely "political" about white Americans gathering Asians like Ravi Shankar (and later the starving children of Bangladesh) into their embrace, it was a politics without a program. Three decades after Ram Dass and others like him went on the "hippie trail" to India, Indian American writer Bharati Mukherjee had a character ask, "how do you protest the war by doing dope on an alien continent?" (Mukherjee 153–154). When radical journalist Ray Mungo took his own journey on the "hippie trail" in Asia, he recalls having a "stunning awareness" of the concurrent slaughter taking place in Vietnam, but does not connect up his own trip with it (489). "Playing Indian" in this new way allowed young white Americans a way to imagine themselves as rebels—tuning out the West, turning on the East—even as they kept a hold on the privileges of white American citizenship.

The turn East more commonly functioned as individual therapy than as collective action: in Vijay Prashad's formulation, India acted as a "fantasy of redemption for the trials of this world" (*Karma* 2). The "movement" of modern American Orientalism, comprised "almost exclusively of white, educated, middle- and upper-middle-class young people" too often devolved—as in the case of the EST seminars—into a program for "ego expansion and self-gratification" (Cox 93, 85). Theodore Roszak and other contemporary commentators were aware that a good deal about the turn East could be explained as "postwar middle-class permissiveness reaching out for a religious sanction, finding it, and making the most of it" (136). Recognizing that there is "no business like religion," Shankar still found himself "offended and shocked" by the "hotch potch" of "yoga and tantra and kama sutra and siddhartha" (*Fresh Air; Raga Mala* 203, 116). Taking note of this "hotch potch," Harvey Cox has suggested that the "greatest irony of the neo-Oriental religious movements is that in their effort to present an alternative to the Western way of life most have succeeded in adding only one more line of spiritual products to the American religious marketplace" (129–130). While some Indian immigrants to the United States capitalized on this developing market for Eastern goods as small-scale entrepreneurs in textiles and religious goods, most of the Karma Cola was being poured by white Americans. A few actual Indian gurus, from the Guru Maharaj Ji (who rented out the Houston Astrodome for a mass rally in 1973) to Bhagwan Rajneesh (who took over a whole town in Oregon in the 1980s), have been able to capitalize on this American desire for Eastern stuff. The latter actually argued that "capitalism simply gives you the freedom to be yourself" as he outfitted himself with a fleet of Rolls Royces (Brown 197).

This successful marketing was itself due to a complicated web of migrations—of capital, people, and goods. Service industry attention had shifted to India in the wake of the Vietnam War as trade in Southeast Asia dried up (Mehta 137). Cheaper air travel made it possible to transport goods more efficiently from South Asia to the United States, and to bring young Americans *to* South Asia to contribute to the turning East synergy (Kim 55). In the mid-1960s young people inside of America were moving in droves to Northern California; Joan Didion described it as a social "hemorrhaging" (84–85). Paths were crossing in interesting new ways; Ravi Shankar himself saw that his own turn West (for which he was roundly criticized in India) was "encouraging dissatisfied youths from the West to flock to India" and other points in Asia (*My Music* 96). Harvey Cox also registered the central paradox in the concurrent turnings East and West: "The most ironic aspect of the whole thing is that it is occurring just as many millions of Asians are involved in an epochal 'Turn West'—toward science and technology" (101). Cox's one mistake is his use of the word "ironic": he should have said "fitting." For decades white Americans had been engaged in a variety of attempts—from the emasculation of Charlie Chan through the mystical nonsense featured on television's *Kung Fu* series (1972–1975)—to tame their concerns about the presence of Asians as economic, religious, and romantic threats (Yang et al.; Chin and Chan).

It is also "fitting" that what most young Americans (and other Westerners) found when they actually journeyed East was the antimodern bliss they expected. Bhagavan Das describes his entry into India in 1964 as being "like walking into a concert that had been playing for five thousand years with seven hundred million people in the band" (3); counterculture hero Timothy Leary wrote similarly of his own visit to Benares, which he called "the holiest city of the Hindus, the site of a non-stop hippie festival for the last 5,000 years" (208). Ray Mungo joined in this chorus when he tried to convey his feelings about reaching Nepal in 1972: "You actually caught the sense of something supernatural in the air . . . you could let your mind go free without fear" (539). This construction of India and Indians as belonging to the past supported the project of incorporating South Asian immigrants to the United States as "contemporary ancestors": the phrase "our contemporary ancestors" was first applied to Appalachian white people in the United States by William Goodell Frost in 1899 as a way of rendering what he saw as their distinctly marginal social place. The mystifying of India as an "ancient" and/or holy place had a similar cultural effect. For his part, Ravi Shankar bemoaned the fact that India had rushed headlong into the technological, commercial, and political world of modernization (*Raga*).

India (and Eastern spirituality more generally) was constantly conflated by young people with the altered states of mind associated with psychedelic drug use. Former Harvard professors Richard Alpert (later Ram Dass) and Timothy Leary were the most important rhetorical practitioners of the East = psychedelic equation. By his own admission, Ram Dass saw LSD as the "avatar" of the kind of higher consciousness that turned him East in the mid-1960s. For Leary, the "Hindu Bibles read like psychedelic manuals," and he also discovered important connections between psychedelics and the Tibetan Book of the Dead" (Ram Dass 14; Ellwood 84, 342n58). Poet Gary Snyder saw psychedelics as a reasonable shortcut: "Those who do not have time or money to go to India or Japan, but who think a great deal about the wisdom traditions, have remarkable results when they take LSD." In short, it is safe to say that a "significant proportion" of those Americans who turned East in the 1960s "were influenced in their choice of religious orientation by experiences induced by psychoactive substances " (Batchelor 9).

Taken together, the individual experiences that linked drug experimentation with India led to some reductive cultural stereotyping. Ravi Shankar, like most of the Indian "gurus" adopted by the hippies, was stridently antidrug—instructing his listeners that the music was enough to get them high (*Fresh Air*). Even so, he was projected by many to be a proto-hippie of sorts, and was described by David Crosby as "always stoned" even though he "never used dope" (Miller 49). In the 1966 movie *Chappaqua,* director Conrad Rooks has a young mentally disturbed man tell a psychiatrist about his first trip on peyote (associated with Native American Indians) and the "vision" he had; immediately the film cuts to a seated Ravi Shankar, playing his sitar. "Then," the protagonist tells us, "I went interior." India, drugs, and a search for "vision" inside are combined here in a way that became increasingly common as the 1960s wore on. Christopher Isherwood's Swami actually felt it necessary to go on television in the late 1960s to describe the difference between his practice and psychedelic drug use (Isherwood 294). For some hippies it was possible to imagine that religious practice might replace drugs: one acolyte at the San Francisco Zen Center explained her motivation for going there as rooted in her desire to stay in the "acid state" at all times (Downing 174). Followers of the Yogi Bhajan, living in New Mexico, even made up new words to the Beatles' "Get Back" to describe the process: "Bhajan was a Yogi, came here from New Delhi, but he didn't smoke no grass. / Said you could get higher on the breath of fire, so we opened up a class" (Law 95).

Imagining Indians as twenty-four-hour-a-day trippers was, at least incidentally, a way of reading them out of the modern world of politics and commerce. When Ray Mungo and other members of the counterculture suggested that just "being in India makes a Westerner feel high" or connecting up their own drug use with Hindu religious concepts, they were participating in a kind of cultural imperialism (518). Converting complex spiritual ideas into packaged goods and soundbites, they reduced an entire subcontinent into a travel brochure and a mail-order catalog. The modern turn East was (and still is) comprised of various, sometimes contradictory stereotypes. When taken together, these images add up to a picture of a population of unthreatening noncompetitors: whether beamingly asexual (as most gurus and Shankar himself were imagined to be—despite all evidence to the contrary) or compellingly attractive, the "Indians" in this portrait were not, on the one hand, motel keepers or new hires in the technology industries, nor, on the other hand, marchers—or rioters—in the street. In other words, they resembled neither the *actual* South Asians coming to this country, nor the radical African Americans (and Native Americans and Puerto Ricans) challenging the dominant social order. Appearing, in Vijay Prashad's apt insight, as the "solution" to the "problem" of African Americans, South Asians had their own complex subjectivities—their personhood—erased (*Karma* 6). Fantasy Indians offered at least some Americans a provisional way out of the cultural and emotional turmoil wrought by Vietnam, race riots, political assassinations, and so on.

It is difficult to find any traces in the dominant cultural record of the late 1960s and 1970s of Indians as *actual* immigrants, facing the challenge of entering a new American world of labor and social relations. One of the striking things about Israel Horovitz's play *The Indian Wants the Bronx* (first performed in 1968, with a young Al Pacino playing a street hood) is that it focuses exclusively on the plight of an Indian immigrant confronting both racism and the complexities of the New York City phone and transit systems. With only three characters, Murph, Joey, and Gupta, the play functions as a sort of dark commentary on one tradition of ethnic humor ("An Irishman, a Jew, and an Indian walk into a bar . . ."). The action of the play involves Gupta trying to find his way to his son's apartment in the Bronx. He speaks little English and Murph and Joey function mostly as his tormentors and as Greek chorus: occasionally they break into a doo-wop-style song that features the line "baby, no one cares" (35). As the play ends, Gupta is speaking into a dead telephone, repeating the few English phrases he has mastered: "How are you? You're welcome. You're welcome. How are you? How are you? Thank you" (35). Rather than having some kind of special direct line to young Americans (or indeed, even to other Indian immigrants), Gupta speaks into dead air. The Indian in America, in Horovitz's vision, is lost, unwelcome, and unprepared to meet the challenges of American life. Horovitz's play was an attempt to reintroduce the subject of Indian immigration and "Indianness" in a realist context. There was little audience for this dark vision of an Indian lost in America. The counterculture, along with some fairly square business people, had already found a home in the United States for Indians. The domestication of "Indianness" promised that the assimilation of the new migrants was an opportunity and not a problem.

The reach and power of the modern turning-East cultural phenomenon was astounding. Simultaneous with Shankar's American stardom and Horovitz's play was the rise of what came to be called "bubblegum" music—a frothy, 45 rpm–based popular music concocted in American studios by "groups" (very often just collections of studio musicians) such as the 1910 Fruitgum Company and the Lemon Pipers. The corporate venture at the heart of this musical movement? Buddah and Kama Sutra, two companies operating under one roof. Neil Bogart, a leading executive for the labels (whose names summarize hundreds of years of Western investment in the East—spirituality *plus* wild sex!) explained the mission of Buddah and Kama Sutra: "It's about sunshine and going places and falling in love and dancing for the fun of it. It's not about war and poverty and disease and rioting, and frustration. . . . It's about the good things in life" (www.bsnpubs.com/buddah/buddahstory.html).

The 1971 benefit Concert for Bangladesh held at New York's Madison Square Garden acted as a kind of punctuation on the modern turn East. Here the iconic spiritual father figure, Ravi Shankar, was joined in a powerful way by the image of the starving child of Bangladesh. While the concert, film, and album booklet contained some minimal information about the occasion for the event (organized by George Harrison and featuring Billy Preston, Bob Dylan, Ringo Starr, and Shankar), the million or more East Bangladeshis murdered by the governing regime in West Pakistan, and the millions of refugees who fled Bangladesh for India, barely crossed the radar. The politics that led to the genocide are nowhere to be found: concert organizer George Harrison himself admitted that the "political side" was not his concern. (Robert Christgau later commented aptly on Harrison's non-stance: "The man who seeks after transcendence wants to avoid the ugly immanent contingencies that taking sides involves" [*Any Old Way* 233]). From the idolization of Ravi Shankar and various other "gurus" of the 1960s that put (mostly young) Americans in the position of children and supplicants, Bangladesh offered an opportunity for the Western audience to flex a little

First World muscle, and incorporate starving children into a vision of how "we" treat deserving Asians.

Karma Coda

"Guru," in contemporary American parlance, no longer makes primary reference to Indian spiritual leaders, or teachers; it has, perhaps, outpaced "karma" as a keyword. In the fascinating evolution of the terminology, "guru" now mostly means "expert"—usually in a business context. *The Guru Guide*™ series, with books on marketing, entrepreneurship, and so on—and "gurus" drawn from the ranks of the "best and/or most popular business writers and thinkers of today"— are only one indication of this transformation (Boyett and Boyett ix). Sometimes the "expert" is depicted as an actual holy man. As Thomas Tweed and Stephen Prothero explain, the "Asian guru perched on the mountain awaiting inquirers had become a ubiquitous caricature in advertising; in one commercial Michael Jordan of the Chicago Bulls climbed a mountain to seek out an Asian holy man, who advised him to drink Gatorade" (1).

The modern American marketplace is filled with Indian (and other "Eastern") stuff. The shelves of natural food markets and the back pages of *Yoga Journal* (just to name two obvious outlets) are lined with Indian-inspired goods. The domestication of yoga (now, typically, Americanized as "power yoga") is only the latest offering in a seemingly endless chain of self-help products and services. A number of actual Asian holy men have jumped on this marketing bandwagon: Yogi Bhajan has been particularly successful, with his Wha Guru Chew, Peace Cereal, and Yogi Tea. The marketing of the East (often combined, as in the 1960s and 1970s, with Native American "wisdom") has traveled since at least the 1980s under the rubric "New Age." The real punctuation for the hippie's turn East, in this light, came not with Bangladesh, but with the Holy Man Jam of 1970, which took place in Boulder, Colorado, and brought together Yogi Bhajan, Swami Satchidananda, other spiritual leaders, and loads of hippies. It stood as the model for later "New Age" gatherings, seminars, and festivals (Law 103).

But with its reliance on mystified pictures of India and Hinduism, the New Age doesn't always look so different from the old one. While Shankar is not a major presence anymore, his role has more than ably been occupied by new gurus like Dr. Deepak Chopra (Prashad, *Karma* 47–68). Pop musicians do not turn to sitars too often anymore (although hip-hop musicians from A Tribe Called Quest to the Fugees have found uses for it), but a whole culture of dance music fans have turned to the East all over again: Goa, a beach area in the Southwest of India, has become the touchstone (and a name) for a subgenre of techno music (Reynolds 175–176; Maira, "Trance-Global-Nation"). Dance music compilations in the late 1990s and early 2000s were regularly packaged with names that made reference to geographical sites and spiritual practices associated with the East. The Buddha Lounge is the name of a gay Asian dance club in West Hollywood, California, *and* a "relaxing" anthology of "multicultural" DJ music (http://www.sequoiarecords.com/902.shtml). At the turn of the 21st century, with South Asians firmly rooted in American soil, it has become somewhat more difficult for white Americans to use them only as a screen onto which they project their own personal fantasies. "India" is now the vehicle of a sort of Western cultural free-for-all that encompasses devotion, parody, commercial exploitation, and scathing critique. For every Bart Simpson seen meditating cross-legged in a satirical cartoon there is still an Alanis Morissette earnestly singing "Thank U" ("thank you consequence / thank you silence / . . . thank you India / thank you providence / thank you disillusionment / thank you nothingness" [Tweed and Prothero 1]).

Perhaps no invocation of India was so complex and hard to read as the name of the band that made "alternative" the dominant rock and roll form of the first half of the 1990s: Nirvana. Leader Kurt Cobain's very public struggles with addiction and mental illness—and his ultimate suicide—retrospectively made the band name seem positively gothic. The band's purposeful desecration of the Youngblood's hippie classic "Get Together" on their song "Territorial Pissings" (1991)—along with its anti-guru "Never met a wise man" lyric—made sharp comment on the whole 1960s turn-East phenomenon. Similarly dark is a live version of the anti-Vietnam War song, "Born in the USA" that Bruce Springsteen released in 2001; unlike the original anthemic full-band hit of 1984, this version uses a slide guitar to sound like a sitar and in doing so neatly connects up the Southeast Asia of the Vietnam War with the South Asia of the late 1960s turn East.

The line between sincere devotion and tribute on the one hand, and minstrelsy and exploitation on the other, remains hazy. When Madonna performed her "Ray of Light" at the 1998 MTV awards with "henna body art on her hands, wrists, and face" and a "new arrangement that drew on the sounds of India," it was possible to see it as either an outgrowth of her own engagement with Eastern spirituality or as an insulting game of dress-up (Gracyk 91). This, of course, raises the specter of the American tradition of blackface. At least two critiques, one from 1968 and one from 1989, have made explicit the connection between blackface minstrelsy and turning East; both pivoted on a rewrite of the 1919 song "Swanee"—a "Dixie" number, written by George Gershwin and Irving Caesar and first performed, in blackface, by Al Jolson. The original song is organized around the line "Swanee, how I love ya, how I love ya, my dear old Swanee." On the cover of *MAD* magazine's hippie parody of 1968, the border features the words "Swami, how I love ya, how I love ya, my dear old swami"; similarly Tuli Kupferberg's song "Swami" goes "Swami how I love you how I love you / Swami Everykinanda" (*MAD about the Sixties*). Separated by more than twenty years, the two song lyrics bring to light, in one bad joke about the modern turn East, the long history of masquerade that lies at the heart of American popular culture. What got lost in translation, of course, as all manner of white Americans made (racial and religious) sense of the East was that the United States was now home to thousands of real-life Indians and other South Asians. Rather than face this new reality, with all of its complexities, many Americans turned instead to the bad old habit of minstrelsy, but this time figured out how to "brown up" rather than "black up."

The cultural history of the changes wrought by the Hart-Cellar Act of 1965 cannot even begin to be written: those changes continue to shape American life—from its demography, to its physical landscape and popular culture. The appearance of Ravi Shankar on the American scene was an augury—a heads-up to white Americans—that they would have come to terms with new populations and their cultural stuff. But while Shankar and all the "karma cola" coming in his wake influenced American culture immeasurably during the Vietnam War and in the years after, the impact on the world of music, ironically, was ultimately negligible. The people who would utterly change American music in these years came from the tiny island of Jamaica. In a fascinating case of cultural imperialism in reverse, these young Jamaicans (mostly in the Bronx and other parts of New York City) helped invent the dominant popular music of the past twenty-five years: hip hop.

CHAPTER 5

South Bronx, 1977

Jamaican Migrants, Born Jamericans, and Global Music

> Throw that beat in the garbage can.
> —The B-52's

> A refugee child, Mariel saved things.
> I was American. I wanted to throw
> everything away.
> —Maxine Chernoff,
> "The Hills of Andorra"

It was difficult, as we argued in the previous chapter, for South Asian Indians to make many inroads into the actual production of culture in the first decades of their mass migration to the United States. White Americans—especially the young hippies who adopted Ravi Shankar and so many other "Eastern" things —helped direct the workings of a cultural marketplace in which Indian stuff was highly valued but Indian people were not granted much space to construct cultural goods. Promoting mythologies about Indians as born mystics and India as a place of unchanging spiritual truth made it possible for many socially powerful white Americans to push "real" Indians out of sight. For some in the counterculture this may have been an "unintended consequence" of a well-intentioned turn East. Nonetheless, it represents a powerful example of how immigrants have been blocked from having full citizenship in the world of popular culture, even by putative sympathizers.

A very different narrative develops when we turn to another important migration, that of Jamaicans, in the post-1965 period. In some ways this is a much more complex story to tell, because it involves some very contradictory lessons about the increasing internationalization of trade and cultural exchange that we have come to call globalization. What is under investigation in this chapter is a moment in the history of colonialism (and neocolonialism) when a shift from outright dominance of Jamaica by England to a more diffuse type of economic and cultural control by the United States opened Jamaicans—and later Jamaican Americans—to all the pitfalls and possibilities available to "global citizens." The central question here has to do with how the "victims" of cultural imperialism (defined here as the coercive exportation of goods and styles), the Jamaican migrants of the 1960s and 1970s, were able to play such a shaping role in the launching of hip-hop music in the United States.

The Jamaican (and "Jamerican") innovations that energized the formation of this new music in the United States represent a fascinating case of cultural takeover of a more powerful entity by seemingly marginalized forces. While African Americans and Jamaican Americans had for decades collaborated on a variety of political initiatives over the course of the 20th century, never before had they engaged in such a focused and sustained process of cultural sharing. One central argument that will be developed here is that Jamaicans came to the United States with an amazing amount of American cultural literacy: Jamaican life had been flooded with American cultural goods starting in the 1950s, and Jamaicans had, throughout the 1960s and early 1970s, created a few crucial and powerful strategies for reconfiguring and recontextualizing that American stuff. From American rhythm and blues to Hollywood Western movies, Jamaicans took the offerings of First World power and changed them from "below." In doing so they embodied one of the most puzzling results of cultural imperialism: as American culture industries spread their influence around the globe, these multinational corporations instructed growing numbers of Americans-to-be about how to "speak" the languages of American popular culture. These adaptations have not been unproblematic: as Deborah

Thomas has cogently argued, Jamaicans have a love-hate relationship with U.S. popular culture and that love-hate relationship is an "integral element" of their identity (248). If Jamaicans—especially Jamaican youths—have found ways to practice "radical consumerism" (a concept Thomas borrows from Daniel Miller), they also have developed deep resentments about living in the economic and cultural shadow of the United States (248, 250).

This complicated dynamic comes quite clear in the case of post-independence Jamaica and with the migrants that left Jamaica to come to the United States in the 1960s and 1970s. Jamaicans had been coming in small numbers to the United States for decades by the time of the Hart-Cellar Act and had exerted a substantial influence on the political life of New York—and the rest of the nation. Black nationalist leader Marcus Garvey established a major following from his base in New York during the 1920s, and a number of other Jamaican transplants to America made important contributions to American political culture. But before 1965 Jamaicans had not played a shaping role in American cultural life. Their numbers were simply too small for this, and their intricate working-out of relations with African Americans made it difficult for them to gain direct access to a non-black American public.

In the 1970s, though, Jamaican Americans managed to enact a major paradigm shift in the American music business. They did so by redeploying cultural approaches that had already been perfected—under conditions of great duress—in Jamaica. These musical strategies relied on a cultural process known as "bricolage," or making new products out of limited resources. Samuel Kinser defines bricolage as a way to make culture for people in difficult circumstances; they "construct their lives and their cultural activity from interchangeable parts, parts which one can make do in many different situations. Since resources are so limited, everything must serve six purposes" (quoted in White and White 151). These musical tactics were used by Jamaicans in Kingston (in a cultural field heavily influenced by the global reach of American popular culture) and in the Bronx (in what has to be seen as an internal colony of the United States). Jamaicans arrived in the United States having already served a sort of cultural apprenticeship through their own consumption and revisions of American popular forms. They would use their experience of American imperialism to become leading innovators in American music and thereby demonstrate that immigrants might now have to be reckoned with not as "contemporary ancestors" (as Indians had) but as guides to the future.

One of the most powerful stories that has been told and retold in histories of hip hop has to do with the American life of Jamaican immigrant Clive Campbell, later known as Kool Herc, and widely credited as the first "Jamerican" to transplant Jamaican music-making techniques in American soil. Kool Herc's biography, even in its barest outlines, holds in it a great deal of crucial information about Jamaican immigration, about the history of colonization that predates it, and about the way that Jamaicans (and Jamaican Americans) have come to exert cultural power in the world—and in the U.S.-centered popular culture industries—far greater than one might have predicted based on the size of the island, its population, and its economic status.

What is usually emphasized in retellings of the life of Kool Herc is his ability, in just ten years' time, to go from an awkward and green immigrant in 1967 to a founding figure of hip-hop music in New York by the late 1970s. Campbell himself has promoted this version of his biography, telling often of how, even though he came to New York from Kingston, a major city, he felt like "a country boy" in America (Chang 72). Attending Alfred E. Smith High School in the Bronx, Campbell found it difficult to fit in, according to some accounts because of his accent, and threw himself into weight lifting: hence the nickname Hercules, later shortened to Herc. Campbell also spent a huge amount of time in these years collecting records and studying audio technology. His collection of tunes and his technological savvy would, within a few years, help Campbell establish himself as the progenitor of a new musical culture.

But it only takes the slightest shift in focus to discover that perhaps the most important historical lesson taught by Clive Campbell has more to do with who he was and what he knew when he got on the plane in Kingston. This young man, Clive Campbell, was already deeply familiar with American culture, and had learned much about the white fantasies of his new homeland from watching *Dennis the Menace* and *Bewitched* on television back home in Kingston and much about musical taste by listening to the radio and the tunes provided by Jamaica's well-established mobile sound systems (Hager 31). Campbell's mother had come to New York before him and sent him records; James Brown and the pop and soul sounds of Motown were favorites (Nelson 16).

The basic insight Campbell developed in the Bronx—or, to be more accurate, adapted from Jamaican musical culture—is that dancers liked it when he extended the "break" of a song as long as possible, most notably by switching back and forth between two copies of the same record. As Campbell tells it, "I was smoking cigarettes and I was waiting for the records to finish. And I noticed people was waiting for certain parts of the record" (Chang 78–79). The technique of breaking down a song and then reconstituting it was familiar to other Jamaicans and fans of Jamaican music. For a few years before Herc's Bronx ascendancy of the mid-1970s, one of the most popular subgenres of Jamaican reggae music was "toasting"—a style defined by the kind of beat collages Herc was working on, with the addition of a vocalist who would rhyme over this new musical track (Kenner 352). (In England, reggae DJ Dennis Bovell was arrested during a skirmish in a club for inciting a riot. During his trial the judge asked what he was saying over the speakers as the violence broke out. Bovell tried to explain that "it was a record where people speak over music or a song." The judge responded by exclaiming, "Do you expect me to believe that people *talk* over records?" Bovell was convicted. [Bradley 425]).

Herc realized very quickly that his audience was not interested in reggae music; to reach them, he needed to create new beats out of more accessible material. As Afrika Bambaataa, another important early DJ puts it, Herc "took the same thing they was doing . . . [in Jamaica] and did it with American records, Latin, or records with beats" (Toop 69). Herc continued to follow the Jamaican model by augmenting the cut-and-mix musical tracks with his own vocals, which often consisted of little more than "shout-outs" to friends in the crowd, or simple and catchy phrases that were part of the current youth lingo ("to the beat y'all," "and you don't stop") (Toop 69). He also practiced the centuries-old technique of call-and-response developed by Africans and their descendants in the diaspora; this is a convenient and effective way to create community among performers and audiences (or preachers and their congregations, or politicians and their supporters). Herc saw that the crowd would stay with him if he left a space in his performance for audience members, for instance, to shout out their own names. Rap

vocalists (soon called MCs—short for mic controller or master of cere-
monies, depending on whom you ask) made this kind of audience participation an integral part of their shows.

Herc was the first important American example of what S. H. Fernando, Jr. has called a new kind of "cultural hero" (33)—the hip-hop
DJ—who combined entrepreneurial drive and artistic vision to introduce innovative soundscapes to ecstatic audiences. Perhaps foremost
among Kool Herc's gifts was his Kingston-bred sense (there born of a
few different kinds of necessity) that music is best enjoyed in public, in
a large crowd, and played as loudly as possible. In interviews Herc has
acknowledged that the whole idea of creating a mobile sound system
was inspired by a man named George (also known as King George),
whom he heard spinning tunes in St. Mary's Parish in Kingston (Toop
4; Chang 68). For his sound system, Herc borrowed heavily from his
father; he even had business cards printed up that read "Father and
Son" (Chang 70). This kind of intergenerational connection was significant to pioneer DJs. Grandmaster Flash (also with roots in the Caribbean) pilfered his father's record collection regularly. In wonderful adolescent fashion (and with obvious psychological dimension), though,
Herc wanted to create bigger sounds than his father's equipment could
provide (Nelson 16). Ultimately, Herc and his crew developed a "massive sound system" that included a state-of-the-art amplifier and huge
speaker columns. Many observers have agreed that "Herc's sound system was so powerful that when he held a block party nobody tried to
compete. He would even occasionally shame Flash in public, demon-
strating the superiority of his set-up over Flash's homemade rig" (Fernando 43; Toop 62) (see fig. 5.1).

If Herc did not have the best hands or eyes—Grandmaster Flash insists that Herc "couldn't mix too well" and relied too much on "needle
drops" instead of the more accurate headphone-based audio cueing
(Toop 62)—he did have great ears. Almost every convincing account of
the early days of rap music suggests that the great DJs had a voracious
appetite for all kinds of music and the ability to repackage it in a plea-
surable way for their listeners. Afrika Bambaataa was perhaps the most
outrageous of the first-generation Bronx DJs, "tricking" African American and Latino audiences into "dancing crazy" to the Rolling Stones,
the Monkees, the theme from *The Pink Panther,* and so on—in doing so

Figure 5.1. DJ Kool Herc was known
for his enormous booming sound
system, inspired by the Jamaican
sound trucks he heard in Kingston
in his youth

instructing them that great beats can be found almost anywhere (Toop 66). Reggae DJs had been finding usable "riddims" all over the place in the years prior to the founding of rap in the Bronx, but Herc was more responsible for introducing the concept to the Bronx than any other DJ. Like his Jamaican forebears—Sir Coxsone, Prince Buster, and others—Herc understood that finding good tunes from which to make variations was a form of cultural capital, a concept we are using here to denote those benefits that accrue to a person with particular skills, educational attainments, and so on. Having first—and sometimes exclusive—use of good beats was an important aspect of the DJ's work. So, again following Jamaican example, Herc would sometimes soak the labels off records so that his competitors would not be able to figure out where he got his beats from (Fernando 33). For Kool Herc, the song "Apache," as performed by an obscure Jamaican disco group, became a signature rhythm of sorts, and a true crowd-pleaser when rappers Coke La Rock and Clark Kent added vocals (Hebdige 138).

"Digging in the crates"—searching for good beats in used record stores, yard sales, and so on—has been enshrined since the first days of rap music as one of the most important tasks for the successful DJ. Clive Campbell was already "digging in the crates" in Kingston, where he found in his father's record collection everything from the au courant vocal stylist Nina Simone, to the country crooner Jim Reeves (Chang 68). Herc added one more crucial factor to his mix of record-collector resourcefulness and the sheer sonic power of the sound system. Herc brought with him to the United States (or rediscovered when he started making music on his own) the Jamaican musical strategy of "versioning." Quite removed from a central impulse in American music-making—and listening—that puts value on "originality" over all other qualities, Jamaican artists had, for some years, been creating "versions" of popular tunes (or "riddims"). Issues of copyright infringement were not germane throughout the years of reggae's rule, because Jamaica was not a signatory to the international copyright agreement. Legal issues aside, musicians in Jamaica have insisted on the premise that taking a musical track and revising it (thus creating a "dub") is its own art form —not a diminished form of somebody else's art. As one musician puts it, "It's not like we stealing anything from anybody. We take a [song] and update it and re-record it." Applying new ideas to an existing track, according to this musician, is a way of "anointing" the song (Hebdige 86). A number of technological innovations added to this mix: reggae performer Dennis Alcapone, for instance, has noted that producer King Tubby used reverb to great effect, making "every song sound rich" (Bradley 314). Kool Herc helped bring this idea—that a new song was always waiting to be born out of an old one—to the Bronx and the rest of the United States, and in doing so, helped found hip-hop music.

DJ Kool Herc's life and career teach numerous lessons to students of immigration and American popular culture about the complicated relationship of cultural imperialism and the arts of the colonized, about the shifting definitions of production and consumption in the age of globalization, and about the ways African Americans and black immigrants to the United States have engaged with each other. To make sense of all this we will have to delve into Jamaican history, U.S. involvement in the Caribbean, theories of globalization, post–World War II American urban demographics, and the relationship of production and consumption in the American popular music business. Doing all this, we will develop a fuller understanding of rap and reggae as mutually constitutive and we might come to appreciate the "miracle" that rock critic Robert Christgau has described: "that one fucked-over little island should prove such a treasure house" (*Christgau's Consumer Guide* 319).

Running from Jamaica/Rocking in America

It takes a lot of history to get Clive Campbell onto the tarmac of the New York airport that had only recently been renamed to honor the memory of John F. Kennedy, the slain American president who had not only written a book called *A Nation of Immigrants,* but had also begun the process of immigration policy reform that would ultimately bring so many Jamaicans to the United States. For a number of reasons, it is a history that cannot be told using traditional immigration history templates, the kind that focus mostly on individual will and need, on the one hand, and state policy on the other. To get a handle on the experience of Jamaicans in New York—whether immigrants or born "Jamericans"—we will have to travel around a triangle that connects the island of Jamaica to two other islands, New York and England. In doing so, it will become clear that Kool Herc's story offers up a powerful lesson in the meanings of post–World War II globalization.

Jamaica was a colony of Great Britain for nearly three hundred years; before that it had been under Spanish control since the time of Columbus. This is not to say that the United States took no interest in the affairs of its Caribbean neighbor; beginning with the Monroe Doctrine of 1823—a declaration of the primacy of the United States in the Western Hemisphere—and intensifying in the decades surrounding the turn of the 20th century, the United States made it clear in a number of ways that it had military, economic, cultural, and political interests in the region. During these years the United States was victorious in the Spanish American War, took control of the Panama Canal Zone, involved itself in the internal politics of Haiti and the Dominican Republic, and purchased the Danish West Indies (now the Virgin Islands). The islands of the Caribbean offered, among other things, relatively cheap labor, easily exploitable markets, and strategic locales for military bases. All three of these factors would become crucial in determining the relationship of the United States to Jamaica (Baptiste 11).

The central fact for understanding Kool Herc's story is that during the World War II era, as Norman Stolzoff writes, "Jamaica's involvement with the United States began to increase at the same time as its political ties to Britain started to decline" (38). One of the great social developments of the immediate post–World War II era is that of decolonization. First came Gandhi's successful leadership of India's liberation struggle in the late 1940s; numerous African, Asian, and Caribbean nations would follow the Indian example in the next two decades. Jamaica's full political independence would not come until 1962, but its political distancing from Great Britain started much earlier. The first steps Jamaica took to shake off the formal colonization imposed by the British were accompanied by the development of a less formal, but similarly imbalanced relationship, with the United States. This relationship was similar to that which obtained in Trinidad and Tobago, where calypso singer Lord Invader sang in the early 1940s of being forced to work for "the Yankee dollar."

Of paramount importance was the establishment of two American military bases—one at Sandy Gully and one at Vernon Fields—on the island. Military personnel brought music with them (particularly American rhythm and blues records); so too did Jamaican migrant workers returning from newly created opportunities to pick fruit in the United States bring cultural goods (records, stereo equipment, and so on) back with them to the island. Working together with the steady stream of American music beamed from Miami radio stations (and later the television programs), these developments insured that American culture would quickly exert influence on Jamaicans.

These early glimmers of this cultural imperialism must, of course, be understood as an adjunct to the neocolonial economic imperialism (and the attendant political control) that the United States—its government and its corporations, the World Bank, and the International Monetary Fund—have ultimately imposed on Jamaica (*Life and Debt*). As Laurie Gunst has explained in her fascinating book about the crime culture that began developing in Jamaica in the 1960s, the island's economy was structured in this era by two industries: bauxite and tourism. For

all of the economic and cultural injuries inflicted by the "heavier" industry, Gunst rightly argues that tourism "was even more socially cor-
rosive." She explains that even though tourism brought "seasonal,
low-paying jobs to a few people who lived in the small towns on the
north coast . . . this work came with a wicked, atavistic fantasy: the
Jamaica Tourist Board wanted white visitors to see the island as the
Old South of *Gone with the Wind*" (*Born* 74). Michael Manley, Jamaica's
prime minister for much of the 1970s and leader of the socialist People's
National Party, recognized that whatever tourism brought to Jamaica, it
took out quite a bit more: "If our socialist programs are allowed to
mature . . . Jamaica could finally become a paradise for Jamaicans, not
just for the tourists" (Davis and Simon, *Reggae International* 174).

The PNP's socialism was not allowed to flourish. Manley had great
ambitions for the island, but his plans were repeatedly undercut by ex-
ternal forces. Lloyd Bradley summarizes Manley's first year in office, in
the early 1970s:

> He introduced a basic minimum wage and legislated for improved
> labour relations; set about renationalizing industries sold off to pri-
> vate ownership by the previous government; launched a nationwide
> literacy campaign; poured money into the ailing health and educa-
> tion services; laid extensive public-housing plans; and initiated a
> scheme to encourage small farms and holdings by providing credit
> facilities for interested parties to buy land from the government or
> large corporations. Consumer confidence was up, as unemployment
> that had been rising steadily through the last few years leveled out
> and started to decline. (282)

These innovations—and Manley's closeness to Cuba's Fidel Castro—
were met with outright hostility by U.S. businesses and the American
government. The nationalization of the bauxite industry led aluminum
companies to withdraw from Jamaica (Stolzoff 101); Manley's socialist
ties caused Jamaica to be "almost frozen out of foreign investments and
loans as a result of U.S.-led directives to the World Bank and the International Monetary Fund" (Stolzoff 101). By the middle of the 1970s the
situation in Jamaica was dire, as Laurie Gunst explains:

The American press painted a harsh portrait of the island, the International Monetary Fund (IMF) devalued Jamaica's currency and destabilized an economy already battered by the oil price shocks of the 1970s, and travel agents discouraged their clients from going to Jamaica, thereby crippling the industry on which the island depended for its survival. And a tide of high-powered weapons flowed like bloody currency from the United States into the hands of political gunmen. (*Born* xviii, 42)

It has also been suggested by a number of credible sources that the CIA helped to destabilize Manley's PNP; by the time of Manley's race against longtime opponent Edward Seaga of the Jamaican Labour Party in 1976, Seaga's name was appearing all over Kingston as CIA-ga (Davis and Simon, *Reggae International* 174). Whether or not the CIA was this directly involved, the fingerprints of the United States were all over Jamaica by the 1980s. The crack economy rooted in the consumption habits of Americans turned Jamaica into a convenient midpoint between Colombia and the United States. The Caribbean Basin Initiative —purportedly an attempt by the United States to boost the economy of the region and stave off communist encroachment—actually served as a further conversion of public sector activity into private ownership. Its effect, overall, was to turn Jamaica, along with many other islands of the Caribbean, into "offshore sweatshops" where cheap labor could be easily exploited. By the early 1980s, Jamaica had the highest per capita foreign debt of any nation in the world (Gunst, *Born* 34; Kuper 18). The Jamaican dollar, which had been exchanged at a rate of 5.50 for each U.S. dollar in 1989, traded in 1995 at 40 to 1 (Chang and Chen 211). The tourist industry now encompassed what has come to be called "sex tourism"—the search for "virile" and available Jamaican men by women from the developed world, what Klaus de Albuquerque, following Calypso singer the Mighty Skipper, calls the search for "the big bamboo" (57).

Since at least the time of World War II, Jamaica has been under a two-pronged attack. While the tourist industry—created and supported mainly by the fantasies and dollars (and pounds and francs and deutschmarks . . .) of white visitors—colonized Jamaican land and created a caricatured version of Jamaican culture, the United States government and its corporations were forcing (commodified) elements of American culture onto the island. U.S. interests in Jamaica had even more far-flung results: they caused widespread migration of rural Jamaicans to the Jamaican urban centers and to the United States. As Philip Kasinitz writes, "the infusion of American capital since the mid-1960s" can be seen to have upset Jamaican labor patterns and contributed to high rates of unemployment and, finally, to large-scale emigration (28–29). Tracking this part of the story will bring us back a little bit closer to Kool Herc and will give us a better sense of what Jamaican poet Louise Bennett meant when she called emigration from Jamaica (in this case to England) "colonization in reverse" (http://social.chass.ncsu.edu/wyrick/debclass/Revers.htm).

The numbers alone are staggering. To understand them it is important to keep in mind two important dates. In 1962 Jamaica declared its independence and Great Britain responded by passing a very restrictive new law that severely limited Jamaican immigration (Reimers 145); and in 1965 the United States passed the Hart-Cellar amendments to an earlier (1952) immigration law. The 1952 Immigration and Nationality Act (known as the McCarran-Walter Act) had stuck with a traditional approach that limited immigration by applying a complicated (and largely racist) formula having to do with national origins. It had been particularly strict with regard to emigrants from "dependencies"—or colonized lands. But Jamaican independence freed its citizens from this ban, and the Hart-Cellar Act created a new math entirely (Ward 75–79; Buff, *Immigration* 68).

Before 1965 emigrants from Jamaica generally went to England. Afterwards they were—statistically speaking—much more likely to go to the United States. In 1967, over 10,000 Jamaicans entered the country legally. (Bob Marley was one of the Jamaicans to come into the United States that year; he worked briefly at a Chrysler plant in Wilmington, Delaware [Davis and Simon, *Reggae Bloodlines* 32].) The number jumped to over 15,000 in 1970 and over 19,000 in 1979. In the 1980s, more than 213,000 Jamaicans came to the United States—some 9 percent of the island's population (Gunst, *Born* 22; Reimers 130; Foner 199; Mandle 55–56). Taking a broader view, it is also worth noting, as Rachel Buff has, that the "foreign-born Black population of the United States doubled between 1960 and 1970, and increased more than two and a half times between 1970 and 1980" (*Immigration* 77). The largest majority of these immigrants settled in New York.

But what did these immigrants "do" to America and what did America "do" to them? Constance Sutton has nicely summarized this immigration dynamic. She notes that Jamaicans and other immigrants from the region have "Caribbeanized" New York, providing not only labor, but also new ways of talking, eating, worshipping, and—most relevant to our concerns—new ways of performing (15–30). A few individual Jamaicans had earlier exerted a major influence on the development of U.S. culture, but it was only the immigrants of the 1960s and 1970s who were able to change, permanently, American styles and institutions.

Jamaicans in New York have also forged "new" identities—as "West Indians" on the one hand, and as "African Americans" on the other (Sutton 19). Their West Indian identity has gained particularly from Jamaican participation in yearly carnival celebrations in Brooklyn—a Caribbean import that was originally the domain of Trinidadians. African American identity is sometimes trickier to negotiate, given that for West Indians entry into the racialized culture of the United States has often meant a step down in status; it has also meant direct competition with African Americans for jobs. Over decades, African Americans had developed unflattering terms for West Indians that included "monkey chasers" and "black Jews." (A Harlem rhyme of the 1920s cruelly suggested that "When a monkey-chaser dies / Don't need no undertaker / Just throw him in de Harlem River / He'll float back to Jamaica" [in Osofsky 134–135].) For these reasons, maintaining a sense of Jamaican identity (sometimes through a vague "Britishness") or inventing a new "West Indian" identity has seemed preferable to a simple identification as "black" (Kasinitz 45–49; Bradley 140).

In the broadest terms, Jamaicans in New York have created a "crossroads" culture: they operate a switchboard that connects up peoples and cultures of the United States, Africa, Great Britain, and Jamaica. The process by which Jamaicans have become Americans (or "Jamericans") is full of triumphant tales of "colonization in reverse," but even the most cursory look at some of the culture created by Jamaicans and

Jamaican Americans during this great exodus to the United States demonstrates that this movement has been met with a large amount of Jamaican and Jamerican ambivalence. This is nowhere expressed more directly than in a 1976 song by the Meditations, an important roots reggae vocal group, called "Running from Jamaica." In slyly indirect fashion, the singers take note that so many are leaving Jamaica and gloat in anticipation, thinking of the time when the Americans (once again?) close the door on Jamaican immigration: "Look who's running from Jamaica / I hope it's forever . . . When the gates is closed we don't want no knocking." The Meditations were likely noticing not only the general volume of Jamaicans leaving the island, but also the way that migration was particularly decimating the ranks of musicians in Jamaica. A few years earlier, reggae singer Paulette Williams had put it a bit more gently when she implored other Jamaicans to stay home instead of going to England or the United States: "If we put hands in hands / We can build a better nation / Instead of going to another island" ("My Island").

Just as migration to England after World War II had cut down on the number of big band players in Jamaica (and led to some interesting creative developments, as we will see), the new migration was having a similar effect: as one reggae historian has put it, for "a while in 1978 it seemed as though the entire reggae establishment had moved to Brooklyn" (Davis and Simon, *Reggae Bloodlines* 212). The island of Jamaica itself has often been construed as a place of exile by many Jamaicans—particularly those who have ascribed to one form or another of Ethiopianism. From the first stirrings of Jamaican Ethiopianism at the dawn of the 20th century, through the radical back-to-Africa movement of Marcus Garvey in the 1920s and the Rastafarian insistence that everything outside of Africa is "Babylon" (inspired by Ethiopian leader Haile Selassie—also known as "Ras Tafarai"), Jamaicans have frequently imagined themselves as people in exile. This gave reggae musicians from the 1960s onward access to a "language" that put migration at its center. The late 1960s was a particularly ripe time for songs about movement: from Bob Andy's plaintive description of the impossibility of making it in a new land in his 1967 song "I've Got to Go Back Home" to Desmond Dekker's 1968 breakthrough hit "Israelites"—which reached number 9 on the U.S. charts in 1969 and is about having to live outside the promised land—Jamaican artists have continually thematized migration in their songs.

One dominant motif that travels through Jamaican popular culture will be familiar to anyone who has read in American immigrant literature or listened to blues music: as enticing as the prospects of migration might be, there is no guarantee of success. The story of the country boy or girl coming to and being defeated by the city is as familiar in Jamaican culture as it is in the United States. When the roots reggae group the Heptones sang "Country Boy" in the mid-1970s about a clueless transplant, they were tapping into a decades-old Jamaican tradition. The main issue, of course, is that if you leave the country, you must ultimately have something to show for it. As one of Laurie Gunst's informants puts it, once you go to the city it "is like you go a' foreign [i.e., overseas]. You cyan' come back unless your pockets full" (*Born* 75). Poet Louise Bennett had illustrated this dynamic years earlier in her parodic 1966 poem "Noh Lickle Twang!" in which she castigates a migrant who has returned to Jamaica from America with nothing to show for it—not even a "little twang"—or American accent: "Yuh mean yuh goh dah America / An spen six whole mont' deh, / An come back not a piece betta / Dan how yuh did goh wey?" (http://www.pacificnet. net/~jaweb/lou-b-01.html). Of course, many of the these unfulfilled desires were created by the products of the American culture industries— first through music and movies, and then later through the products brought in via cable television, video cassette recorders, and the Internet—and by the examples set by American tourists.

Here and there it is possible to find an outright embrace of emigration to the United States in Jamaican and Jamerican culture. Perhaps most surprising is to find that ten years or so after recording "Running from Jamaica" the Meditations released a celebratory song called "Rocking in America" (1988). With absolutely no irony, and a musical introduction that stitches together "Yankee Doodle" and "Pomp and Circumstance" (perhaps to signify the movement from rebellion to graduation—or in this case, full acceptance), the Meditations sing about a country "big enough for everybody." (A quick look into the history of this group results in an easy answer raised by the question of how we get from "Running from Jamaica" to "Rocking in America." One member of the group, Chris Wilson, was committed to staying in Jamaica, while two others moved to the United States. As Wilson puts it, "I had no hopes from living in America. I thought they should come back to Jamaica to live" [The Meditations, *Deeper Roots*]).

Born Jamericans Rule

The ambivalence that has continued to structure Jamaican migration to the United States is captured well by the name of a dancehall reggae/hip-hop group, Born Jamericans. By calling themselves Born Jamericans the duo naturalizes the fact that an entire second-generation culture of Jamaican Americans has grown up in New York City since the 1960s; mixing Jamaican and American music, they offer up some of the fruits of that culture. But a note of complexity enters when the name of their first album, *Kids from Foreign,* is taken into account. The use of "foreign," the all-purpose Jamaican term for "not Jamaica," reminds us that Jamaicans in New York live in a constant relationship (or at least an implied constant relationship) with Jamaicans on the island.

All born Jamericans, as well as first-generation transplants from the island, also live in a constant relationship with the dominant culture's definition of who they are, a fact that explains a good bit of the ambivalence Jamaicans and Jamaican Americans have expressed about immigration to the United States. It is no surprise to find a slightly sardonic tone in a 1992 song by rap-reggae artist Shinehead called "Jamaican in New York" (a rewrite of Sting's 1987 "Englishman in New York"). In this song Shinehead changes most of Sting's lyrics—but not the lines that go "I'm an alien / I'm a legal alien." In Sting's hands, this declaration is little more than an ironic comment on the slight differences—the "manners" that "maketh" a man—that separate him from the Americans around him. Shinehead's rewrite sharpened and contextualized his own feelings of alienation with the key line, "We're not the only ones with guns." The mention of guns here is certainly meant as a reference to the panic surrounding Jamaican criminality in the 1980s.

One of the major ways that Jamaicans crossed the American radar in the Reagan years was through their role in the crack cocaine trade. Laurie Gunst explains that these years saw an "outlaw exodus to the American promised land" during the 1980s (*Born* xiv). Groups of Jamaicans with roots in the slums of Kingston organized into "posses" (a name taken from American Western movies) and became significant players in the international cocaine trade in the 1980s. According to one Drug Enforcement Agency report, by the late 1980s, Jamaicans were controlling around 40 percent of the drug trade in the United States (http://www.cocainefacts.org/pages/jamaica_traffickers.html).

This fact alone, though, cannot explain the hysteria surrounding the appearance of Jamaican drug gangs in the United States. Coverage surrounding the trial of Delroy Edwards in New York in 1989 makes this clear. The *New York Post* summarized the feeling of the times in its usual succinct fashion, with a huge headline: "JAMAICAN GOT CITY HOOKED ON CRACK" (Gunst, *Born* 159). This tapped into old (and not so old) American fears about immigrants as carriers of disease and mayhem: it was only a few years before this that Haitians were being blamed for bringing AIDS to the United States, and there is a time-tested tradition of arguing that tuberculosis and other communicable diseases come from immigrants. In short, American government officials and media figures pinned a whole complex of anxieties about increased drug use in the Reagan era onto Jamaicans.

When Edwards was convicted, the reporter for the *New York Times* made it clear that the prosecutor had made a convincing case that the Jamaican man was the first dealer to sell crack on the streets of New York. As with the quest in the 1980s to find the single figure responsible for bringing AIDS to America, many Americans were searching for an easy explanation for a complicated social problem (Shilts; Buder B1). The extreme violence of the Jamaican drug gangs made this scapegoating easy: reports suggested that in addition to public executions, gang members sometimes dismembered and boiled their victims as well. One magazine report called the posses "clannish, cunning, and extraordinarily violent" and full of "enthusiasm for . . . torture and murder" (Morgenthau 21–22).

Law officers and government officials picked up on the same Western-movie lingo that the posses themselves favored. One Alcohol, Tobacco and Firearms (ATF) agent described the unsettled nature of gang competition in Brooklyn by calling it "still the Wild West"; an agent in Miami warned that the Jamaican posses "better get out of Dodge City" (Gunst, "Johnny" 568; Gonzalez 26). Shinehead commented more neutrally on the posses, using the same Western motif in his song "Gimme No Crack" (1989) as he described the cocaine dealers entering a city as if they were replaying the gunfight at the O.K. Corral: "It was a cold and rainy Sunday morning / when the baseheads rolled in town / . . . No one dared try to take them / No one shared with them a spliff / No one dared challenge the strangers with the base pipes on their wrist."

The racist dimension of the media response to the Jamaican drug gangs should not be overlooked. One 1988 *Newsweek* article described the presence of Jamaican drug dealers in a small West Virginia town, essentially reconfiguring immigration as attack: "A Jamaican Invasion in West Virginia" was the title, and it only got worse from there (Miller 24). Author Mark Miller described the "tidy clapboard houses and neat apple and peach orchards on land George Washington surveyed centuries ago"—presumably to figure out how many shacks for enslaved African Americans would fit there—that seemed "far from the mean streets usually patrolled by drug gangs." The Jamaicans had come to Martinsburg first as migrant fruit pickers, but they ignored the structural imperatives of migrancy that should have instructed them that it was time to move on and stayed instead to become drug dealers. Worst of all, in the house of one crack dealer, a picture was found of a "former homecoming queen posing half nude, pieces of crack lying about her. According to law-enforcement authorities, she later gave birth to a baby fathered by the dealer" (Miller 24). Here, another old anti-immigrant bias—"they're ruining our women"—is being deployed. In the first few decades of the 20th century, a "white slavery" scare implicated Jewish and Chinese men in particular as exploiters of young white women (see chapter 1).

The *Newsweek* writer indulges in a kind of hysterical language about Jamaicans that was fast developing in the late 1980s. One *U.S. News and World Report* story suggested that "Jamaican gang members are among the hardest to track because they change names and appearances so often" ("A Gang Member's Story"). Discussions about the crack epidemic of the 1980s tended to deny the complicated calculus of global contact and conflict in favor of a simpler math of good immigrants and bad immigrants. Numerous observers have explained that Jamaicans became crucial players in the crack economy largely because of their original location: as Don Robotham put it in an article in the *Jamaica Gleaner* in 2001, "Sections of West Kingston have become a major axis of the international cocaine trade from Colombia to London and elsewhere" (jamaica-gleaner.com). And others, including Winston Rodney of the eminent roots reggae band Burning Spear, have decried how (relatively) quickly Jamaicans have been turned from "good" to "bad" immigrants. While getting the dates of Jamaica–United States immigration slightly wrong ("In the early fifties and sixties and seventies / America stretched forth her hands and welcome us all") in the 1999 song "Statue of Liberty," Burning Spear's point is hard to miss: "Yes we built and now they refuse us / Yes we clean it and now they refuse us." Outlining the many jobs Jamaicans have filled in the United States (fruit picking, hospital work, domestic service), Burning Spear then makes what now seems like an incredibly prescient (if invidious) comparison: "We have no intention to bomb threat / No intention to hijacking."

Jamaican artists have for a long time been aware that the political and cultural meanings of Jamaican immigration to the United States have to be understood as part of the complex web of individual, governmental, and corporate activity we now call "globalization." Even in a parodic song like "Crack in New York," sung by Culture, another roots reggae mainstay, it is made clear that what seems like a local problem (the popularity of crack in New York) is really part of a global system. In this song, leader Joseph Hill sings almost gleefully—if obliquely—about how a surprising early 1980s alliance between socialist leader Michael Manley and the United States government ("Operation Buccaneer") that was aimed at eradicating marijuana production in Jamaica ended up opening up the crack market. Operation Buccaneer, it should be noted, was largely a failure: as Lloyd Bradley notes, it was aimed at curtailing the huge amount of marijuana exported, but by the end of the 1980s Jamaica was still sending some $2 billion worth of the drug to the United States (470).

The governments of Jamaica and the United States failed to see how this oversimplification (i.e., "bad stuff coming from Jamaica must be stopped") ignored how even a small island could become a major player in the global economy; perhaps all the United States government wanted out of the plan, anyway, was to gain leverage in Jamaica it could then use to destabilize Manley's government (Bradley 470). For too long, the movement of people, culture, and contraband into the United States has been mystified by those keepers of "the official story" who want to divert attention away from the difficult facts of globalization. Saskia Sassen has written as clearly as anybody about the ways that the old language of immigration (privileging individual will, linear movement, and so on) has obscured the workings of globalized activity (xxxi). As Sassen writes, migrations "do not just happen; they are produced. And migrations do not involve just any possible combination of countries; they are patterned" (56). It is worth quoting Sassen at length, because her comments bear directly on how Kool Herc ended up in New York, and why he had the effect he did:

> In the 1960s and 1970s the United States played a crucial role in the development of today's global economic system. It was a key exporter of capital, promoted the development of export-manufacturing enclaves in many Third World countries, and passed legislation aimed at opening its own and other countries' economies to the flow of capital, goods, services, and information. The emergence of a global economy . . . contributed both to the creation abroad of pools of potential emigrants and to the formation of linkages between industrialized and developing countries that subsequently were to serve as bridges for international migration. Paradoxically, the very measures commonly thought to deter immigration—foreign investment and the promotion of export-oriented growth in developing countries—seem to have had precisely the opposite effect. (34)

In short, as Sassen explains, the massive migration of Jamaicans to the United States in the 1960s and 1970s can only be explained by looking at British disinvestment from the Caribbean, and American military and economic interest. Upsetting traditional rural modes of existence in Jamaica, American businesses and government officials helped create an "urban reserve" in Jamaica that would soon migrate to the United States (41).

As discussed earlier, the United States has been engaged in the process of "undeveloping" (or "underdeveloping") the Jamaican economy since at least the time of World War II. And Jamaica was not the only target: one need only take the briefest detour into the history of Trinidadian music to find a pointed response being created by calypso artists—from Lord Invader to Mighty Sparrow—who recognized that their homeland was being exploited for raw materials and finished cultural goods (Hebdige 40–41). One question that must continually be tracked has to do with what these culture bearers from developing lands get for their labors; as George Lipsitz and others have explained, members of advanced industrial nations have frequently enjoyed consuming the products of "hinterland" colonies (4–5). As early as 1888 a missionary publication titled *Jamaica's Jubilee* somewhat gleefully suggested that America was "a giant whose increasingly capacious stomach will always be enough to demand all that little Jamaica can produce" (quoted in Thomas 43).

But what happens when these "colonists"—now migrant workers and immigrants—go on the move? Can they become the most expert analysts of their birth culture and their new home, the most influential artists? What sorts of cultural and political alliances might these migrants to the United States form? (One account of a concert by Culture on a Native American reservation slyly argues that leader Joseph Hill went over well with the crowd because he was speaking "indigenous North American to indigenous North American" [Weber].) Roy Simón Bryce-Laporte has made the case that we need to understand New York City not as the center of the world for Caribbean migrants but as either a "northern frontier" or a "pole in a circular migratory stream" (68). Kool Herc, for instance, was ready to create his new art in New York because Americans had been coming to Jamaica for decades (as missionaries, as soldiers, as business people) and bringing with them American cultural "stuff"; meanwhile, Jamaicans had been coming to the States as migrant workers and bringing American goods back home with them (Stolzoff 36). By the time Kool Herc physically landed at Kennedy Airport, he had already been "internationalized."

Louis Chude-Sokei calls the new cohort in New York, London, and so forth, "a postcolonial underclass navigating a global network of immigrant communities" (217). Dub poet and reggae performer Linton Kwesi Johnson said it more sharply in an interview when asked whether signing with Island Records gave him an international base: "Island did not give me an international base from which to operate. [The] fact that I'm a black person from the Caribbean who lives in Britain means that I have an international base. Y'know?" (Davis and Simon, *Reggae International* 163).

As early as 1964, and the New York World's Fair of that year, the Jamaican government and culture industries tried to cash in on this internationalism. That fair, perhaps best remembered for the "Unisphere" that dominated the visual landscape, had as its central theme "Peace through Understanding." But the real focus of the billion dollars' investment made in the fair was industry: planner Robert Moses wanted, above all, to highlight human beings' "achievements on a shrinking globe in an expanding universe." The display of those achievements was underwritten and capitalized on by major American corporations—from Disney to U.S. Steel to IBM (http://naid.sppsr.ucla.edu/ny64fair/map-docs/buildingfair.htm). The Jamaican government also sent a contingent to the fair whose aim was simple: to encourage tourism to the island. Jamaican music was featured prominently at the fair, and it is here that the story gets interesting.

Edward Seaga, then Jamaica's culture minister (and later the bitter rival of Michael Manley), wanted to send ambassadors to the fair who would seem enticingly "different" to the audiences there while not seeming frighteningly "other." Instead of sending a hardcore ska act such as the Skatalites, Seaga featured Byron Lee and the Dragonnaires—essentially an uptown, society dance band. Ska music was a hybrid of Caribbean music (calypso especially) and American jump blues and rhythm and blues that was just taking off in Jamaica; Lee's band called the music it was playing "skalypso" (Bradley 136). The Jamaican government also sent Millie Small (soon to have a big British hit with "My Boy Lollipop"), Jimmy Cliff, and Prince Buster, along with the Dragonnaires. The Skatalites—whose space-age name, a contraction of "ska" and "satellites" was meant to emphasize their modernity and global appeal—were seen as too "rude" for the fair goers. (The Skatalites did cut a song called "World's Fair" with Stranger Cole and Ken Boothe on vocals. They captured nicely the central purpose of the fair, with the lines, "Took my baby to the World's Fair / Let her choose all she need there.")

The real focus, however, was on ska as a dance; hoping to cash in on the demand for new dance steps (following in the wake of the Twist, just to name one), the Jamaican government sent along Carol Crawford, "Jamaica's 1963 Miss World, to provide an easily accessible ska demonstration" (Bradley 136). The idea, as Lloyd Bradley explains, was to present ska as one more activity tourists might participate in when visiting Jamaica. The government also wanted to forge stronger economic ties with the U.S. record industry, and again Lee was the key figure; he had already contracted with Atlantic Records to distribute their product in the Caribbean, and now Lee made a deal to have Atlantic distribute his first U.S. release, *Jamaica Ska* (137).

Ska did not find a broad-based American audience but it did have some important international effects. In Britain it energized a "rude boy" culture of self-styled outsiders who found inspiration in ska tales of anti-authoritarian rebels. Ska—as music and as posture—would exert a shaping influence on the British punk of the mid to late 1970s. In the United States, ska caught the interest of a few key music industry figures, most notably Curtis Mayfield, who coproduced a compilation *The REAL Jamaica Ska* that was inspired by the Jamaican World's Fair visit (Bradley 138). His involvement with this ska project nicely highlights the circle of influence that defines the globalized relationship of Jamaicans to the more "developed" worlds of London and New York. The Jamaican vocal groups that were finding their voices in the world of ska were heavily influenced by Mayfield's own Chicago vocal group, the Impressions. Bunny Wailer (who formed the Wailers along with Peter Tosh and Bob Marley) put it most succinctly when he described the earliest performances by the Wailers as an "impression of the Impressions" (Stephens 175). More materially, Danny Sims, an American producer, promoter, and booking agent—for Curtis Mayfield, among others—became an important figure in shaping the music and early career of Bob Marley (Bradley 403).

But the entire challenge of newly independent Jamaica figuring out what "product" to export to the United States (and the world) is a slippery issue. Albert Murray has provocatively called African Americans the "omni-Americans"—another way of saying that people of African descent in the United States have made a major virtue out of a chilling necessity: they have incorporated all of the most significant American styles and stances into their own new aesthetic. It is tempting, in this light, to call post–World War II Jamaicans "omni-Westerners." Coming out of one kind of colonization (British rule) and negotiating a new kind (American economic and cultural imperialism), Jamaicans busily created not just a culture of their own, but an entire approach to culture that ended up at the heart of the hip-hop aesthetic. This approach —anthropologists call it "bricolage"—is one that favors recombination over originality, powerful displays of style and savvy over "authenticity," and above all an amazing regard for the usefulness of any and all "raw" materials. Kool Herc's real achievement in this light was one of translation rather than invention: his insight was that the practices of Jamaican DJs were portable, not site-specific. To put it another way, it does not matter whether or not Kool Herc was the first person ever on American soil to play records loudly in public and create new songs by mixing the sounds found on those records; rather, what is most important about Kool Herc was his ability to sell Jamaican strategies to American fans and his ability to inspire other small-scale entrepreneurs (i.e., other DJs) to do the same.

Wild West Indians

Jamaicans, in New York and Kingston, had long been creating culture through this cut-and-mix method. It is an approach that forces us, as Norman Stolzoff has argued, to go beyond what he calls the RAP paradigm (records-artists-producers) (xxi). Jamaican (and Jamaican American) musical production cannot be understood, in short, by focusing on discrete products. Instead, process must come to the fore. For years before Kool Herc's appearance on the New York scene, Jamaican DJs had been taking seemingly "finished" products—other records—and fashioning them into something new. This "retreat" from the dancehalls to the studio, as Stolzoff puts it, represented a fascinating case of fans becoming artists (91). David Toop has nicely summarized the cultural meanings of this process as articulated in early rap by suggesting that DJs and MCs were "half-way between consumers and performers . . . and their response to packaged music was to violate it with cutting and mixing" (115).

Cut-and-mix has been discussed in a multitude of scholarly contexts; Dick Hebdige, for one, has called his book about Caribbean music *Cut 'n' Mix*. Many commentators agree that the meanings of the end product of cutting and mixing (if there can be said to be such a thing) cannot be determined by reference to the practice itself. That is to say, a DJ who combines two different tracks to make a new one might love both songs used, hate both songs, love one and hate one, be indifferent to both, and so on. What seems most important to establish is that the DJ has found some use for the original products and chooses to demonstrate mastery through a careful (or sloppy) redeployment of the source elements. Often a DJ communicates her or his superiority to the original product by using it; perhaps more common is the recontextualization of the original as a way of paying homage. In the case of Jamaican and Jamerican cut-and-mix, stakes get even higher as we consider the racial and national dimensions of the cultural work being done. When Desmond Dekker sang his saga of outlaw "rude boys" shooting and looting in a "shanty town" he began with a repeated invocation of "007"—James Bond's number. Given that the first James Bond movie, *Dr. No*, was released in the year of Jamaica's independence (1962) and was set in Jamaica (at least sort of), it is impossible not to hear Dekker's opening lyric as a kind of ironic rewrite of Bond's "naughty-but-necessary" approach to justice. This kind of racialized reformulation is all over Jamaican and Jamerican music—and nowhere more consistently than in the dozens of performances that use the American West and, more to the point, Western movies, as source and subject.

There is no need to go into much detail about the centrality of the Western in American life: as film, literature, and music, the Western has, for some three centuries, helped Americans understand themselves (and explain themselves to others). Since at least the 1960s, Jamaicans have employed Western imagery to enact their own dramas of rebellion and belonging. As Norman Stolzoff explains, many young Jamaican performers in the 1960s "superimposed the drama of the Wild West onto their familiar ghetto landscape, modeling themselves after the cowboys on the movie screen" (82). Cowboys, not Indians. This is the first clue that some sly reversals are being promoted here.

As consumers/producers of popular music, Jamaicans (and later Jamericans and other African Americans) have demanded the right to say where they go in the script. To put this another way, it seems just as possible that young Jamaicans would have, all along, identified with Native Americans—not with the white/Anglo cowboys who represent the (oppressive) dominant majority. But it is no surprise, really, that Jamaicans would stitch themselves in as cowboys: at the movies, that is where most of the power lies. If one is going to indulge in counterhistorical (not to mention counter–present day) fantasy, one might as well make it good. Jamaican music in the late 1960s and 1970s is filled with performers with names like Colonel Josey Wales, Clint Eastwood, Butch Cassidy, and Johnny Ringo, and songs that use "Western" sound effects and storylines; the Skatalites recorded a number of Western movie themes, and DJ I Roy has a whole song (1973) about his viewing of the Sidney Poitier–directed Western *Buck and the Preacher* (1972). The absurd end of all this came with a 1991 song by the Pinchers called "Bandalero," a song that consisted simply of a list of "Western" sounding names and words—"El Paso," "gringos," "Zorro," and bizarrely, "Al Pacino" (Chang and Chen 198).

Occasionally the use of the Western by Jamaican artists has had manifest political content—as with Bob Marley's "I Shot the Sheriff" (1973). Marley has been quoted as saying, "I want to say 'I shot the police' but the government would have made a fuss so I said 'I shot the sheriff' instead . . . but it's the same idea: justice" (http://www.bobmarley.com/songs/songs.cgi?sheriff). But even without Marley's explicit political point, the overall meaning of Jamaican "Westerns" has been clear; Louis Chude-Sokei describes the Jamaican revision of Westerns as "allegorical representations of America's dreams of itself . . . rewritten with a pen soaked in the blood of colonialism, slavery, and black ghetto style" (320). The Jamaican "posses" that would ultimately act out their own gunfighter dramas in the United States certainly got many of their ideas from the movies. As Laurie Gunst puts it, these "island desperados are the bastard offspring of Jamaica's violent political 'shitsem' (as the Rastafarians long ago dubbed [the "system"]) and the gunslinger ethos of American movies. They are a Caribbean cultural hybrid: tropical bad guys acting out fantasies from the . . . westerns [and other movies] . . . that play nightly in Kingston's funky movie palaces" (*Born* xv).

The movies, of course, have their own agenda. One of the most fascinating demonstrations of how dominant and oppositional readings can come into conflict is offered in the hugely important 1973 film, *The Harder They Come*—the movie that launched Jimmy Cliff as an international star. In the movie, Cliff plays Ivan, a character loosely modeled on a Jamaican outlaw of the 1940s named Rhygin (also known as "Alan Ladd" and "Captain Midnight") (Gunst, *Born* 49). Ivan has migrated to the city to find his fortune as a reggae singer, but soon is leading a life of crime. Early in the movie he watches a Western and begins to pattern himself after the hero; instructed by another audience member that the hero cannot die in the first reel, Ivan begins to live out a fantasy rooted in his vision of himself as a Western hero. If he doesn't die in the first reel, nor does he make it out of the movie alive (Gunst, *Born* xxi). A year later, Mel Brooks would make a whole movie (*Blazing Saddles*) whose generative joke is the visual one of seeing a black man as a cowboy/sheriff; in *The Harder They Come*, Jimmy Cliff convincingly acts out some of the ways that fantasy could have appeal for "downpressed" Jamaicans (see fig. 5.2). A few years later, in 1976, Bob Marley would play with the same imagery. Appearing at the Smile Jamaica concert soon after being shot (perhaps as a result of his support for Michael Manley), Marley ended his show by rolling up his sleeve "to show his wounds to the vast crowd. The last thing they saw before the reigning king of reggae disappeared back into the hills, was the image of the man parroting the two-pistoled draw of a frontier gunslinger, his head thrown back in triumphant laughter" (Davis and Simon, *Reggae International* 79).

While Hollywood has, from the time of the Ku Klux Klan–glorifying *Birth of a Nation* (1915) onward, frequently told darker people that they are marginal, inhuman, ugly, and so on, Jamaican musicians demonstrated some ways for black people to arm themselves with the same weapons used against them. Consuming Western imagery and then converting it into anti-authoritarian expression is a significant cultural move on the part of Jamaicans in the post-independence period. The Western imagery made its way into hip-hop culture in the 1980s as well

Figure 5.2. The 1973 movie *The Harder They Come*
revised American Western movies to fit the contemporary Jamaican urban scene

—mostly in fashion, but also in Kool Moe Dee's anti-gun song "Wild,
Wild West" (1987). The use of "posse" language by Jamaican gangs also
became central in the hip-hop world—most of all as a signifier of unity
(Forman 176–183). If movies (such as 1981's *Fort Apache, the Bronx*)
would continue to articulate a tired cowboys versus Indians formula
where the darker people always have to be the Indians, Jamaican, Jamerican, and African American artists found some interesting ways to
turn the tables.

The final twist, perhaps not surprisingly, comes with a few acts offering a metacommentary on the whole of this "Western" cultural history: one move has been to insist on the reality of black cowboys. Here we find Jamaican reggae artist Eek-a-Mouse, who took on the persona of the Black Cowboy on a 1996 release and concert tour (DJ Duke Reid was doing this decades earlier at dances in Jamaica [Hebdige 63]), and the Toronto-based Reggae Cowboys, who combine reggae, rhythm and blues, and country and western as they sing of neglected African American and Native American heroes (www.reggaecowboys.com). Most striking is their self-identification (in a 1999 song) as "Wild West Indians." Making what, in retrospect, seems like an obvious joke, the Reggae Cowboys also have a serious point to make about who can be a hero in a "Western." Roots reggae artists Burning Spear sharpen the anti-colonial political point in their 2000 song "Sons of He": "The Wild West is in our face / Let's not play the cowboys."

Ring the Alarm

Using scraps of available culture—or any sized piece, really—to fashion a new culture has always been at the heart of reggae and hip-hop culture. What Rob Kenner has written of reggae is equally true of hip hop: calling it the "most versatile, least predictable form of music on earth," Kenner goes on to explain that reggae producers can "absorb and reconfigure any sound, from breaking glass to passing gas" (352). Each use of a "found" sound indicates playful and resourceful willingness to foreground one's own consumption processes; this is what led I Roy to rant about a movie he saw and call the result a song and led Afrika Bambaataa to "trick" his audiences by playing snippets of the most unlikely songs (the Monkees!) to keep the beat going. It is only an exaggeration in degree, but not spirit, to say that every hip-hop song is a palimpsest—one song recorded over another.

Rap and reggae—and all the hybrid forms growing out of their merger—begin, then, with someone's good taste (Stolzoff 54). From the Jamaican selectors (DJs) of the 1950s and 1960s, to Kool Herc and Grandmaster Flash (who often explains that his career started in his father's record collection), the most important founding figures have made it clear that success as a producer of music must begin with developing as a savvy consumer (Stancell 116). There is something radical in this development: under capitalism, consumption is supposed to be an endlessly repeating endgame—you buy it, you eat it, it's gone. Then you buy another. Unless it has gone out of style. But Kool Herc brought with him from Jamaica a fascinating challenge to this system, one that suggests a way out of the age-old dilemma of how to have one's cake and eat it too.

What is fascinating is that what Kool Herc brought from Jamaica— essentially booming sound systems and the practice of making new records from old—developed out of scarcity, not plenty. In 1950, as Kevin O'Brien Chang and Wayne Chen explain, a basic home stereo would cost a full year's salary for the average Jamaican. Additionally, migrant workers returning from the United States were bringing back popular American records, thus creating a demand for an appropriate social space in which to share them (119). For years, professional musicians had been emigrating to the greener pastures of labor in postwar Great Britain, making it all the more unlikely that a homegrown system of live performance would develop (Hebdige 62). Gussie Clarke has also explained that Jamaican radio was completely taken over by American rhythm and blues and Trinidadian calypso in the 1950s and that this conservatism led listeners to sound systems that were willing to play newer (and more homegrown) sounds (Bradley 305–306). The sound system directors were small-time entrepreneurs who brought music to people who could not afford to buy it—or play it back—themselves (Davis and Simon, *Reggae Bloodlines* 14).

In the 1950s a few of them, most notably Coxsone Dodd, studied the "personality" DJs then so popular in the United States—who augmented the usual introduction of songs and sponsor announcements with a run of "jive" patter—and imported that concept, thus laying the groundwork for later DJ records (Toop 39). Those Jamaican DJ records would, of course, provide a crucial model for the first generation of American rap DJs (Szwed 9). How quickly Jamaican DJs turned a "lack" (the dearth of live bands, of homemade Jamaican records, and so on) into a lot!

At the dawn of the 21st century it is now a commonplace to assert that Kool Herc's innovation was such a success that it is no longer really possible to separate out rap and reggae. The techniques brought to the Bronx by Kool Herc were just the start; converging thematic concerns, some shared repertoire and rhythms/riddims borrowed back and forth, and actual collaborations between rap and reggae artists all conspired to make it seem as if Kingston and New York, rap and reggae, were overlapping circles and not separate spheres. By the late 1980s and through the 1990s it became increasingly difficult to find the dividing line between rap and reggae (now mostly represented on the American scene by "dancehall"—which frequently featured staccato beats, gravelly voiced male leads, and violent imagery). Richie Daley, a member of the reggae group Third World, described the late-century situation somewhat poignantly, as he noted that there "is nowhere to cross over to anymore" (Jahn and Weber 242). *Village Voice* journalist Elena Oumano declared the same point as an axiom: "Heads [i.e., insiders] know that reggae dancehall is Jamaican hip hop, and hip hop with its template lifted from old-time Jamaican sound system dances is American reggae."

Contemporary reggae artists are certainly clear about how closely tied rap and reggae are: DJ Papa San suggests that "the only difference between rap and DJ [meaning dancehall] is the accent," while DJ Tony Rebel describes rap and reggae as being "from the same family, and they went off in different directions, and now they're getting back together again." Jamaican-Canadian reggae artist Patra and pioneering DJ U Roy argue more strongly that rap is just the American form of reggae (Jahn and Weber 24, 66, 39, 135). There is nothing mystical about the hybrid: as music industry insider Maxine Stowe has explained, the fusion has grown from the simple fact of Jamaican Americans and African Americans living "side-by-side, giving parties, and black American kids going to these parties" (Jahn and Weber 173).

In our own time it is impossible to say for sure whether Haitian American Wyclef Jean, for instance, should be understood as a rap or a reggae artist. From his early career with the Fugees (with Pras and Lauryn Hill, who made her own interesting hybrid music and married a son of Bob Marley), Jean has made it increasingly difficult to separate out the parts of his music that come from New York, Kingston, Port-au-Prince, and so forth. His production of Beenie Man, the Jamaican dancehall artist, has further muddied the waters.

With his complex musical and lyrical approach, Jean is following a precedent set by a number of key rap and reggae players. On the rap side, no one has been more important in bringing "Jamaicanness" (in the vocal delivery, riddims, and lyrical matter of his own music and in promoting and producing Jamaican artists) to rap than KRS-ONE, originally the leader of Boogie Down Productions. With Boogie Down Productions KRS-ONE released a few of the earliest (1986–87) rap-reggae fusion songs and helped launch Jamalski, whose 1993 release, *Roughneck Reality* (like Shinehead's early work) elaborated on the same basic formula. BDP's own *Live Hardcore Worldwide* (1991) was perhaps the most influential of all the "first generation" attempts to bring rap and reggae stylings together.

Less appreciated but equally significant in some ways were the Fu-Schnickens, who combined the vocal particularities of rap and reggae (along with some stunning "nonsense" syllables) so seamlessly on two early 1990s records that they sometimes sound as if they have invented a whole new language: to adapt Motown's famous 1960s motto, we might call it "the sound of young Black America." A case can be made that the two Fu-Schnickens records (*F.U. "Don't Take It Personal"* [1992] and *Nervous Breakdown* [1994]) represent the insane apotheosis of Kool Herc's Jamerican innovation. Foregrounding their West Indian roots, the Fu-Schnickens begin from the premise that rap and reggae are unified. With music borrowed from all over the place (most striking is their use of "Ring the Alarm," originally a Jamaican dancehall hit for Tenor Saw [1985]) and rhymes in patois, Spanish, "standard" English, and African American vernacular that feature a dizzying combination of references to American culture—Bugs Bunny at the center, but also Daffy Duck, rapper Rob Base, *Leave It to Beaver,* Bruce Lee, boxer Gerry Cooney, and on and on—the Fu-Schnickens took the Jamaican practice of recontextualization to lengths at once absurd and deeply meaningful. As critic Robert Christgau has put it, they balance "B-movie fantasy against everyday brutality without denial or despair" (*Christgau's Consumer Guide* 110–111). From Kool Herc's Bronx to the Fu-Schnickens' Brooklyn (and later, the Wu-Tang Clan's Staten Island

and then the rest of the globe), marginalized young people have continually figured out how to redraw the maps handed to them and customize the standardized products forced on them.

The fruits of Kool Herc's simple yet profound act of transplantation are impossible to track completely; if Kool Herc had been a gardener, it would be as if his one graft had grown into a lush forest. How stunning that this started in the South Bronx, compared by Ronald Reagan during a 1980 campaign visit to Dresden after World War II and called "Vietnam" by some residents. The South Bronx, isolated by the construction of the Cross Bronx Expressway in the 1950s, a feat of social engineering that led inexorably to deindustrialization. The South Bronx, abandoned by the middle class in the 1960s and the 1970s. The South Bronx, wounded since at least the late 1960s by increasing gang violence. Wracked by fires (some say 30,000 from 1973 to 1977 [Chang 15]) set on behalf of absentee landlords, and damaged by a citywide blackout in 1977 (Hager 43; Fernando 2). At least two players in the emerging scene, Grandmaster Caz and Disco Wiz (a Latino DJ also known as Louie Lou), suggest that the blackout was a crucial moment in the development of the culture: according to Grandmaster Caz, the redistribution of wealth (i.e., the looting of turntables and other electronics gear) that took place during the blackout "sprung a whole new set of DJs." Disco Wiz agrees, suggesting that before the "blackout, you had about maybe five legitimate crews of DJs. After the blackout, you had a DJ on every block" (Fricke and Ahearn 132–133).

In this era of apparent physical and cultural degradation, a cadre of young immigrants and their African American fellow travelers were busy creating a new culture—one whose key elements included sound, dance, visual art, and technological innovation. If the South Bronx looked like "Fort Apache" to many outsiders (and even plenty of residents), looks were deceiving. New cultures are often described with spatial metaphors—"underground," "avant garde," and so on. This reminds us that even if official commentators could not see it, the South Bronx was teeming with cultural life in the 1970s.

Marshall Berman did notice this, as early as 1984, in a *Village Voice* article. Here, Berman took note of the "physical and social destruction" of the Bronx that began with "the construction of the Cross Bronx Expressway." But even as Berman mournfully surveyed the mindless "urban renewal" that so changed the Bronx, he also insisted that there was "cultural creativity in these ruins": "The South Bronx subculture of rappers, break dancers, subway graffitists, poets, and assorted workers in a multitude of media is one of the most vibrant and creative cultural scenes anywhere today" (18, 25). Wondering, rhetorically, how so much cultural activity could emerge from such unlikely conditions, Berman answers his own question. Relating the cultural ferment of the South Bronx to older traditions of what he calls the "literature of urbicide," Berman describes young people who "have had to stretch all their faculties to find new ways to define themselves, to connect with each other, and to relate to the world" (22). The early hip-hop disc jockeys did this by recontextualizing a Jamaican musical strategy—cut and mix—and transplanting it onto the American urban landscape.

Perhaps no one did this with such stunning artistic verve in the 1970s and early 1980s as Afrika Bambaataa, who grew up in the Bronx River Houses. Afrika Bambaataa lived on the ground floor of one of the Bronx River project's dozen buildings. According to Jayson Byas, who became a follower of Bambaataa, "the center of Bronx River was like a big oval. The community center was right in the middle and Bam used to live to the left of it. He used to play his music, and I would ride my bike around all day. . . . He was like the Pied Piper" (Chang 89, 92–93). According to Bambaataa, the Bronx River Community Center was "one of the original hip-hop big spaces—hundreds of people could fit in at one time" (Fricke and Ahearn 46; Chang 89–95). Other "big spaces"— the gym at the Smith Houses, for instance—were "personalized and transformed" as New York's young African Americans, Afro-Caribbeans, and Latinos planted this music into the only soil they had (http://www.jayquan.com/charliea.htm).

Willing to become a new kind of American, a "Jamerican" as his symbolic descendants would put it, Kool Herc made not only a new identity for himself, but also helped shape a new culture. Kool Herc's innovative application of Jamaican sound system techniques to the New York scene (different from Kingston with respect to fan demands and expectations, musical palette, music industry organization, and so on) is a good example of what sociologists, literary critics, and historians mean when they talk about "reformulating" ethnic identity or even "inventing" new ethnicities in the United States (Kasinitz; Sollors, *In-*

vention). Jamaicans like Kool Herc, especially those of the 1.5 generation as he was (born in Jamaica but came to the United States as children), are faced with myriad choices having to do with identity, from what to call oneself—Jamaican? West Indian? Caribbean American? Black?—to how to dress, walk, and listen to—and create—music.

Mary Waters studied how Caribbean migrants to the United States negotiate all of these issues and found, interestingly, that it is mainstream, middle-class migrants who are most likely to hold on to a fierce sense of national identity and pride. Working-class migrants like Clive Campbell more commonly forge "hybrid" identities—in short, as "Jamericans"—whether born or made. Waters has made it clear that many West Indians in New York lived with hybrid identities—"situational, multilayered, and socially constructed identities"—long before they migrated to the United States. But once in New York, these Jamericans (and other West Indians) have remade the city (Waters 329). They have, as so many sociologists have put it, contributed to the "Caribbeanization" of New York (Waters 39; Sutton). Hip hop is one major area of activity where "Caribbeanization" has exercised its power; one could look at other forms of street culture (parades especially), domestic service, and hospital work to find other obvious examples.

The hip-hop pantheon is full of key players—Biggie Smalls, Busta Rhymes, Canibus, Slick Rick—who trace their roots to Jamaica, an island, as Rob Kenner has noted, that is smaller than Connecticut (353). But more important by far than any literal concept of "lineage" connecting Jamaica to the United States, or Jamaican music to American music, is how Kool Herc and his cohort—the Jamericans—revolutionized the music business in the United States. In the process they taught a huge number of Americans to honor their cultural history, to recycle, to use what they had to get what they needed. As Bunny Lee, a reggae producer, has said of dub maker King Tubby: "He could make music outta the mistakes people bring him—like every spoil is a style to King Tubby" (Bradley 314). Ending this chapter where it began—with the epigraphs—it is worth reiterating that perhaps the greatest gift of the "Jamericans" was their willingness to save things, never to "throw that beat in the garbage can." Their stunning cut-and-mix approach to making culture inspired major artistic developments, not only in popular music, but also in visual and literary expression.

CHAPTER 6

Cyberspace, Y2K

Giant Robots, Asian Punks

> Let the market go and it will bring us the future.
>
> —Steven E. Miller,
> author of *Civilizing Cyberspace,*
> characterizing "net idealism"

> "They" is a fluid concept.
>
> —Zinester Mimi Nguyen

A Nation of Newcomers

The cultural offerings of hip hop—a celebration of hybridity, a focus on "border" as a place and "border crossing" as a constant state, an exploration of the aesthetics of juxtaposition—energized, not surprisingly, an attendant anxiety about protecting borders. Interestingly, one important site where that anxiety was articulated shared with the hip-hop aesthetic a technological craving. We are referring here to the spate of science fiction movies made from the late 1980s through the early 2000s that present the frightening possibility of alien invasion by extraterrestrial beings (of which the movie *Men in Black* and the TV show *Roswell* are examples).

There has been, over the years, ample academic focus on science fiction movies, especially those made during the Cold War, as fantasy expressions of very real dread: *Them!* (1954), *The Fly* (1958), and *The*

Amazing Colossal Man (1957), for instance, each organized around a scientific accident that causes mutation, speak to fears about nuclear capacity and what it could mean. With the Cold War ostensibly over, the genre of science fiction turned new attention toward an old staple: the threat of an alien invasion, a possibility famously able to terrify a "real" radio audience when Orson Welles broadcast *War of the Worlds* in 1938. (A 9/11 movie version of *WOTW* was released in 2005.) Not only did the numbers of alien-invasion movies increase, but during the 1990s these films often contained manifest signals that space "aliens" were stand-ins for the more mundane, terrestrial sort. The beginning of this generation of science fiction movies was signaled by 1988's *Alien Nation,* an unusually self-conscious film set in a future in which extraterrestrial immigration is a given, and Americans are forced to come to terms with this new challenge to their "melting pot" ideals. Although an imagined "alien" spaceship could presumably touch down anywhere, *Alien Nation,* significantly, is located in Los Angeles, one important and central site where the implications of "real" border crossing are continually being worked out—as the so-called zoot suit riots showed. *Alien Nation* continually reminds its audiences that reality stands just behind the fantasy, through references to the fact that the "aliens" are often willing to perform jobs that the "humans" won't do, through deliberately clichéd discussions about whether interracial romances are acceptable, and so forth.

Alien Nation was followed by a host of movies and television series that mined the same territory. The decade when the hip-hop nation reached a peak of influence—and the "new" immigration accounted for fully one-third of the United States' population growth—saw a flurry of science fiction representations on screens large and small of invading hordes. In various ways, these movies tended to associate the manifest invasions they worried about with the "invasions" some American institutions were processing. *The Faculty* (1998) is set in a public school (site of English-only language battles) while in *Visitors in the Night* (1995) the embattled protagonists' last name is English. *Predator* (1987) is set in Central America; its sequel, *Predator II* (1990)— barely sublimating—then "migrates" to Los Angeles. (When Arnold Schwarzenegger, star of the *Predator* movies, was elected governor of California, the sublimation faded even further.) *The Arrival* (1998) locates the threat in Mexico; *Crossworlds* (1996) invokes that border in its name alone. The slapstick *Mars Attacks!* (1996) parodies open-door policies and multicultural ideals: the invaders mouth platitudes about friendship, thereby lulling overly hospitable politicians into a vulnerable state, and then, cackling, open fire once they are close. *Invasion* (1997) worries that humans could be turned into aliens themselves; *Invasion!* (1999), jokingly connects the alien attack to the closing down of the town's factories. The cult TV series *X-Files* presented stories about an impending alien takeover, in which an international conspiracy plans to turn all humans into aliens (and then into a slave race). In *Puppet Masters* (1994), the aliens are literally parasites (who look like slugs and attach themselves to people's necks). All of these movies (and more!) directed audiences' attention toward the perils of an incursion by outsiders, but perhaps most interesting in light of the accomplishments of hip hop's founding fathers is the organizing principle of *Dark City* (1998); that movie creates an invading race called the Strangers, who are a threat to humanity because of the special power of their memory. This very partial list is intended to give a sense of scope to this burst of "alien" stories. We will now focus briefly on one movie and one television series that emerged as particularly influential and successful: *Independence Day* (1996), and *Buffy the Vampire Slayer* (1997–2003).

Our introduction begins with the ending of *Men in Black II*; we point out that the movie deliberately stitches itself into iconic immigration history with a crucial scene involving the Statue of Liberty. What more recognizable symbol exists of the "classic" immigration explored by gangster movies in the 1930s—a useful touchstone to invoke when seeking to soothe or express anxieties about a newer immigration? The movie version of *X-Men* (2000) likewise capitalizes upon the powerful symbolic value of the Statue of Liberty in its final struggle, which takes place in, on, and around the statue. *Independence Day* begins where these two end. Its opening shot is of the statue—which, during the course of the movie, will crumble into the harbor, signaling the end of the promise inscribed there in the poem by Emma Lazarus ("give me your tired, your poor, your huddled masses yearning to breathe free") while showing at the same time that it is the hostile migrants themselves who are to blame.

Independence Day opened to the most successful week in the entire history of movies. By the time its run was over, it had become the top-grossing movie of 1996 both in the United States and worldwide, and was the sixth top domestic grosser of all time (Rogin, *Independence Day* 12). Directed by Roland Emmerich and starring rapper-turned-actor Will Smith and Jeff Goldblum, the movie, according to Michael Rogin, was made with full military cooperation and with an endorsement by former presidential candidate Bob Dole, who had emphasized in his campaign the supposed "depravity" of Hollywood. In short, *Independence Day* is one popular cultural text whose connection with real-world politics was clear from the very beginning.

The film posits that a fleet of alien ships is hovering over the United States. At first their intent isn't clear to everyone, and the U.S. president enlists the help of linguists and technical experts to try to communicate with them, sending messages of friendship. Eventually, of course, it becomes plain that the ships are part of an invasion, and the president turns his attention to figuring out how best to fight back the attack. Patriotic ideals come to fruition as black (Will Smith's fighter pilot), Jewish (Goldblum's computer expert), and WASP (the president) heroes work together against the "new" outsiders, presented in the form of hideous creatures from beyond Earth's borders. Stereotypically enough, the black character provides physical bravery and strength, the Jewish character provides intellectual capability, and the WASP provides nobility of purpose and humility of bearing, coupled with an old-fashioned "can-do" attitude.

This alliance prevails against the odds, and the aliens are beaten back (although the United States suffers some serious losses along the way, including entire cities). *Independence Day* shares the positioning of spunk and smarts against threatening hordes with the TV series *Buffy the Vampire Slayer,* which debuted the next year. *Buffy* did not achieve the same level of commercial success as *Independence Day,* but it was taken seriously by a huge number of cultural commentators, and quickly garnered a loyal and vocal cult following. In the show, which ran for seven seasons—all of which are now good sellers on DVD—a group of California teenagers (and later in the series, young adults) from the fictional town of Sunnydale must constantly discover their own powers and competencies in order to push back, for another day, the constantly invading outsiders. Structurally speaking, the show shares its chief conceits with *Independence Day*, only here the hostile "aliens" are pictured as various supernatural, folkloric figures: vampires, demons, ghosts, the occasional ancient goddess.

Both critical detractors and fans of *Buffy the Vampire Slayer* have made claims that the show is "about whiteness." Indeed, given the composition of the show's cast, especially during the first five years, it would be very hard to argue otherwise. As Jon Stratton has pointed out, although Sunnydale is supposed to be located less than a two-hour drive from Los Angeles—which in 1990 became a "majority minority" population—not only is it "implacably" white, but none of the major (human) characters have "names that would suggest central or eastern European origin, or even southern European origin for that matter" (Stratton 180). (There is one Jewish character, Willow Rosenberg, who is not played by a Jewish actor and who is presented as vigorously assimilated.)

As with *Alien Nation*, it makes sense that *Buffy* would be set in California, the locus of a process that had begun in the 1990s to be called (generally with an alarmist tone) the "browning of America." The "browning of America" was the name of a *Time* magazine cover story in 1990, which referred to census information indicating that by 2056, the United States would be a majority non-white population, and that the single fastest-growing ethnic group was Latinos. Even more than the representations of aliens who come from above, through the air, *Buffy the Vampire Slayer* is fixated on a literal border crossing: Sunnydale's high school is built on a "hellmouth," through which the vampires, demons, and other alien creatures, characterized by their soullessness, are constantly trying to cross. In Buffy's world, the good guys are marked by the goods available to them and their habits of consumption—the stylish clothing worn by the teenagers was the subject of much discussion throughout the show's entire run. Markedly, then, the tropes of the 1930s gangster movies are here reversed, or perhaps more aptly, retired. No longer is the immigrant's ascent marked by his or her access to consumer goods; instead, his lack of caring about clothes sets him off as undesirable. And as Buffy and her friends, never wearing the same outfit twice even when unemployed, defeat Sunnydale's hellmouth version of illegal aliens, they know that theirs cannot be a conclusive victory. They can only stave off the invasion for another day.

Sometimes explicitly (*Alien Nation*) and sometimes more metaphorically (*Buffy the Vampire Slayer*), then, 1990s science fiction took note of the fact that the story of American immigration had changed again and worried about what the new immigration would mean for the way America looked, worked, and played. In this way, these sci-fi works are the direct descendants of the gangster movies of the 1930s—without the clear invitation to root for the immigrants. But in addition to marking a familiar xenophobic anxiety, these movies and television series also represent a sea change in the way immigration itself would be understood in the popular imagination. Narratives of the "classic" European immigration that gave rise to the gangster movies tended to proceed in a recognizably linear format: from "Old World" to "New World," from greenhorn to sophisticate, from yokel to urbanite.

The futuristic locus of these latest musings on immigration reveals that this pattern has changed. Immigrants are no longer forced to represent the American past. Instead, they represent the future. The insistently technological quality of the Jamaican hip hoppers revealed the beginnings of a new answer to the question, "What are immigrants doing to America?" as the conventional portrait must expand to accommodate brain drain, the high-tech industry, and immigrant figures like the techno-savvy Indian character in the hit workplace revenge comedy, *Office Space* (1999). The opportunities for cultural innovation that would become available to immigrants and their children in the age of the Internet extended the cut-and-mix principle far beyond its original social location (South Bronx/music). Young Asian Americans were particularly drawn to amplifying the cross-cultural and multimedia artistic attack pioneered by the Jamericans: their contributions to cyberculture in the 1990s and beyond demonstrated an amazing cultural literacy and a demonstrable willingness to use whatever was at hand (or "at mouse") to advance their artistic and political agendas.

Looking Ahead

On the eve of the 21st century, a group of young Asian American writers launched a creative endeavor that seemed to invoke and make use of the current popular culture fixation on "alien" invasions. These writers announced, tongue partially in cheek in keeping with the aesthetic of sincere irony that characterizes the so-called Generation X, their re-creation of "a monster." The announcement was made on the Internet (at www.gidra.net). It was drafted by a group calling themselves the "editorial recollective" of *Gidra,* a self-published monthly newsletter launched thirty years earlier by a group of UCLA students who had wanted a forum where they could address the particular concerns and issues facing Asian Pacific Americans in the Vietnam War era. The name *Gidra* was taken from a Japanese movie; "Gidra" was an invading monster.

The writers and editors of the new *Gidra* declared with a flourish their intention to create a publication that would provide a way to "get off our collective asses, look ahead and define the world of tomorrow." The circumstances of *Gidra*'s moment of rebirth—from the idealism and bravado demonstrated by its writers, to its relatively low profile on an Internet positively cluttered with Web sites produced by volunteer labor—encapsulates a number of important directions in which popu-lar culture (especially popular print culture) had developed since the original *Gidra* ceased publication after five years. Toward the end of the 20th century, the number of noncommercial "amateur" publications like the new *Gidra,* known as "zines," swelled so quickly and to such a degree that it became common for commentators to use rhapsodic— or alarmist—words such as "revolution," "epidemic," "explosion," or "chaos" to describe the appearance on the scene of this radical cultural expression that swiftly involved millions of writers and readers, but remained largely underground, independent of the institutions that generally prop up (and influence) American publishing: corporate me-dia, advertising, the academy, the government.

Zine publication locates itself in stark and staunch contrast to the mainstream publishing world. "Against the studied hipness of music and style magazines, the pabulum of mass newsweeklies, and the pos-turing of academic journals, here was something completely different," marveled Stephen Duncombe in his introduction to his book on zines and alternative culture (1). Zine publishers seldom earn any money from their efforts, and frequently don't manage to break even, either. They are motivated by passion, not profit; they tend to forgo flawless production in favor of "homemade" flavor; they are mostly publicized by word-of-mouth (and, if paper, distributed from hand to hand); and their raison d'être is to give voice to the intimate and the oddball, rather than the trendy and the conventional.

As intimate as zine publishing undeniably can be, these publications are no less consequentially the product of international, national, and local processes that have radically altered the technological landscape, and along with it the entertainment industry, as well as the relationship of audiences to that industry. An understanding of the import of these zines takes us through military history and through the history of the technological innovations inspired by military demands. Those demands created the Internet, which has now traveled from its origins inside the war machine all the way to the sex lives (and other personal arenas) of its users. And Asian American young people (women in particular) have found in zines a remarkably congenial venue for self-expression and self-definition: scores of zines are devoted to the talents, cultural needs, and political realities of Asian Americans.

This chapter explores zines created by Asian Americans on paper and on-line as process and as product, as grassroots network and as artifact. Delving into military history, the history of technology, and literary history, among others, we will investigate some of the ways that zines have been able to come to terms with the remarkable complexity of meanings carried by the term "Asian American." Unlike the case of Ravi Shankar, whose star presence, we argued, allowed a generation of white Americans simultaneously to endorse and fend off the implications of the "new" immigration from Asia, the exploration of "Asian American" that concerns this chapter takes place from within Asian American communities.

Of central concern here will be the fate of "bodies" and "race" in virtual reality, where some claim that the physical has become all but irrelevant. The question of American identity has been bound up in how physical bodies are evaluated, regulated, and interpreted, by institutions and by individuals, and much scholarship (including that in previous chapters of this book) has traced out the ways in which social meaning is attached to perceived physical characteristics as bodies are racially and sexually marked. What does all this mean in cyberspace, where no actual bodies are to be seen? This chapter focuses on the careful deployment by a generation of Asian American writers of deliberate and purposeful *construction* of the body: of stereotypes and antistereotypes, of codes of behavior and decorum, of strategic affiliations and denunciations, and ultimately of Asian American identity. These constructions, coupled with a historical acceleration of technological accessibility, have been manipulated to create a wide-open, compelling cultural opportunity for immigrants, the children of immigrants, and the grandchildren of immigrants in which social stereotypes, generational conflict, personal ambition, intragroup relationships, and gender politics are contested and presented.

Who Is Asian American on the Internet?

Amy Ling defines "Asian American" in a poem as "Asian ancestry/ American struggle" (1). This couplet captures the duality of experience, the divided heart, that Ling feels characterizes the lived experiences of Americans with Asian ancestry. She continues in this vein to describe a "tug in the gut" and "a dream in the heart"—definitions that are wonderfully evocative, but elusively (and purposefully) nonconcrete. Indeed, the *feeling* of being Asian American, the varied and internal processes by which that name acquires particular meaning, for all its ineffability, is actually much easier to pin down than it is to formulate an answer that refers to a map. While Asia is the world's largest continent, accounting for more than a third of the world's land mass and two-thirds of the world's population—including some 140 different nationalities—the term "Asian American" has been mostly used to refer to American immigrants from certain Asian nations, but not others. Furthermore, the term's application has not been entirely consistent, so that "Asian American" can include one list of ethnic groups in the federal census, another list of ethnic groups in a college's Asian American Studies curriculum, yet another list in the political rhetoric of an activist organization or an elected official, and so on. And when it comes to individuals choosing how to identify themselves, there is an even broader range of usage: some consider themselves to be Asian

American while others do not, even though they or their parents have immigrated to the United States from a country on the continent of Asia. Finally, the meaning of the term has changed over time to suit the rhetorical demands of different cultural moments.

Asian American zine publishing reflects this complexity. A majority of these zinesters do use the word "Asian" or "Asian American" (instead of exclusively using narrower categories such as "Korean American"). But when more specific identifiers are added, or when "guest books" (open forums some Web creators place on their Web sites, so that people who have "visited" the site can comment) are examined, it becomes plain that "Asian American" has been embraced as a way to self-identify by Americans of certain backgrounds, while other Americans with Asian ancestry choose different ways to identify themselves. On the pages (Web and print) under consideration here, "Asian American" seems to include backgrounds that are Japanese, Chinese, Korean, Vietnamese/Cambodian/Laotian, Filipina/o, and sometimes South Asian (Indian, Pakistani, Nepalese, Bangladeshi). In contrast, writing by Arab Americans or Armenian Americans, for example, does not surface when Asian American search engines are used to navigate the Internet, and does not tend to use "Asian American" and related language as descriptors of its content or creators.

In addition to being constituted by a large number of nationalities, the term "Asian American" is further complicated by the fact that it can refer to immigrants, their children, their grandchildren, or even subsequent generations. Since the mid-1800s, when Chinese workers came to build the cross-continental railroad, multiple generations of Asian immigrants have made their way to the United States; and from the very beginning, Asian immigration was linked to restriction and racial anxiety. In fact, the notion of controlling immigration based on ethnic and national factors was born in xenophobic fear of Chinese immigrants: welcomed at first as a source of cheap labor, Asian immigrants were soon the subject of pressures to stop the influx of workers. The Chinese Exclusion Act, passed in 1882, denied admission to Chinese laborers, and subsequent laws in the next two decades further extended the act. The Chinese Exclusion Act also made explicit a provision that had been invoked vaguely since the first American naturalization law of 1790 announced that only "free whites" could naturalize: no state court or court of the United States was permitted to "admit Chinese to citizenship."

The rhetoric surrounding this legislation identified the Chinese and Japanese as forever alien, as "heathens," as so immutably different from white Americans that they could never assimilate into American society and adopt "American" ways. It was here that the precedent was set that immigration to the United States was something that could and should be regulated by the government based on group definitions. This approach to controlling who entered the United States represented a significant departure from earlier notions of immigrant desirability based on individual qualifications. The exclusion of Asian immigrants from American citizenship culminated in 1924, when the Immigrant Restriction Act declared that "no alien ineligible for citizenship" could be admitted to the United States.

Restrictions against Asian immigration began to loosen somewhat following World War II. The Chinese Exclusion Act was repealed, and the 1952 McCarran-Walter Act, while restrictionist in nature, nonetheless gave token quotas to all Asian countries. In 1945, the War Brides Act allowed wives and children of members of the American armed services to enter the United States, without being subjected to evaluation by racial or national criteria. These moves are generally considered to represent a progressive wedge in anti-Asian exclusion; however, historian Rachel Buff has recently pointed out that such measures actually opened up systematic opportunities for a kind of sexual imperialism, in which United States military men created personal circles of influence, which they then claimed as "American" and incorporated into the United States ("Marrying In"). Buff's groundbreaking analysis reveals a power dynamic within Asian immigration, acted out on a sexual and domestic plane, that Asian American zine creators took up in force a half-century later.

Large-scale immigration from Asia did not begin again until 1965, when the so-called new Asian immigration followed the liberalization of the quota system under the Hart-Cellar Act (see chapter 4). By 1970, Asians were the fastest-growing group of immigrants to the United States. By 1980, nearly half of all immigrants to the United States came from Asia.

The "new" immigration would completely change the nature of Asian American communities, which previously had been made up largely of Chinese and Japanese Americans. Now, the variety of Asian groups expanded; soon, the fastest-growing Asian ethnic groups in the United States were those previously not represented. The "new" Asian immigrants came from South Korea, the Philippines, Cambodia, Laos, Vietnam, India, Pakistan, Bangladesh, Singapore, and Malaysia.

The "new immigration" was marked by two visible groups of immigrants. First, in contrast to the earlier generations, came what historian Reed Ueda has called "a human capital migration" of highly educated professionals and technical workers (65). These elites from India, the Philippines, China, and Korea worked in health care, technical industries, and managerial positions.

The "new" immigration also brought waves of low-skilled and poor immigrants from Asia. One million refugees from Northeast and Southeast Asia came to the United States from the end of World War II to 1990. Chinese refugees fled to the United States following World War II. The devastation of the Vietnam War brought refugees from Cambodia, Vietnam, and Laos (including minority subgroups such as the ethnic Chinese from Vietnam and the ethnic Hmong from Laos and elsewhere). Unlike the Chinese railroad workers of a century earlier, these "new" immigrants were planning to stay permanently in the United States. They therefore naturalized in large numbers, brought extended families to the country, and formed new Asian communities as well as transforming and revitalizing older ones.

The history of Asian immigration gives some sense of how complicated and fraught the definition of "Asian American" can be. The idea of a pan-Asian identity, implied by the term "Asian American," dates back to the political activism of the 1960s; the term was first used as an organizing tool to facilitate discussions about issues of racism in the United States and issues of global politics in Asian countries, such as the recognition of China, the Vietnam War, the presence of American military rule in South Korea, and so forth. (Indeed, the original *Gidra* also was born out of the anti–Vietnam War movement, and stressed the movement's particular importance for Asian Americans; articles such as "GIs and Asian Women" and "The Nature of GI Racism," for instance, addressed the implications for race relations in the United States of the

U.S. Army's tactic of dehumanizing Asians—particularly Asian women —as a way to create psychological conditions that would allow the killing of the Vietnamese.)

The geopolitics of Asian immigration to the United States is, therefore, responsible for the very notion that there is such a thing as "Asian American" identity. In the various countries of origin, an "Asian" identity would not be primary; people might identify as "Korean" or "Chinese" or "Indian" or, even more likely, according to even more specific categories of religion, caste, region, and so forth. While there are certainly cultural as well as environmental similarities among various Asian nations, lumping together the dozens of group identities with origins on the huge continent can obscure much more than it explains. But as part of the compound "Asian American," "Asian" gains relevance and specificity as a social or cultural identifier. In large part, this is because of the way that "mainstream" American vision has categorized Asians from without, and speaks to the status of "other" conferred upon them; after all, "Asian" still has not fully replaced the word "Oriental," formerly the general term and rejected during the 1960s and 1970s as reflecting a colonialist mentality. ("Oriental" means "Eastern," having to do with the East. Since directions are relative, the word "Oriental" betrays Eurocentrism; in other words, Asia is east of whom?) In short, while there is a big difference—not to mention many miles— between, say, a Buddhist from rural China and a Japanese Hawaiian, or between someone from the Indonesian islands and someone from Kazakhstan, that distance has tended to be collapsed in the public imagination once these immigrants arrive in the United States. (This conflation has at times occurred against the efforts of Asian immigrants themselves, as during World War II, when some Chinese wore buttons stating "I'm Chinese, not Japanese," and still faced abuse or ostracism.)

But immigrants from the various Asian countries also have had their own reasons for embracing an Asian American identity. A kind of judicious essentialism (the belief or at least profession that the category "Asian American" has innate, defining features exclusive to that category) can facilitate the cultural empowerment that permits Americans like the editors of *Gidra* (in both incarnations) to speak of an "Asian" experience in the first place—not to mention building the solidarity that could allow for Asian representation in elected bodies of government. Thus, while individual Asian countries and cultures are often singled out in Asian American zine culture (*Bamboo Girl* targets the Filipina/o community, for instance, while *Half Korean* speaks to Korean intermarriage), more often zine writers bolster the symbolic ethnicity of "Asian American"—symbolic, because of its rhetorical and deliberate nature, but nonetheless possessed of real-world implications. The authors of on-line zine *generationrice* (www.generationrice.com) explain how they chose the name for their zine in a way that underscores the symbolic power of an Asian American identity:

> Rice is the one thing that binds all Asian ethnicities together; the one thing that is common regardless of location, culture, language and religious beliefs. *generationrice* is trying to reach this generation that is looking, or in the process of looking, for an identity. Whether it's "full," "pure," "half-half," "hapa," "mutt," or "mixed," *generationrice* wants to do its part and bring every group together.

Singer/songwriter Chris Iijima further explains the dynamics at play in "the process of looking" for an identity that serves a political purpose:

> We were able to construct an APA [Asian Pacific American] identity precisely because our shared experience as Asians in America—always cast as foreigners and marginalized as outsiders—allowed us to bridge ethnic lines and allowed a platform and commonality to engage and understand other people and their struggles. You ask whether there is an "authentic" Asian American sensibility. Asian American identity was originally conceived to allow one to "identify" with the experiences and struggles of other subordinated people—not just with one's own background. (Ling 320–321)

Iijima's words, and the *generationrice* mission statement, emphasize that Asian American identity is a deliberate and motivated thing: experiential rather than biological, grounded in the present as much as or more than in the past. In this light, the category "Asian American" is as ambiguous as it is strategic. For Asian American cyberzine writers, the ambiguity, especially in combination with the decentered reality of cyberspace, would prove to be artistically liberating.

Where Did Cyberculture Come From?

The technological innovation upon which cyberculture is built was, as is often the case with new technologies, an outgrowth of military research. In other words, the wars and international conflicts that were responsible for the mass migration of Asians to the United States after 1965 also provided the impetus for the research that led to the creation of the Internet. The germinal idea of the Internet was first conceived some thirty years ago by the RAND Corporation. RAND, the United States' foremost Cold War think tank, was trying to answer a particular strategic question: How could United States authorities communicate with each other following a nuclear war? The problem was that any network would be shattered by a nuclear bomb, and furthermore, the network's central command station would be an obvious target for attack. So RAND's scientists came up with a network that was assumed to be vulnerable at all times—but would work anyway, since there would be no central station, and no single path of communication. If part of the network should be inoperable, the information would simply travel via an alternative route.

In 1968, the Pentagon's Advance Research Projects Agency funded a large, ambitious project to explore the concept of a decentralized network. High-speed computers were to be the stations in this network (called "nodes"); the first station was installed at the University of California, Los Angeles in 1969. In the next few years, more stations were added. These stations were able to transfer large amounts of data very quickly and could be programmed remotely from the other stations. Although this feature was a boon for researchers, it did not take long for it to become clear that most of the computer time on the network was being used not for research or collaboration among scientists, but for personal messages.

The computer mailing list was invented early on, allowing the same message to be sent to large numbers of network subscribers. Thus, almost from its inception, creation of a mass audience was key to the Internet's appeal to huge numbers of users. This was an important step toward the proliferation of cyberzine writing, for it contains the seeds of the technology that provides e-zine writers with an almost unlimited readership.

Throughout the 1970s and 1980s, more and more social groups acquired powerful computers. It became increasingly easy to connect
these computers to the growing network, turning them into new
"nodes" in the system that would come to be called the Internet. The
software belonged to the public domain (no one owned the rights and
it was widely available), and the leadership was fully decentralized as
originally planned by RAND. Connecting cost little or nothing, since
each station was independently maintained. Quickly, anarchically, and
unevenly, the Internet network mushroomed, and by the 1990s, Internet connection was a necessity for many businesses, "computer literacy" became a requirement for college education, and "personal computers" found their way into more and more homes, in the United
States and elsewhere.

The decade of the 1990s saw the fastest growth of the Internet,
which was expanding at a rate of 20 percent per month. Moving outward from its original base in military and scientific arenas, the Internet established itself in educational institutions of all levels (including
preschool), libraries, businesses of all kinds, and, of course, personal
residences. Since any computer with enough memory needs only a mo-
dem and phone line to be added to the network, the Internet continues
to spread more and more rapidly, on an increasingly global scale.

The chaotic nature of the Internet's spread has gifted it with a
uniquely democratic potential. By comparing the Internet to the English language, Internet historian Bruce Sterling stresses the very basic
cultural significance of the Internet's easy access:

> The Internet's "anarchy" may seem strange or even unnatural, but it
> makes a certain deep and basic sense. It's rather like the "anarchy"
> of the English language. Nobody rents English, and nobody owns
> English. As an English-speaking person, it's up to you to learn how
> to speak English properly, and make whatever use you please of it
> (though the government provides certain subsidies to help you learn
> to read and write a bit). Otherwise, everybody just sort to pitches in,
> and somehow the thing evolves on its own, and somehow turns out
> workable. And interesting. Fascinating, even. Though lots of people
> earn their living from using and exploiting and teaching English,
> "English" as an institution is public property, a public good. Would

English be improved if "The English Language, Inc." had a board of directors and a chief executive officer, or a President and a Congress? There'd probably be a lot fewer new words in English, and a lot fewer new ideas. (Sterling)

Indeed, it is not uncommon for zine writers to claim that they began their zine because they could not find publications that suited their own cultural needs. Sabrina Margarita of *Bamboo Girl*, now in her thirties, launched her zine for this reason:

It started in 1995, and I pretty much started launching it because I could not find anything reading material-wise that I could relate to. Because most of the items that dealt with feminism or queer identity weren't really geared toward women of color. So I had to search for items that dealt with women of color. However, when I did, I did not find anything that was very supportive of the feminist or queer communities. In particular, I was looking for Asian American publications, and most of these only addressed upwardly-mobile professionals. Which totally did not include me. (Margarita interview)

Because of her needs as a reader, Sabrina Margarita started handing out copies of her zine, which is in print format, creating an accompanying Web site that both publicizes and complements the zine. Initially, she made up about a hundred photocopies of each issue and distributed them to her friends. A few years later, in 2001, she had a circulation of about three thousand, was working with about five or six contributors in each issue, and sold the zines by mail and also in some bookstores. In 2005, a decade after she first launched *Bamboo Girl*, Sabrina Margarita is still publishing the zine. Its Web presence has become more and more elaborate, with frequent updates, digital photographs, and interactive features such as a guestbook; the Web presence is also increasingly central to the zine's calling.

Sabrina Margarita's experience in deciding to create *Bamboo Girl* shows how in Internet publishing the lines become thoroughly blurred between consumption (or audience) and production (or writer)—with the democratic access to the Net acting as conduit from one to the other. Another example can be drawn from Kristina Wong's e-zine, *Big*

Bad Chinese Mama. The site features parodic biographies and photos of fake mail-order brides. At first, the twenty-three-year-old Wong used her own photograph and ones she collected from her friends. Now, she says, she receives and posts pictures mailed to her from women around the country and beyond (Wong interview).

That the Internet is, as Sterling puts it, "headless, anarchic, million-limbed" also has concrete and particular influence on what Web zines look like. There are millions of public files that can be accessed and downloaded (transferred to the computer one is using) easily and in a matter of moments. In other words, zine writers can look around the Internet and find a seemingly endless supply of elements they can add to their zines: photographs, artwork, language, music, and more can be included with a simple cut-and-paste. And zine writers with just a little more hardware and a few more computer skills can easily scan into the computer images or sounds of their choosing (which other people, after visiting the site, can in turn download to their own computers).

A result of this cut-and-paste smorgasbord is that many cyberzines take their shape and their energy from the contrasts and juxtapositions of the collage. The vast world of the Internet has encouraged zinesters to develop the style of bricolage, already important in print zines. But using the Internet, the collage can include many more forms (animation, music, live video clips, etc.). Cyberzines can also make their collage multilayered through the use of hypertexting, by which a highlighted word or image, "clicked" with a computer mouse, jumps the reader to another screen from within the first one. Readers can jump back and forth among hypertexted pages, potentially creating endless combinations of pages, images, and sounds. In addition, highlighted links can also take readers to other users' sites, which might be similar or relevant to the original zine (as in Mimi Nguyen's list of feminist and Asian American Web sites linked to her zine *Exoticize My Fist*), or might simply be a site the original Web writer likes (as in Kristina Wong's list of other sites that happen to tickle her fancy, linked to her site *Big Bad Chinese Mama*). Hypertexting is a basic tool of Internet navigation; considered not only as a tool but as a new *form*, it has revolutionized literary output by adding layers of associative "thickness" to a previously linear enterprise.

As artistic strategies, both bricolage and hypertexting find their power in juxtaposition and constant recontextualization. Words, sounds, and images circulate endlessly (at least in theory), acquiring new layers of meaning, as they carry the associations and meanings from previous usages with them into their new contexts. One of the richest expressions of this cut-and-paste is the art of sampling (as discussed in chapter 5) in hip-hop music, wherein musical, spoken, or other sounds previously recorded are included within the rap song. The result is a wholly new frame of reference for the sample—and also an affirmation of shared cultural experience, because in order to understand the new song fully, a listener must remember and recognize the sample.

Because the artistic mandates of bricolage inspire its practitioners to seek new elements to borrow or include in all sorts of places, the strategy is an extremely congenial form for artists and writers who want to express and encompass the process of globalization. The Internet has connected up different parts of the world in a powerful new way: images, words, and so forth can flow across borderlines in more directions and faster than ever before. For those interested in studying the cultures of immigration, this ability has also been revolutionary, because it challenges the relevance of a particular focus on movement—on departures and arrivals, on the boats, feet, airplanes, and even spaceships that have so long acted as metonyms for the immigrant experience. Indeed, the practices of the Internet call into question Mikhail Bakhtin's concept of chronotopes, around which we have structured the case studies that make up this book, for the process of importing and exporting cultural bits from all around the globe can lead to a Web zine that contains content that originated almost anywhere and at any time. (Among other things, this has made policing speech much harder to do, as Internet users can simply visit Web sites hosted in other countries.)

The aesthetics of bricolage, in which originality and newness are not primary values, but recirculation, reproduction, and reinterpretation are, is a hallmark of an economic and artistic system called postmodernism. Economically speaking, "postmodern" refers to a system that does not depend chiefly upon industry and production (as did the "modern" or Fordist economy) but rather on information technologies and service-based jobs: work in offices rather than factories, marketing of experiences rather than goods, and relying upon the rapid transfer of information made possible by fax machines, cellular phones, photo-copiers, overnight mail services, and, above all, the Internet. When used in reference to culture, "postmodern" generally refers to an aesthetic system that privileges the audience's role in creating meaning; celebrates the popular; and produces works of art by "ceaselessly re-shuffl[ing] the fragments of pre-existing texts, the building blocks of older cultural and social production, in some new and heightened bric-olage" (Jameson 96) with the result that fixed meaning is problematized or fragmented. Thus, the Internet—with its rapid processing of infor-mation—is both product of, and medium for, the postmodern sensibil-ity, which, in turn, speaks for and to an increasingly global economy.

Another hallmark of the postmodern sensibility is a fascination with the body as changeable and socially constructed. This fascination has manifested itself in a variety of ways, including a ferocious surge in popularity of plastic surgery, body piercing, tattooing, and the like, es-pecially on the part of young people who grew up in the postmodern era. (In the case of body piercing and tattooing, the popularity points not only to a notion of the body as shapeable, but also to the process of globalized culture, as these practices have been widely practiced for a long time in other, "developing" countries.) In this regard, the Internet inserts a fascinating twist: what can we say about the idea of the body (as a place where cultural texts may be inscribed) in a circumstance where it is essentially removed? How do bodies function at all, and what do they mean, in cyberspace?

In the world of the Internet, ethnic publishing, such as Asian Amer-ican e-zines, presents a fascinating contradiction. In the first place, bodies are a major way in which definitions of ethnicity or race get written (and read), and therefore a certain amount of exploration of what makes an Asian American body is unavoidable. Zinester Mimi Nguyen, in her on-line zine *worsethanqueer,* meditates at some length about the range of ways her Asian body can "mean" depending upon what sort of hairstyle she is wearing:

All through high school I had "natural" long black hair. A white man approached me in the park one day, told me he must have been an "Oriental" man in a former life, because he loves the food, the culture, and the women. At the mall a black Marine looked me up and down and informed me he had just returned from the Philippines, and could he have my phone number? . . . I cut off all my hair and damaged it with fucked-up chemicals because I was sick of the orientalist gaze being directed at/on me. (http://www.worsethanqueer.com/slander/hair.html)

Nguyen continues to explore the complexities of hair in a racialized setting: Can bleaching black hair imply self-hatred? What does it mean to dye your hair green? Does hairstyle have anything to do with politics?

But despite the urgency of Nguyen's descriptions of how her body has looked at various times, and what physical changes she has made to her appearance, there is no real corporeality to the medium in which she registers her complaint. One thing that makes the Internet possible is that place has no literal meaning, and that neither users nor information need be located in a fixed position. Furthermore, it is an Internet tradition of sorts to use that lack of physicality to create, and re-create, various identities according to whim, so that "a central utopian discourse around computer technology is the potential offered by computers for humans to escape the body" (Lupton 479). In chat rooms, for instance, men regularly log on as women or women as men, users invent entire personas for themselves, including made-up physical descriptions, and people have "virtual sex":

> Role-playing sites on the Internet . . . offer their participants programming features such as the ability to physically "set" one's gender, race and physical appearance, through which they can, indeed are required to, project a version of the self which is inherently theatrical. Since the "real" identities of the interlocutors . . . are unverifiable . . . it can be said that everyone who participates is "passing," as it is impossible to tell if a character's description matches a player's physical characteristics. (Nakamura, "Race in/for Cyberspace" 712)

Nakamura goes on to point out that when white people create Internet personas that are non-white, Asian personas are by far the most common—and the way these personas are drawn tends to reiterate and reinforce a handful of very recognizable racial and ethnic stereotypes, such as the submissive woman or desexed (or regendered) man (714).

For some Asian American zinesters, then, bodies are an obsession because sex and sexuality have been so central to the process of marginal-
izing and commodifying Asian Americans.

Where Did Zines Come From?

The world of zines is incredibly varied, so that most definitions will
tend to be inadequate. Until fairly recently, zines were part of a cultural underground; self-produced and haphazardly distributed, they
were driven by mission rather than business plan, and, although their
focuses could literally be on any subject, they generally shared a contempt for big-business publishing, a celebration of the quirky and the
confessional, and a respect for the open expression of unpopular tastes
and ideas.

At the present, zines can be divided into two basic categories: print
zines and cyberzines (also called e-zines). Paper zines range from hand-
written sheets, stapled, photocopied, and mailed to friends, to elaborately produced publications created by editors with skills in desktop
publishing and sold in alternative bookstores and even some big chain
stores (such as Tower Records). An important means of distribution and
publicity are the zine festivals held on college campuses and in many
cities. Cyberzines run a similar gamut: some of the designs are visually
spectacular and make use of video clips, digital photographs, links to
other sites, and so forth, while others are essentially text-only rants.
While there are still hundreds of paper zines being published, cyberzines are proliferating even faster, because they are even cheaper to
produce, there is no need to worry about distribution at all, and the
potential audience is practically limitless.

The name "zine" is not directly descended from the more common
"magazine," as might be supposed. Instead, the antecedent for "zine" is
"fanzine," a term that originated in the 1930s to describe cheap period-
icals that published science fiction stories. The growth of the popularity of science fiction coincided with the surge in popularity of the mim-
eograph machine, with the result that the 1930s, 1940s, and 1950s saw
a boom in self-publishing of these fanzines, which began to contain

not only science fiction but also comics, fantasy stories, mysteries, and other popular forms of writing. These fanzines produced some writing that left an indelible mark on the popular cultural landscape. For instance, in the third issue of *Science Fiction,* published in 1932, Jerome Siegel and Joe Shuster introduced their Superman character.

The tradition of self-publishing was further developed during the 1960s, when activists in a number of grassroots organizations began publishing their own newsletters and alternative newspapers across the United States. In addition to *Gidra,* some of the more prominent alternative papers of this era included the *Berkeley Barb,* the *Los Angeles Free Press,* and Detroit's *Fifth Estate.* The era of the 1960s also added underground comix (most famously represented by cartoonist R. Crumb) and music fanzines to the mix. (The word "comix," as opposed to the more common "comics," generally refers to a body of work associated with the 1960s counterculture and comprising the "scene" of underground/independent art, while "comics" refers mostly to newspaper strips and comic books produced by the major publishing companies such as Marvel and D.C. It must be noted, though, that these categories are extremely permeable, and at this point the two spelling variants indicate a difference in emphasis, rather than discrete groupings.)

The late 1970s and 1980s saw the birth of punk subculture as a reaction against the incorporation of rock and roll music into big business, at the expense of its rebellious nature and musical frisson. As Greil Marcus put it, with the introduction of punk,

> Very quickly, pop music changed and so did public discourse. A NIGHT OF TREASON, promised a poster for a concert by the Clash in London in 1976, and that might have summed it up: a new music, called "punk" for lack of anything better, as treason against superstar music you were supposed to love but which you could view only from a distance; against the future society had planned for you; against your own impulse to say yes, to buy whatever others had put on the market, never wondering why what you really wanted was not on sale at all. (2)

Hundreds of publications such as *Punk,* took a philosophical and aesthetic stand against the bland seamlessness of corporate popular culture by developing a publishing style that fit the punk credo of DIY (or Do It Yourself). In this light, it is important to emphasize that the unpolished, nonprofessional style of zines is a positive statement, rather than simply a condition of not being able to do a "better" job. The style of DIY (and its offshoot, "indie" or independent) continues to represent a multilayered critique of the popular culture industry: its motivations, its methods, and its material.

This outspokenly oppositional stance, in the words of R. Seth Friedman (the first compiler and reviewer of zine writing), gave zines in the 1980s "the heart of a music fanzine but the character of an underground comic" (12). The lessons of punk, coupled with the proliferation during that era of cheap copy-shop chains such as Kinko's and the introduction of personal computers and printers into a mass number of homes and workplaces, led thousands of people to create their own idiosyncratic zines. And the distribution of the zines also dovetailed with the philosophy of DIY: authors generally handed them out, or mailed them out themselves after receiving a request and money to cover postage. Even more notably, zine writers often offered a trade instead of a price tag: you send me a copy of your zine, and I'll send you a copy of mine. The result is a kind of cultural swap meet that undeniably has its utopian qualities in its ability to create a community of zine producers and consumers without being ruled by the marketplace.

Of course, producing a DIY zine requires a large amount of commitment on the part of the authors. Holly Tse, at thirty years of age and while working a full-time job, spent from forty to sixty hours producing each issue of *AsiaZine,* which comes out every three months (Tse interview). Tse's dedication is not unusual. Sabrina Margarita of *Bamboo Girl,* for instance, not only makes time to publish her zine and maintain its Web site, but she also runs an e-mail mailing list for "updates" between issues.

Why Asian Americans? Why Zines?

"Zines have been very good for young Asians," declares a female college student who helped to organize a zine conference at her Massachusetts college. Lorial Crowder of *BagongPinay,* an e-zine with the stated goal of producing a "positive representation for Filipinas on the Internet," agrees: "It [the zine movement] has been really important, a major voice for us" (personal communication; Crowder interview). Given the power and frequency of such anecdotal testimonials, it is worth considering concretely what it is, exactly, about the form that has proven to be such a congenial means of expression for Asian American youth.

A statistical look at who uses the Internet accounts for some of it. Asian Americans are "the most wired group in America," Lisa Nakamura has pointed out, creating what Nakamura has dubbed a "little-known digital divide" between Asians and all other ethnic groups (Nakamura, *Cybertypes* 23–35). Coupled with the fact that in large numbers Asians also perform the cheap labor that makes wide use of the Internet possible in the first place, this gives Asian Americans a significant, and edgy, relationship to the computer culture. But practical concerns alone do not fully explain why Asian American writers would find cultural opportunity in the Internet. The aesthetic mandates of zine publishing have turned out to serve some particular needs of young Asian Americans.

Asian American zines—paper and electronic—flowered at a time when Asian culture reached the American mainstream in a big way. At the turn of the 21st century, Hong Kong action movie actor Jackie Chan became an American star with his crossover hit *Rumble in the Bronx* (1995), which grossed $28 million during its first release. Americans spent millions of dollars on products from lunchboxes to trading cards to T-shirts touting figures from Japanese animation (most notably Pokemon, the Powerpuff Girls, and Yu-Gi-Oh). Karaoke became a popular pastime for white Americans across the United States and grew into a multibillion dollar industry. "Japanimation" on television and at the movies broke from its cult status and gained widespread appeal. Girls of all ages began sporting clothing and makeup emblazoned with the resoundingly cute cartoon portrait of the Japanese product trademark "Hello Kitty."

It is no coincidence that zine production, with its antiprofessional stance and its edgy aesthetic, would snowball at precisely this cultural moment of crossover and cooptation, or that its writers and Web mas-

ters would voice a nearly continuous appeal to "keep it real" by resist-
ing commercial polish and by defining and describing Asian culture
from within. *Gidra,* for instance, refers directly in its inaugural issue
to the glut of "slick, full-color, high-fructose eye syrup publications"
about Asian culture that fill the newsstands (http://www.gidra.net/
Spring_99/bring_it_back.hmtl). Similarly, the two young writers of *Hi-
Yaa!,* June and Phung, refer to the plethora of elaborate Web sites that
exoticize Asian culture as a motivation for starting their own zine
(http://www.hi-yaa.com/index2.html). The relatively democratic nature
of zine publishing has facilitated this kind of self-expression to an unprecedented degree.

An important touchstone in Asian American zine publishing reveals
unusually clearly this tension between commercial and DIY, between
mainstream and marginal. This is the case of *Giant Robot,* launched in
1994 by Martin Wong and David Nakamura. *GR,* a quarterly zine of
Asian American pop culture that comes out of Los Angeles, began as a
photocopied affair with a run of 450 copies. *GR* quickly came to exem-
plify what would be known as "GenerAsian X," growing so rapidly
that the editors claimed a circulation of 12,000 by the ninth issue. Over
the years of its production, *GR* has taken on a wide range of subjects,
including Asian squatters in New York City, Margaret Cho's stand-up
comedy, the Asian American Power Movement of the 1960s and 1970s,
Asian haircuts, Asian junk food, and a skateboarding trip by the editors through an abandoned World War II internment camp.

With *Giant Robot* firmly established as a critical and commercial success, a fascinating kind of self-backlash occurred. Issue 17 came out
on time in 1999. A photograph of comic Margaret Cho, the first Asian
American star of a TV sitcom (*All-American Girl*), graces the cover,
along with a bar code for scanning by large retailers. The perforated
subscription blank offers a credit card payment option. Advertisers
tout products ranging from books, videos, and CDs to toys and skate-
board gear. In many important ways, the zine maintains its in-your-face
stance: headlines scream "milk farts," "sluts and bolts," and "eat bugs."
Even so, this is a journal with high production values, a big budget,
and wide distribution.

But Wong and Nakamura, it seems, missed something about the indie
aesthetic to which self-produced zines generally hew. They created a

second zine they called *Robot Power,* a raggedy spin-off of *Giant Robot* billed as "Issue 17.5." (This inaugural issue was followed by subsequent releases, which are released after each issue of *Giant Robot.*) *Robot Power* looks very different from its parent: no glossy paper, no color graphics, staples instead of glued binding, and much less advertising (especially by bigger companies). In short, the homemade quality of zines is clearly part of the point, and Wong and Nakamura's ambivalence about leaving it behind speaks to a central dynamic between the commercial and the "folk" in the electronic era.

Zines, then, have proved to be an especially hospitable forum for the cultural needs of Asian American youth because of the way they allow young people to "talk back" to a cultural industry turning huge profits by selling Asian things. It has also been important that zines, and the punk aesthetic generally, tend to be organized in gleeful opposition to decorum and propriety. In other words, zine publishing has "worked" so well for Asian American youth because it is uniquely successful at providing a means of expression that flies directly in the face of the "polite Asian" stereotype. For young people chafing under the label of "model minority," the slaphappy world of zine culture is a significant opportunity for opposition. An example is *Dead Fish Online Magazine: An Asian Online Zine.* In addition to the disgusting title (and the illustration that accompanies it), the zine has a banner across the bottom of its home page that declares, "Warning: we are not experts on anything, so complain to someone who cares."

Similarly, Lela Lee's character Angry Little Asian Girl (first presented on-line in 1998) refuses in various comic strip adventures to be anyone's nice girl—and found a surprisingly large and loyal audience along the way (see fig. 6.1). This intentional refusal to be polite can be quite emphatic, as illustrated by the many, many references to shit, farts, and comic sex that crop up in the zines. Much artwork by Kristina Wong, of *Big Bad Chinese Mama,* for instance, pivots on the rejection of being a silent "good girl." Wong reproduces the Japanese cartoon character "Hello Kitty," an extremely cute kitten drawn with no mouth who appears on a huge number of products, with a caption reading "What Hello Kitty would say if she had a mouth." Word balloons show the dainty feline saying, "Who's up for a threesome?" or "Who are you calling a pussy?" (see fig. 6.2).

Figure 6.1. (*top*) Lela Lee's Angry Little Asian Girl and
friends
Figure 6.2. (*bottom*) The secret life of Hello Kitty™

As these young Asian Americans have it, the notion of "model minority" is both limiting and condescending in the way it seeks to con-
gratulate Asians for knowing their place and buying into the American dream. By focusing on well-off young people who make it to Ivy
League colleges, the "model minority" myth leaves out or penalizes
Asian immigrants who are struggling against great challenges—language barriers, poverty, racism—and whose future is not assured. A
new stereotype emerges, one that encourages anti-Asian backlash as
well as misrepresenting the diversity and complexity of Asian America.

The "model minority" myth also praises (if backhandedly) Asian
Americans at the expense of other so-called minority groups, most notably African Americans, thereby making Asian American social mobility complicit in racism—a bitter stance indeed for the many zine
writers who clearly identify themselves with African American cultural practices, especially hip-hop culture. This dynamic has led Mia

Tuan, in her book on the Asian American ethnic experience, to frame the fate of Asians in the United States as stretched between two poles: "forever foreigners or honorary whites."

Thus, although not all zines are explicitly political (as are *Gidra* or *Asian American Revolutionary Movement Ezine,* among others), the zines overwhelmingly share an emphasis on attitude, revealed through direct and belligerent addresses to the reader, use of slang and sarcasm, pugilistic graphics (frequently featuring a person punching or kicking directly at the reader's face), and so forth. This quality of "attitude" is hard to define or pin down, but it is nonetheless central to the rich world of Asian American zine writing. "Attitude" is the means by which Asian American zine writers give their publications what Michael Denning would call "accent"—a symbolic and rhetorical device by which they mark themselves as immigrants, children of immigrants, or grandchildren of immigrants struggling toward a nuanced understanding of American identity (Denning, *Mechanic Accents* 3–5). "Attitude" includes a range of tactics by which zine writers loosen themselves from inadequate categories such as conformist "American" or traditional "Asian."

The Asian American youth "attitude" is transmitted across a variety of styles or forms of zine production. *Gidra* makes use of words and expressions associated with hip-hop culture, quoting rapper KRS-ONE and announcing, "Gidra's back. Spread the word, yo" (http://www.gidra. net/Spring_99/bring_it_backq.html). *AsiaZine* uses sly wordplay; its slogan "Get oriented!" is at least a triple pun, with each meaning mocking an aspect of the (nonetheless) urgent construction of Asian American identity, which is an organizing principle for the zine (see fig. 6.3). The title of *Hi-Yaa!* also reminds us of the multiplicity of identity: the authors expand "Hi-Yaa" into "Hi, Young Asian Americans!" while the name simultaneously reiterates the stereotypical sound made in kung fu movies—or by small children playing at kung fu (see fig. 6.4).

Many zines by and about Asian American women use zine "attitude" to confront dominant images of Asian women in popular culture: the submissive geisha girl, the China doll, the Indian princess. Zinester

Figure 6.3. (*opposite, top*) Multiplicity of identity as parody on ASIA 'ZINE
Figure 6.4. (*opposite, bottom*) In your face (literally) attitude

Angry Asian	Asian in Denial	Banana/Coconut	Asian FOB	Politically Correct Asian
Very angry about how Asians are viewed by Western society. Has big chip on shoulder and goes on and on about "Asian pride" and "elevating our race".	Usually grew up in a predominantly White neighbourhood. Pretends to be White. Does not acknowledge that they are Asian.	Yellow/brown on the outside, white on the inside. Generally raised in a Western society, but has experienced the quirks of being raised Asian. Does not deny heritage.	Fresh Off the Boat. Usually spent formative years in an Asian society. Holds onto Asian values and attitudes. Limited influence by Western attitudes (except for shopping).	Generally raised in a Western society and as such, is highly influenced by Western ideals of political correctness. Quick to judge others about judging others based on skin colour.
Personal Mantra: "If you don't see things my way, you are anti-Asian, you f**king a**hole!"	**Personal Mantra:** "I am White. I am White. I am White."	**Personal Mantra:** "I used to wish I was White, but I'm mature and grown up now. I have the best of both worlds."	**Personal Mantra:** "Everything Asian is far superior to everything Western."	**Personal Mantra:** "I do not make distinctions regarding race. This is a bad thing to do."
Buzzwords/ Phrases: "Asian pride", "f**k you", "you dumb sh*t", (any grammatically incorrect expletives)	**Buzzwords/ Phrases:** "If they live here, they should speak the language." "My friends think I'm more White than they are."	**Buzzwords/ Phrases:** "It's ok when I make (insert nationality here) jokes because I'm (insert nationality here)."	**Buzzwords/ Phrases:** "Are you (insert nationality here)?" "How come you don't speak (insert Asian language here)?"	**Buzzwords/ Phrases:** "eracism", "we all bleed the same colour", "let's all get along", "perpetuating stereotypes"
Social Interactions: Hangs out only with other Asians in a big group. Has a confrontational attitude and looks for racism in every gesture.	**Social Interactions:** Will only hang out with White people. Avoids other Asians like the plague. May talk to other Asians in Denial, but will never be caught dead in a group of Asians.	**Social Interactions:** Has friends who are Asian and friends who are not. However, is always aware of the racial dynamics of the group.	**Social Interactions:** Friends are all Asian. Has a "stick-together" mentality. Will hang out with someone solely because they're Asian even if they don't really like them	**Social Interactions:** Hangs out mostly with other Politically Correct Asians. Has a few token White friends. Makes a point to not notice race.
Thoughts on Lucy Liu: "She's a sell-out."	**Thoughts on Lucy Liu:** "I think she sucks. I prefer Calista Flockheart."	**Thoughts on Lucy Liu:** "I heard she's a bitch." OR "Way to go! Another Asian in mainstream media."	**Thoughts on Lucy Liu:** "I secretly admire her, but publicly look down on her because she is not truly Asian."	**Thoughts on Lucy Liu:** "She perpetuates the dragon lady stereotype."
Thoughts on ASIA'ZINE: "Your 'zine sucks. You don't know anything about Asian pride."	**Thoughts on ASIA'ZINE:** None, as an Asian in Denial would never read this 'zine.	**Thoughts on ASIA'ZINE:** "I laughed my ass off."	**Thoughts on ASIA'ZINE:** "This is not true."	**Thoughts on ASIA'ZINE:** "People are ridiculed everyday because of their skin color or ethic back ground. This is shit, and you shouldn't publish it." (Actual quote, spelling errors and all)

Figure 6.5. "I will be what they fear most," says zinester Mimi Nguyen

exoticize my fist.

Mimi Nguyen writes, "Now I will be what they least expect. I will be scary. I will be other than the stereotype of the model minority, the passive Asian female" (http://www.worsethanqueer.com/slander/hair .html). Nguyen sets out to confront notions of what an Asian American woman should be, and makes clear in various mission statements that this is her intent. "Go ahead," dares a self-portrait on the Web site, in pugilistic pose. "Exoticize my fist" (see fig. 6.5).

Likewise, Lela Lee's *Angry Little Asian Girl* turns cuteness inside out —and in the process, has attracted a lot of attention, inspiring Lee to create more defiant characters (other Angry Little Girls). And sometimes, when zine writers begin to take their thoughts to the public, the confrontation happens automatically, as when Holly Tse of *AsiaZine* found that her first choice of titles for her zine—InvAsian—was taken already—by a porn site.

On the Internet, pornographic images abound that hawk the stereotype of the physically small, submissive Asian woman as sex slave, or the emasculated Asian man. (It is worth pointing out here that pornography is the industry that was able to make the Internet profitable.) There has been much academic attention focused on the *gender* implications of pornographic images, but little of it focuses on the *racial* or *ethnic* implications of pornography. This is surprising, since pornography has long been one of the most prominent cultural locations where racial fantasies are created and played out—much more starkly and for a larger audience than, say, the entire Fox television network. Perhaps the intense feelings engendered by the *gender* debate over whether pornographic images contribute to the oppression of women, or whether antiporn stances can actually harm women by contributing to state regulation of their bodies, has made it difficult for other questions about porn to be heard. For the purposes of argument, we would like to consider racially themed pornography as a thriving form of minstrelsy: the enactment of racial stereotypes and fantasies in a performative context for the purposes of entertainment, presumably of nonmembers of the group being portrayed. (The same argument might be advanced about the *gender* fantasies in some porn.) We raise this with cognizance of all the complicated power dynamics the word "minstrelsy" implies: can there ever be power gained from wearing the minstrel mask? Are all such performances historically coercive, or can they be undertaken voluntarily? How does being paid—or needing to be paid—change the equation, if at all?

If one types "Asian women," or even more, "Asian girls" into an Internet search engine, the search will yield a few zines or political sites—and a vast number of porn sites promising women who are "mysterious," "exotic," and "submissive." Many Asian American zines are in dialogue with the racial aspect of Internet porn. Several zinesters express a kind of annoyed weariness at still having to harp on what one writer referred to as the " 'I'm not a geisha' protest," while Web sites like the one maintained by the porn star Annabel Chong—who caused a stir by filming "the biggest gang-bang in history," in which she had sex with 251 men in ten hours—strive to emphasize agency and humor in the sexualized Asian body. Nonetheless, the zinesters admit, the notions of what it means to be an Asian woman purveyed in standard pornography remain ubiquitous. Sabrina Margarita has received drawings sent without apparent malice to her *Bamboo Girl* of Asian men having sex with white straight men; Holly Tse, editor of *AsiaZine,* points out that even a purportedly Asian-oriented Web site, Click2Asia.com, registers under its umbrella literally hundreds of porn-swapping and sex-oriented clubs that advertise young Asian women (Margarita interview and Tse interview).

In this light, the most daring and oppositional aspect of Kristina Wong's *Big Bad Chinese Mama* might be the fact that she publishes photographs of Asian and Asian American women—all looking ugly on purpose. This completely flies in the face of what Asian women are "supposed" to do with their bodies—or what any women are supposed to do with their bodies, as the multimillion-dollar cosmetics industry attests. The captions accompanying the photos of young women making absurd faces, picking their noses, sitting on the toilet, or sticking out their tongues refer to the cultural expectations they are working to thwart: "Not quite a lotus blossom, but the next best thing," one reads. Another, cleverly, offers a haiku: "I know my purpose / my life is but to serve ME / get your own damn beer" (http://www.bigbadchinesemama. com/meredith.html). With her zine, Wong deliberately tries to inter-cept readers expecting one of the many Internet sites promising Asian mail-order brides or Asian women interesting in dating white men. (In an interview, she confessed to publicizing her zine on genuine porn and "dating" sites.) Upon arriving at Wong's Web address, readers are greeted with a photograph of Wong eating cheese doodles with her mouth open, grimacing as grotesquely as possible. "Sorry Guys, did I ruin the mood for ya?" reads the caption under her photo. Wong writes:

> This is my mail order bride website. This is just like many sites you have seen before but better. Why is it better? Because I have gath-ered lovely "Oriental Creatures" from all over the world, who are just as sweet and pretty as me. They will show you just how demure Asian women REALLY are. These women know how to treat a perverse Western gentleman like yourself. (In fact, they will give you such quality treatment that you might find yourself screaming and run-ning to tell your friends or local law enforcement about how their "Ancient Ass Kicking Technique" took you by storm.)

It's not subtle—but then neither are the hints on www.an-asian-wife.com: "Would you like a wife who never complains, nags or refuses sex? One who devotes her life to making you happy?"

What Have Zines Done to Pop Culture?

The many and varied print and cyberzines that have been produced and distributed in the last few decades provide a goldmine of valuable materials for cultural observers. In the case of Asian American youth, Web writing represents a place where they are prominent and visible as cultural producers. Scholars, editors, book publishers, and the like have started to take note of the zines' significance in American cultural history. Entire academic conferences have been devoted to analyzing zines as a cultural phenomenon.

But zine publishing brings challenges as well as opportunity to those who would study them. Their guiding aesthetic, as well as the conditions of their production, make them hard to study. In the first place, there are so many, both on-line and in print, that systematic approach to the material is practically impossible. Furthermore, the zines often have irregular production schedules (frequently tied to the amount of free time the producer has) and short lives: it's impossible to know even approximately how many are in existence at a given time, and a particular title might disappear altogether without warning. Finally, zines can change their names frequently, at the whim of the author(s) or to convey a new message.

The challenges posed by zines extend beyond the practical: they call into question some fundamental tenets of the American cultural hierarchy while upending practices of the popular culture industry. Perhaps the most fundamental challenge is to the system of cultural value. There is still a dominant ideal that what's valuable must be lasting, as indicated by the word "classic." (Although the marketing of the "instant classic" in our consumer age could be seen as making the notion of "lasting culture" irrelevant.) In order to evaluate zines, "disposability" must replace "lasting" as a key concept.

Disposable culture has practical implications for scholars as well, as most of the zines (paper or electronic) still are not archived, certainly not in ways that are accessible to the public. The creator of *Bamboo Girl*, for instance, maintains the zine's entire run in her apartment (Margarita interview). Several projects are underway to archive the Internet historically, but because these undertakings must preserve each and every change that marks the entire Web, the forest may very well be hidden by the trees, and how to find particular material remains elusive especially since some places of Internet production, such as bulletin boards, cannot be reached by the usual search engines. This means, simply put, that it can be hard to get one's hands on a particular run. While there are now some collections that excerpt zine writing, these are, of course, partial and biased. And because of the sheer volume of zines, it's hard to make a case for the importance of any particular one; rather, analysts must read a large enough number of them to get a sense of general currents—while managing not to slight individual artistry.

The grassroots nature of zine production and distribution also resists the academic frame. The "indie" aesthetic flies in the face of the "great artist" vision of literature—although many of the zines themselves are intensely personal. Distribution of the zines has also attempted to remain outside of the culture industries. Early zine writers describe handing out copies to strangers who caught their attention on the bus; while some zines are carried by some bookstores, the majority of them change hands much more informally. And with cyberzines, individual sites can be linked to other sites at will, and do not require an apparatus of distribution beyond the technology to access the Internet. Therefore, incorporation of this body of work into the story of American culture will necessitate a revised value system. Finally, since many zinesters use computers or copy machines at work to produce their zines, the interrelationships among culture, work, and leisure must be reevaluated.

To shed some light on the dramatic ways in which zine writing has transformed popular culture, this chapter has focused largely on a particular hallmark of cyber-publishing: what could be called decentered, anarchic, independent, outsider, and democratic. The final, key question about the future of cyberzines will be whether this productive chaos continues to characterize Internet relationships. Will the possibility of "empowerment through connectivity" (Weinstein and Weinstein 213) cede to the demands of an increasingly regulated technological marketplace? Has the Internet as a (relatively) free and playful space for expression already given way to the Internet as ultimate achievement and perpetuator of cyber-capitalism? The number of creative and heartfelt zines on the Internet continues to grow every day, but so does the number of pop-up ads, spam e-mail messages, and on-line megastores. In short, whatever opportunities the Internet may offer to individuals and groups in search of a workable identity, it can also take away, with its ability to co-opt, to commodify, to package and resell.

Afterword:
Chelsea, 2006

Wandering Popular Culture

Our story ends with a different West Side Story, as we walk around the "lower West Side" of Manhattan—in the neighborhood that has been known as "Chelsea" ever since Captain Thomas Cook established his home on the block that now stretches from 9th to 10th Avenues between 22nd and 23rd Streets and named it after a soldiers' hospital near London. We are taking ourselves on a disorganized but motivated popular culture tour. Aware of Chelsea's history as a magnet for immigrants, we try to keep in mind how the neighborhood (just south of the Hell's Kitchen section that provided the setting for *West Side Story*) was, in the 19th century, a major settlement area for Irish immigrants who then became the core constituency of the Tammany Hall political machine. Since the 1950s this neighborhood, sandwiched between the gay mecca of the West Village and the even more economically prohibitive Upper West Side, has become at least 15 percent Latino and almost 10 percent Asian, reflecting in part the paradigm shifts rooted in the 1950s and 1960s that we have discussed in chapters 3 through 6.

But it is not evidence of these world-historical demographic shifts that we are after. Our goals on this walking tour are less lofty and, perhaps, more macabre. Two important Chelsea sites are particularly on our minds, one that still exists (the Hotel Chelsea), and one that has been demolished—but that is no problem, because it is aura we seek. The "absent" presence we are hunting is the old RKO Theatre, at 23rd and 8th. Constructed in the immediate post–Civil War period, the building was bought in 1869 by financiers "Jubilee Jim" Fisk and Jay Gould. The two renamed the site (previously Pike's Opera House) as the Grand Opera House, and Fisk made sure that it hosted performances that were appropriate for performer Josie Mansfield, his lover. The Opera House also provided Fisk and Gould a place to hide during the panic of Black Friday (in 1869) after they tried to corner the market in gold. Fisk was later shot to death by Edward Stokes (in an argument over their shared interest in Mansfield) and his body lay in state in the lobby of the opera house (*WPA Guide* 153). This opera house-turned-movie-theater was finally torn down in 1960 to make room for a 2,820-unit housing cooperative constructed by the International Ladies' Garment Workers Union (http://www.mcny.org/collections/abbott/a148-a.htm).

Our other death-tour site, the Hotel Chelsea, still stands. A major node of international bohemianism, the Chelsea has provided beds to an amazing array of writers, musicians, and visual artists, from Dylan Thomas to Bob Dylan, and has inspired songs, books, and films too numerous to mention. By the time British punk rocker Sid Vicious (of the Sex Pistols) stabbed his girlfriend Nancy Spungen at the hotel in 1978, the Chelsea had long been established as a seedy hotbed of creativity and danger. Finding the Chelsea in relatively good form, we were also pleased to be reminded that just across the street (at 225 West 23rd Street) stands the headquarters of the Communist Party of the United States (the CPUSA)—another important site for historians of internationalist cultural activity in New York.

Having finished with our planned itinerary, we are now wandering aimlessly through the cold streets of Chelsea, thinking about hot drinks. Rounding the corner onto 9th Avenue we see a sign for NF Hardware, Inc. On the long side of the corner storefront, the entire window is filled with row upon row of *matryoshki,* or Russian nesting dolls. This display of lacquered wooden dolls is somewhat startling, because a quick look inside reveals this to be a fairly nondescript hardware store. Our internationalist interest is piqued: indeed, as soon as we enter we hear a customer asking the (Russian) owner of the store where she can find a certain kind of bathtub plug.

But what can we make of this surprising appearance of *matryoshki*? What tale might the nesting dolls tell about immigration, globalization, and commodification? Russian nesting dolls have become, over the past hundred years or so, an iconic representation of Russian folk art. They date back to the late 19th century, and are modeled on an earlier Japanese form of miniaturist art. Drawing from a woman's name popular in prerevolutionary rural Russia ("Matryosha"—with its own roots in the Latin for "mother"), the *matryoshka* can be a terribly elaborate production. The finest ones are hand-painted and can feature as many as twenty dolls-within-dolls. Representing motherhood and fertility, the *matryoshki* have continued to serve as an important emblem of Russian folk culture, even as their paintings have come to include Russian political figures and world popular-culture icons. In the Soviet Union, in the 1980s, foreign currency shops were full of the *matryoshki,* which were obviously a popular item for tourists to bring home.

In the hardware store in Chelsea, there is quite an amazing variety to be found. Some are "traditional"—the collection that has each doll painted like a rural woman wearing a brightly colored headscarf, with flowers on her dress and in her hands. Some of the *matryoshki* have high-art motifs, such as the ones with each doll patterned after a different Chagall or Kandinsky painting (the Russian man running the hardware store informs us that he knows Kandinsky's nephew, who, he says, runs an art gallery a bit farther uptown). The owners of the store are Russian immigrants with a definite artistic bent. They seem eager to show off the *matryoshki,* and they present them to us with evident pride as genuine Russian folk art. It is unclear how many of the dolls they sell: this is, after all, a hardware store.

In some ways the form of art here (the nesting doll) is much more important than the content (Disney's Lion King, say). A good number of the *matryoshki* at the hardware store depict figures drawn from American popular culture: Star Wars characters, lots of Disney, Bart Simpson and family, Madonna in five different iterations. A quick check on eBay confirms that Russian nesting dolls are enjoying a second life of sorts —as ambassadors of popular culture (and not only American: on eBay you can order "James Bond" nesting dolls that picture each of the actors who has so far played 007 in the movies). These dolls with Western popular culture figures are also widely available in post-Soviet Moscow and St. Petersburg, and are manifestly being marketed to Americans: it seems unlikely that Russians will be lining up to buy Derek Jeter *matryoshki*.

The fact of these dolls—in Chelsea, in Moscow, on the Internet— offers a particular kind of punctuation mark for our investigations in *Immigration and American Popular Culture*. While we happened upon this set of nesting dolls in Chelsea in a store owned by Russian immigrants, their cultural currency has clearly developed outside small-scale Russian immigrant entrepreneurial endeavors. The first (and perhaps too) obvious thing to note here is that in this era of "globalization" the actual movement of people that once defined and shaped cultural change will matter less than the constant worldwide transfer of capital, goods, and images. As we have discussed at a few moments in the book—most notably in chapters 4 and 6—the cultural landscape of the United States is now as much the product of flows of imagery, information, and goods, as it is the product of world-historic population shifts. As noted, some of the most influential theorists of globalization have tried to develop new vocabularies to reckon with these changes: Arjun Appadurai's theory of global "scapes" (ethnoscapes, mediascapes, and so on) has been especially influential in reconceptualizing a new world where national boundaries and traditional sources of identity formation have given way to a worldwide web of economic and cultural activity that spans the virtual and the real.

What should also be clear is that the appearance of the hardware store *matryoshki* acts as one index of a major "war" that we have not yet considered directly in this book: the Cold War. While much in these pages has been concerned with questions of how "hot" wars (World War II and the war in Vietnam above all) have produced the central features and expressive practices of the American popular culture industries, it has been less clear that most of this activity operated in the two-superpower landscape of the Cold War. Our initial foray took us into the "old" immigration culture of the immediate post–World War I era; every other chapter here is wrapped up in the process by which the United States came to be the dominant global power—not only in the political and military senses, but also in terms of cultural dominance. The heart of this book, then, has been concerned with those years, from roughly the early 1940s through the early 1990s (from the zoot suit riots to the science fiction alien movies of the 1990s), during which the United States, in direct competition with the Soviet Union, aimed—in Southeast Asia, in the Caribbean, in Europe and in Latin America—to develop its influence through the agency of popular culture.

The "cultural front" of the Cold War has come under increased scrutiny in the past decade or so. Penny von Eschen's book *Satchmo Blows Up the World* (2004) is only one of many recent attempts to evaluate the organized attempts of the United States government to use "culture" as an ambassador: the complexities of race (i.e., African American jazz musicians sent overseas to promote the American way of freedom and democracy that they do not have full access to at home) in this Cold War project are well noted by von Eschen. Official cultural efforts of the U.S. government—not only acknowledged ones under the auspices of the State Department but secret missions of the CIA as well—were joined, of course, by all manner of other entrepreneurial efforts to spread American goods and politics around the globe.

With the end of the Cold War (usually marked as coming in 1991, but augured by changes throughout eastern Europe in 1989) has come an even fuller elaboration of American global power. The painted dolls of Chelsea show us one important "face" (or faces within faces!) of this new cultural flow. Joining the decades-old process of exporting American cultural goods overseas comes a novel marketplace activity: the "rebranding" of international folk (and commercial) cultural products and styles as American. This is not, of course, a completely new assault: anyone who ate Chinese food in an American suburb in the 1970s, for instance, can tell you how American consumers have exerted pressure in the marketplace to make sure that the cultural stuff of the "other" be at once thrillingly exotic but not too different from our usual fare. What is new is how these previously scattershot acts of Americanization have become part of economies of scale—from chains of "power" yoga studios to taco burgers on public school lunch menus.

Immigrant entrepreneurs, as we see with the proprietors of the NF Hardware store in Chelsea, will continue to act as a conduit for goods and styles from their home cultures into the American marketplace. The end of the Cold War has meant that along with the political reorganization of Europe, parts of Asia, the Middle East, and other areas has come a new ability of American popular culture interests to incorporate commodities and styles that previously were "protected" from U.S. interventions by a counterbalancing Soviet power.

But Bart Simpson's face painted in the place that used to feature a Russian peasant woman should not lead us to conclude that the end of the Cold War means that the United States' military/political/industrial might will translate simply or easily into a univocal and uncontested control over the world of popular culture. One of the most interesting contemporary challenges to this hegemonic (and homogenizing) power comes from another recent transplant from the former Soviet Union who has landed in downtown New York City: Eugene Hutz, leader of the "gypsy punk" band, Gogol Bordello.

Hutz's life story, as he has promoted it on record and in interviews, reads as a sort of primer on the post–Cold War migrant condition. Hutz has invented a "gypsy" identity for himself and for his band that deploys mobility and hybridity as the ultimate sources of cultural strength. Born in Ukraine, and uprooted by the Chernobyl nuclear disaster at age fourteen, Hutz moved through refugee camps in Austria, Italy, Poland, and Hungary for three years with his family, discovering there a melting pot (multiple ethnicities within Russia and Yugoslavia, and so on) that prepared him well for his arrival in America (La Briola). While Hutz claims to be a descendant of gypsies known as the Sirva Roma, what seems more important than any "real" bloodline connection is his discovery of placelessness as the emblematic post–Cold War condition.

Resettled with his family in Vermont ("the last place I wanted to go" [La Briola]), Hutz began working out a persona and a plan for a band that would answer the rhetorical questions laid out later in the liner notes of one of his records: "Where the fuck is, for example Gypsy-disco-punk for the after party. Where is Arabic-dub-sextura and where the fuck is the soundtrack for a Balkan train robbery?" (J.U.F.) Gogol Bordello features members from Moscow, Ukraine, Israel, and Florida and makes music that Hutz calls "immigrant punk": "an orchestra of fucking immigrants jamming in A minor" (Combs). Hutz speaks clearly about his desire to have Gogol Bordello act as a counterforce, to offset "this big kind of movement of sameness that's in the world now, not only in America. . . . It's like if you land in any airport, and it's kind of full of same crap. It's not even the same crap of different brand. It's like same brand of the same crap." Gogol Bordello's role, he says, "is presenting people with something that's so drastically different, that it's gonna play against the program of fucking sameness" (La Briola).

On its 2005 release, *Gypsy Punks: Underdog World Strike,* Gogol Bordello make it clear that they are coming for America's children. *Gypsy Punks* (with the second "y" in Gypsy represented as a slingshot) begins with "Sally," a song about a "fifteen year old girl from Nebraska": "Gypsies were passing through her little town / They dropped something on the road, she picked it up . . . / And cultural revolution right away begun!" The whole record tells a story about "Gypsies"—the new immigrants of the post–Cold War era—that imagines these characters finding one another all over America and forming "a little punk rock mafia" ("Immigrant Punk," on *Gypsy Punks*). The mission, as Hutz hollers in "Think Locally Fuck Globally," is to start a "Gypsy punk revolt" (*Gypsy Punks*). Critic Robert Christgau has summarized Gogol Bordello's mission well, explaining that they "valorize their half-imposed marginalization by reaching out to fellow jetsam from other international backwaters where Islam is an everyday thing" (Christgau, "Gypsy Punks" (*Christgau's Consumer Guide*).

This new world culture that Hutz envisions, "be it punk, hip-hop, or be it a reggae sound" is "all connected through the Gypsy part of town"—which is to say everywhere and nowhere in particular ("Underdog World Strike," on *Gypsy Punks*). The brash confidence of *Gypsy Punks* acts as a promise that Gogol Bordello will not stop until they have made gypsy (and punk) converts of all who hear them: "Let your Girl Scouts lip-synch / about the freedom / Just the way you like them, / but soon enough you'll see them . . . / in a different part of town" is how Hutz puts it in "Underdog World Strike." The music of Gogol Bordello is constantly on the go; the accordion alone will at one moment sound like it is playing eastern European wedding music, then Colombian cumbia, after which it will seem to imitate the melodica of Jamaican dub.

Gogol Bordello's gypsy cosmopolitanism is an "act," of course, a new kind of masquerade that insists that popular culture still offers space for consequential challenges to the corporate control of the senses and imaginations of all citizens. As the whole band takes on the identity of "gypsies"—among the least remembered victims of the Nazi genocide—the immigrants and Americans of Gogol Bordello stand as a fascinating hint of what might yet come in post–Cold War American popular culture.

APPENDIX: TIMELINE

Prepared by Daniel Rodriguez

1790 Congress establishes two-year residency requirement for naturalization.

1819 Congress establishes reporting on immigration.

1845 Potato famine in Ireland leads to mass immigration of Irish to the United States.

1848 Mexican-American War ends and United States gains huge amount of territory that previously belonged to Mexico.

Major failed revolutions in Europe lead to new waves of immigration to the United States, particularly from Germany, which sends nearly one million people over the next decade.

1849 California gold rush leads to mass immigration from China.

1850 United States population reaches 23.2 million. Over two million (9.7% of total) are foreign born.

1881 Czar Alexander II assassinated in Russia.

1882 May Laws and anti-Semitic activity in response to czar's assassination leads to mass migration of Jews to the United States.

Chinese Exclusion Act bars Chinese laborers from entering the United States and denies naturalization to Chinese in America.

1886 Statue of Liberty is unveiled.

1893 Worlds Columbian Exhibition in mounted in Chicago.

1898 Spanish-American War. United States occupies Puerto Rico.

1900 Foraker Law declares Puerto Rico a "non-incorporated American territory."

United States population reaches 75.9 million. More than 10.3 million (13.6% of total) are foreign born.

1901 Polish American anarchist Leon Czolgosz assassinates President William McKinley.

1903 Immigration Act of 1903 provides for the exclusion and deportation of resident aliens for reasons of previous criminal convictions or anarchist beliefs/affiliations.

Statue of Liberty is engraved with a poem by Jewish poet Emma Lazarus, making it a symbol of the United States as an immigrant nation.

1904 Chinese exclusion laws are reaffirmed and made permanent.

1907 "Gentlemen's Agreement" between Japan and the United States results in sharp restriction of Japanese allowed to emigrate to the United States.

1908 Israel Zangwill's *The Melting-Pot* presented on the American stage.

1910 Mann White Slavery Traffic Act aimed at ending the importation of women for the purpose of prostitution, but makes it much more difficult for single women to immigrate to the United States.

Outbreak of Mexican Revolution drives thousands of Mexicans to the United States.

1914–18 World War I halts a period of mass migration to the United States.

During World War I, "temporary" Mexican farm workers, railroad laborers, and miners are permitted to enter the United States to work.

1915 Genocide of Armenians living in Turkey leads to massive wave of Armenian survivors to the United States.

1917 Jones Act is passed, giving all Puerto Ricans U.S. citizenship, and decreeing English to be the official language of the island.

The Immigration Act of 1917 imposes a literacy requirement on all immigrants. All immigrants sixteen years of age or older must demonstrate the ability to read a forty-word passage in their native language. The Act further limits Asian immigration.

Barred Zone act prohibits Indians from immigrating to the United States.

1919 Act of October 16 makes present membership in "subversive" organizations grounds for deportation or exclusion.

In what became known as the Palmer Raids, over 10,000 suspected anarchists and communists are arrested. Most are eventually released, but 248, including a large number of Jews, are deported to Russia.

The Eighteenth Amendment to the U.S. Constitution, known as Prohibition, makes the manufacture, transport, import, export, and sale of alcoholic beverages illegal.

1920 First large wave of Puerto Rican migration to the United States is reported in the 1920 Census.

1921 The Quota Act sets an annual immigration ceiling of 350,000. New nationality quotas are instituted, limiting admissions to 3 percent of each nationality group's representation in the 1910 census. The law is designed primarily to restrict the flow of immigrants coming from eastern and southern Europe.

1922 In *Ozawa vs. United States,* the Supreme Court declares Japanese immigrants ineligible for naturalization.

1923 *Abie's Irish Rose* is a hit on Broadway.

Thind case reaches the U.S. Supreme Court; Court decides Indians are not white, and could not become U.S. citizens.

1924 The Immigration Restriction Act (Johnson-Reed Act) reduces the annual immigration ceiling to 165,000. A revised quota reduces admissions to 2 percent of each nationality group's representation in the 1890 census. Virtually all Asians are denied entry.

Congress creates the Border Patrol.

1925 Jamaican activist Marcus Garvey is convicted of mail fraud, and after serving two years in federal prison, is deported to Jamaica.

1926 Attacks against Puerto Ricans provoke riots in East Harlem.

1927 *The Jazz Singer,* starring Al Jolson, is released.

National Origins Act passed (taking full effect in 1929), further institutionalizing the quota approach to immigration restriction

1930 In India, Mohandas Gandhi marches to seacoast to harvest salt, as part of a civil disobedience campaign against British colonial rule.

Little Caesar, starring Jewish actor Edward G. Robinson, is released and becomes the first major gangster movie.

1931 *The Public Enemy,* starring James Cagney, is released.

1932 *Scarface,* starring Jewish actors Paul Muni and George Raft, is released.

1933 "Good Neighbor Policy" is established, whereby the United States opposes armed intervention by any other foreign power in the Western Hemisphere.

Prohibition is repealed.

1934 The Philippine Independence Act confers commonwealth status on the islands, reclassifies Filipinos as aliens, and limits Filipino immigration to fifty per year.

1937 Ponce Massacre takes place in Puerto Rico. Police kill twenty pro-independence Nationalist activists.

Japanese invasion of China; beginning of undeclared war that lasts until 1945 and leads to greater numbers of Chinese immigrants to the United States.

1939–45 World War II. An estimated six million Jews are murdered in Nazi concentration camps, in addition to hundreds of thousands of homosexuals, communists, handicapped persons, and Gypsies. The United States refuses to alter the terms of the 1927 National Origins Act in order to allow for a greater number of European Jewish immigrants during this period.

1940 The Alien Registration Act calls for registration and fingerprinting of all aliens, and includes past membership in "subversive" organizations as grounds for deportation or exclusion.

1941 United States enters World War II after the Japanese attack on Pearl Harbor.

1942 Hearst newspapers on the West Coast attack Japanese Americans and fuel a public outcry for Japanese exclusion. Executive Order 9066 puts 110,000 Japanese and Japanese Americans in ten internment camps in the United States.

Sleepy Lagoon murder case results in mass arrests of Mexican and Mexican American youths in Southern California.

Prompted by labor shortages, the United States institutes the bracero program, allowing Mexican nationals to temporarily work in the United States, primarily in the agricultural industry.

1943 In Southern California, thousands of soldiers and sailors attack Mexicans and Mexican Americans throughout the summer in what become known as the "zoot suit riots."

The Magnuson Act of 1943 repeals the Chinese Exclusion Act of 1882, establishes quotas for Chinese immigrants, and makes them eligible for U.S. citizenship.

Jazz musician Cab Calloway wears a famous white zoot suit in the movie *Stormy Weather*.

1945 World War II ends. Yalta conference marks beginning of Cold War.

1945–46 The War Brides Act and the G.I. Fiances Act allows immigration of foreign-born wives, fiancé(e)s, husbands, and children of U.S. armed forces personnel.

1945–60 250,000 Holocaust survivors arrive.

1946 In July, Congress passes a bill allowing for naturalization of Indians and Filipinos.

1947 After 163 years of British colonial rule, India gains its independence.

In Puerto Rico, Operation Bootstrap (the Industrial Incentives Act), a plan for economic development through rapid industrialization, is

initiated. The plan transforms the economy of the island, and between 1947 and 1957 a yearly average of 48,000 Puerto Ricans leave
the island, primarily for New York.

1948 Mohandes Gandhi is assassinated in New Delhi by Hindu radical.

Under the Displaced Persons Act, entry is allowed for 400,000 persons displaced by World War II. However, such refugees must pass a
security check and have proof of employment and housing that does
not threaten U.S. citizens' jobs and homes.

1950 United States population reaches 150.2 million. More than 10.3
million (6.9% of total) are foreign born.

1950–53 Korean War. Truman orders the U.S. invasion of North Korea.
After three years, and almost two million dead, a ceasefire is declared in July 1953.

1951 The bracero program is formalized as the Mexican Farm Labor
Supply Program and the Mexican Labor Agreement, and will bring
an annual average of 350,000 Mexican workers to the United States
until its end in 1964.

Oscar Handlin publishes *The Uprooted.*

1952 The McCarran-Walter Act allows immigration from South and
East Asia, but with quotas of one hundred immigrants per country,
compared to the national origin quotas of the Immigration Act of
1924, which gave European countries a much higher quota.

Puerto Rico officially becomes a "commonwealth" of the United
States.

1953–56 Operation Wetback: The U.S. Immigration Service deports
more than 3.8 million Mexicans, most without deportation proceed-
ings. Many U.S. citizens of Mexican descent are also (illegally) deported.

1954 Ellis Island closes, marking an end to mass immigration.

In *Hernandez vs. Texas,* the Supreme Court recognizes Latinos as a
separate class of people suffering profound discrimination, paving

the way for Latinos to use legal means to fight discrimination in the United States.

The film *Salt of the Earth,* depicting the labor struggles of Mexican American miners in New Mexico, is released. As the filmmakers were blacklisted, the film is primarily shown outside the United States.

Four Puerto Rican nationalists stage an armed attack on the U.S. House of Representatives. Five congressmen are wounded.

1956 California's alien land laws are repealed, finally allowing Japanese and Chinese immigrants to own land.

1957 *West Side Story* opens on Broadway.

1959 Cuban revolutionaries, led by Fidel Castro, successfully oust dictator Fulgencio Batistsa and begin enacting a series of far-reaching reforms. Thousands of Cubans begin leaving the island for the United States.

The Capeman murders two in New York City.

1961 The film *West Side Story,* depicting rival Puerto Rican and Anglo street gangs in 1950s New York, is released to wide acclaim. Most of the actors depicting Puerto Ricans are Anglo actors in "brownface."

The film *The Young Savages* is released.

Construction of Berlin Wall begins.

1962 César Chávez organizes the National Farm Workers Association (NFWA) in Delano, California.

Jamaica gains independence from Great Britain.

Cuban missile crisis.

1964 The bracero program is repealed, as the Border Industrialization Program establishes the first *maquiladoras,* and mass employment of cheap labor along the Mexican border by U.S. companies begins.

World's Fair in New York.

1965 Immigration Act abolishes nationality quota system established in 1924. Although the act establishes an overall ceiling of 170,000 on immigration from the Eastern Hemisphere and another ceiling of 120,000 on immigration from the Western Hemisphere, no numerical limits are placed on the immediate relatives of U.S. citizens who may become legal immigrants.

U.S. military presence in Vietnam is greatly expanded.

The Voting Rights Act is passed.

Malcolm X is assassinated in Harlem's Audubon Ballroom.

1967 The Beatles go to India.

Clive Campbell moves from Jamaica to New York.

Indian sitar master Ravi Shankar performs at the Monterey International Pop Festival.

United Farm Workers calls for a nationwide grape boycott.

Human Be-In in San Francisco.

Loving vs. Virginia does away with last state anti-miscegenation law.

1966–68 Boogaloo has its heyday as a popular music.

1968 Martin Luther King is assassinated in Memphis. The murder triggers riots in over one hundred cities.

1969 The Young Lords Party, a Puerto Rican political organization modeled after the Black Panther Party, is established in New York.

First decentralized computer network system is installed at the University of California, Los Angeles.

1971 Bangladesh charity concert at Madison Square Garden in New York.

1973 The Nuyorican Poets Café is founded in the Lower East Side of New York City.

Pedro Pietri publishes *Puerto Rican Obituary*.

The movie *The Harder They Come* is released.

On January 27, the United States signs Peace Accords with North Vietnam.

The film *Badge 373* is released.

Bruce Springsteen's album *The Wild, the Innocent, and the E Street Shuffle* is released.

1975 As a result of the Vietnam War, over 130,00 Vietnamese, 70,000 Laotians, 10,000 Mien, and 60,000 Hmong people emigrate to the United States.

1976 Work is begun on the Great Wall of Los Angeles, California's longest mural.

1977 Blackout in New York City.

1978 Worldwide immigration ceiling introduced. A new annual immigration ceiling of 290,000 replaces the separate ceilings for the Eastern and Western Hemispheres.

1979 Political upheaval and civil wars in Nicaragua, El Salvador, and Guatemala contribute to large migrations of refugees to the United States.

1980 Refugee Act creates a system of dealing with refugees that is separate from regular immigration procedures. The annual ceiling on traditional immigration is lowered to 270,000, and the president is authorized to establish an annual limit on the number of refugees who may legally enter the United States.

The Mariel Boatlift brings over 125,000 Cubans refugees to the United States.

1981 The movie *Zoot Suit* is released.

1986 The Immigration Reform and Control Act declares an amnesty for all undocumented immigrants who can prove continuous residence since January 1, 1982, legalizing the status of millions of immigrants. Also created sanctions prohibiting employers from knowingly hiring undocumented immigrants and increased enforcement at U.S. borders.

1989 Berlin Wall falls.

1990 The Immigration Act of 1990 increases total immigration under a flexible annual cap of 675,000, but ends the unlimited immigration of immediate relatives of U.S. citizens. The act revises all grounds for exclusion, amending the McCarran-Walter Act of 1952. Immigrants can no longer be denied admittance on the basis of their political beliefs or associations.

Germany is reunified.

1991 Warsaw Pact ends. Soviet Union is dissolved.

1994 NAFTA, the North American Free Trade Agreement, comes into effect. The U.S./Mexico border sees a massive increase in population as *maquiladoras* are rapidly built up in the region.

On the same day NAFTA goes into effect, the Zapatista National Liberation Army stages an armed uprising in the southern Mexican state of Chiapas.

In November, Californians pass Proposition 187, banning undocumented immigrants from receiving public education, welfare, or health-care benefits.

1995 *Bamboo Girl* zine is launched.

1996 Immigration Act of 1996 greatly expands border enforcement efforts, and makes it possible for the U.S. Border Patrol to refuse entry or deport immigrants without the guarantee of legal process.

President Clinton signs Welfare Reform Bill that eliminates many benefits, such as food stamps and Supplementary Security Income, for legal immigrants and eliminates virtually all state and federal benefits for undocumented immigrants.

1998 California voters pass Proposition 227, banning bilingual education and English-as-a-second-language programs.

1999 *AsiaZine* launched online.

2000 *Bigbadchinesemama* launched online.

U.S. population reaches over 281.4 million; 31.1 million (11.1% of total) are foreign born.

Note: All population figures come from the U.S. Census Bureau, Population Division. In 1850 information about the nativity of people in slavery was not collected and the assumption was made that all of these African Americans were native born.

WORKS CITED

WRITTEN TEXTS

Amburn, Ellis. *Buddy Holly: A Biography.* New York: St. Martin's Press, 1996.

Appadurai, Arjun. *Modernity at Large: Cultural Dimensions of Globalization.* Minneapolis: University of Minnesota Press, 1996.

Appel, Allan. *High Holiday Sutra.* Minneapolis: Coffee House Press, 1997.

Asbury, Herbert. *Gangs of Chicago* (1940). New York: Thunder's Mouth Press, 2002.

———. *Gangs of New York* (1927). New York: Thunder's Mouth Press, 2001.

Ayala, Cristóbal Díaz. "A Tale of Two Cities: A Revolution in Puerto Rican Music, 1916–1939," liner notes to *Lamento Borincano.*

Ayres, Edward Duran (1942). "Edward Duran Ayres Report," reprinted in *Readings on La Raza: The Twentieth Century,* 127–133. Ed. by Matt S. Meier and Feliciano Rivera. New York: Hill and Wang, 1974.

Bakhtin, Mikhail. *The Dialogic Imagination: Four Essays.* Ed. by Michael Holquist. Trans. Caryl Emerson and Michael Holquist. Austin: University of Texas Press, 1981.

Baptiste, Fitzroy. "United States–Caribbean Relations from World War II to the Present: The Social Nexus," in Palmer, 7–52.

Baraka, Amiri. "Beginnings: Malcolm," in *Somebody Blew Up America and Other Poems,* 3–5. Philipsburg, St. Martin: House of Nehesi, 2003.

Batchelor, Stephen. Foreword to *Zig Zag Zen: Buddhism and Psychedelics,* 9–11. Ed. by Allan Hunt Badiner. San Francisco: Chronicle, 2002.

Bell, David, and Barbara M. Kennedy, eds. *The Cybercultures Reader.* New York: Routledge, 2000.

Bender, Steven. *Greasers and Gringos: Latinos, Law, and the American Imagination.* New York: New York University Press, 2003.

Berger, Meyer. "Zoot Suit Originated in Georgia; Busboy Ordered First One in 1940," *New York Times,* June 11, 1943, 5.

Berman, Marshall. "Roots, Ruins, Renewals: City Life after Urbicide," *Village Voice,* September 4, 1984, 18ff.

Bhudos, Marian. "Culture Shock," *Yoga Journal,* May/June 2002, 88–93, 164–167.

Bingham, Theodore. "Foreign Criminals in New York," *North American Review* 188, no. 3 (1908): 383–394.

Boyett, Joseph, and Jimmie Boyett. *The Guru™ Guide to the Knowledge Economy: The Best Ideas for Operating Profitably in a Hyper-Competitive World.* New York: John Wiley & Sons, 2001.

Bradley, Lloyd. *Bass Culture: When Reggae Was King.* New York: Viking, 2000.

Braunstein, Peter, and Michael William Doyle. *Imagine Nation: The American Counterculture of the 1960s and '70s.* New York: Routledge, 2002.

Briggs, Laura. *Reproducing Empire: Race, Sex, Science, and U.S. Imperialism in Puerto Rico.* Berkeley: University of California Press, 2002.

Browder, Laura. *Slippery Characters: Ethnic Impersonators and American Identities.* Chapel Hill: University of North Carolina Press, 2000.

Brown, Mick. *The Spiritual Tourist: A Personal Odyssey through the Outer Reaches of Belief.* New York: Bloomsbury, 1998.

Bryce-Laporte, Roy Simón. "New York City and the New Caribbean Immigration: A Contextual Statement," in Sutton and Chaney, 54–73.

Buder, Leonard. "Jury Convicts Man as Chief of Drug Ring," *New York Times,* July 26, 1989, B1–2.

Buff, Rachel. *Immigration and the Political Economy of Home: West Indian Brooklyn and American Indian Minneapolis, 1945–1992.* Berkeley: University of California Press, 2001.

———. "Marrying In: War Brides Policy as Imperial Policy, 1945–1965," paper delivered at the American Studies Association Annual Meeting, October 2002.

Calloway, Cab, and Bryant Rollins. *Of Minnie the Moocher and Me.* New York: Thomas Y. Crowell, 1976.

Capp, Al. *The World of L'il Abner.* New York: Farrar, Straus and Young, 1953.

Cassini, Oleg. *In My Own Fashion: An Autobiography* (1987). New York: Pocket, 1990.

Chang, Jeff. *Can't Stop Won't Stop: A History of the Hip-Hop Generation.* New York: St. Martin's, 2005.

Chang, Kevin O'Brien, and Wayne Chen. *Reggae Routes: The Story of Jamaican Music.* Kingston: Ian Randle Publishers, 1998.

Chávez, César, and Jacques Levy. *César Chávez: Autobiography of La Causa.* New York: W. W. Norton, 1975.

Chin, Frank, and Jeffery Paul Chan. "Racist Love," in *Seeing Through Shuck.* Ed. by Richard Kostelanetz. New York: Ballantine, 1972.

Christgau, Robert. *Any Old Way You Choose It: Rock and Other Pop Music, 1967–1973.* Baltimore: Penguin, 1973.

———. *Christgau's Consumer Guide: Albums of the '90s.* New York: St. Martin's Press, 2000.

————. Review of *Gypsy Punks: Underdog World Strike* (found at www.robert christgau.com).

Chude-Sokei, Louis. "Postnationalist Geographies: Rasta, Reggae, and Reinventing Africa," in Potash, 215–227.

Clarens, Carlos. *Crime Movies: An Illustrated History.* New York: W. W. Norton, 1980.

Cofer, Judith Ortiz. *Telling the Lives of Barrio Women.* New York: W. W. Norton, 1993.

Cohen, Rich. *Tough Jews: Fathers, Sons, and Gangster Dreams.* New York: Simon & Schuster, 1998.

Colón, Jesús. *A Puerto Rican in New York and Other Sketches* (1961). New York: International, 1982.

Combs, Seth. "Gogol Bordello's Army of Immigrants" (found at http://westword .com/Issues/2002-09-26/music/music2_full.htm).

Cosgrove, Stuart. "The Zoot Suit and Style Warfare" (1984), in *Zoot Suits and Second-Hand Dresses: An Anthology of Fashion and Music,* 3–22. Ed. By Angela McRobbie. Winchester, Mass.: Unwin Hyman, 1989.

Cox, Harvey. *Turning East.* New York: Simon and Schuster, 1977.

Coyote, Peter. *Sleeping Where I Fall: A Chronicle.* Washington, D.C.: Counterpoint, 1998.

Crowder, Lorial. Interview with Rachel Rubin. July 25, 2001, and October 17, 2001.

Cruz, Victor Hernández. *Red Beans.* Minneapolis: Coffee House, 1991.

Das, Bhagavan. *It's Here Now (Are You?): A Spiritual Memoir.* New York: Broadway Books, 1998.

Davis, Stephen, and Peter Simon. *Reggae Bloodlines: In Search of the Music and Culture of Jamaica.* New York: Anchor Press/Doubleday, 1979.

————. *Reggae International.* New York: R & B, 1982.

de Albuquerque, Klaus. "In Search of the Big Bamboo," *Transition* 77 (8.1) (n.d.): 48–57.

Deloria, Philip. *Playing Indian.* New Haven: Yale University Press, 1999.

Denning, Michael. *Cultural Front: The Laboring of American Culture in the Twentieth Century.* New York: Verso, 1996.

————. *Mechanic Accents.* New York: Verso, 1987.

DeRogatis, Jim. *Kaleidoscope Eyes: Psychedelic Music from the 1960s to the 1990s.* London: Fourth Estate, 1996.

Desser, David. "The Cinematic Melting Pot: Ethnicity, Jews, and Psychoanalysis," in *Unspeakable Images: Ethnicity and the American Cinema,* 379–403. Ed. by Lester Friedman. Chicago: University of Illinois Press, 1991.

Didion, Joan. *Slouching toward Bethlehem*. New York: Farrar, Straus and Giroux, 1968.

Doctorow, E. L. *Billy Bathgate*. New York: Harper and Row, 1989.

Downing, Michael. *Shoes Outside the Door: Desire, Devotion and Excess at San Francisco Zen Center*. Washington, D.C.: Counterpoint, 2001.

Duany, Jorge. *The Puerto Rican Nation on the Move: Identities on the Island and in the United States*. Chapel Hill: University of North Carolina Press, 2002.

Duardo, Richard. *Zoot Suit* (1978). In *Chicano Art: Resistance and Affirmation, 1965–1985*, 264. Ed. by Richard Griswold del Castillo, Teresa McKenna, and Yvonne Yarbro-Bejarano. Wight Art Gallery, University of California Los Angeles, 1991.

Duncombe, Stephen. *Notes from Underground: Zines and the Politics of Alternative Culture*. New York: Verso, 1997.

Edwards, Holly. *Noble Dreams, Wicked Pleasures: Orientalism in America, 1870–1930*. Princeton: Princeton University Press, 2000.

Ellison, Ralph. *Invisible Man* (1952). New York: Vintage Books, 1972.

Ellwood, Robert. *The 60s: Spiritual Awakening*. New Brunswick, N.J.: Rutgers University Press, 1994.

Ettinger, Roseann. *Psychedelic Chic: Artistic Fashions of the Late 1960s and Early 1970s*. Atglen, Pa.: Schiffer, 1999.

Fernando, S. H., Jr. *The New Beats: Exploring the Music, Culture, and Attitudes of Hip-Hop*. New York: Anchor Books, 1994.

Flores, Juan. *From Bomba to Hip-Hop: Puerto Rican Culture and Latino Identity*. New York: Columbia University Press, 2000.

Flynn, Joyce. "Melting Plots: Patterns of Racial and Ethnic Amalgamation in American Drama before Eugene O'Neill," *American Quarterly* 38.3 (1986): 417–438.

Foner, Nancy. "West Indians in New York City and London: A Comparative Analysis," in Sutton and Chaney, 117–130.

Forman, Murray. *The 'Hood Comes First: Race, Space, and Place in Rap and Hip-Hop*. Middletown, Conn.: Wesleyan University Press, 2002.

Frank, Thomas. *The Conquest of Cool: Business Culture, Counterculture, and the Rise of Hip Consumerism*. Chicago: University of Chicago Press, 1997.

Fricke, Jim, and Charlie Ahearn. *Yes Yes Y'All: The Experience Music Project Oral History of Hip-Hop's First Decade*. New York: Da Capo, 2002.

Fried, Albert. *The Rise and Fall of the Jewish Gangster in America*. New York: Holt, Rinehart, and Winston, 1980.

Friedman, R. Seth. *The Factsheet Five Zine Reader: The Best Writing from the Underground World of Zines*. New York: Three Rivers Press, 1999.

Fuchs, Daniel. *Three Novels by Daniel Fuchs: "Summer in Williamsburg," "Homage to Blenholt," "Low Company."* New York: Basic Books, 1961.

Gabler, Neal. *An Empire of Their Own: How the Jews Invented Hollywood*. New York: Crown, 1988.

"A Gang Member's Story: True Confessions," *U.S. News and World Report*, January 18, 1988, 29.

Gardaphe, Fred. "A Class Act: Understanding the Italian/American Gangster," talk given at the Humanities Institute at Stony Brook, February 2004.

Garebian, Keith. *The Making of West Side Story*. Buffalo: Mosaic, 1998.

Garman, Bryan. *A Race of Singers: Whitman's Working-Class Hero from Guthrie to Springsteen*. Chapel Hill: University of North Carolina Press, 2000.

Gilman, Sander. *The Jew's Body*. New York: Routledge, 1991.

Glasser, Ruth. *"My Music Is My Flag": Puerto Rican Musicians and Their New York Communities, 1917–1940*. Berkeley: University of California Press, 1995.

Glazer, Nathan, and Daniel P. Moynihan. *Beyond the Melting Pot: The Negroes, Puerto Ricans, Jews, Italians, and Irish of New York City* (1963). Cambridge, Mass.: MIT Press, 1970.

Gómez-Peña, Guillermo. *Dangerous Border Crossers: The Artist Talks Back*. New York: Routledge, 2000.

Gonzalez, David. "Drug Gangs: The Big Sweep," *Newsweek*, October 24, 1988, 26.

Gracyk, Theodore. *I Wanna Be Me: Rock Music and the Politics of Identity*. Philadelphia: Temple University Press, 2001.

Griffith, Beatrice. *American Me* (1948). Westport, Conn.: Greenwood, 1960.

Grosfoguel, Ramón. *Colonial Subjects: Puerto Ricans in a Global Perspective*. Berkeley: University of California Press, 2003.

Gunst, Laurie. *Born Fi' Dead: A Journey through the Jamaican Posse Underworld*. London: Payback Press, 1995.

———. "Johnny-Too-Bad and the Sufferers," *The Nation*, November 13, 1989, 549, 567–9.

Guterman, Jimmy. *Runaway American Dream: Listening to Bruce Springsteen*. New York: Da Capo, 2005.

Hager, Steven. *Hip Hop: The Illustrated History of Break Dancing, Rap Music and Graffiti*. New York: St. Martin's, 1984.

Hall, Stuart. "Encoding/Decoding," in *Culture, Media, Language: Working Papers in Cultural Studies, 1972–79*, 128–138. London: Hutchinson, 1980.

———. *The Hippies: An American "Moment."* Birmingham, U.K.: University of Birmingham Press, 1968.

Handlin, Oscar. *The Newcomers: Negroes and Puerto Ricans in a Changing Metropolis*. Garden City, N.Y.: Doubleday, 1962.

Hansen, Miriam. *Babel and Babylon: Spectatorship in American Silent Film.* Cambridge, Mass.: Harvard University Press, 1994.

Hebdige, Dick. 1987. *Cut 'n' Mix: Culture, Identity and Caribbean Music.* New York: Routledge, 1990.

Hollander, Anne. *Sex and Suits: The Evolution of Modern Dress.* New York: Kodansha International, 1994.

Horne, Gerald. *Class Struggle in Hollywood, 1930–1950: Moguls, Mobsters, Stars, Reds, and Trade Unionists.* Austin: University of Texas Press, 2001.

Horovitz, Israel. *The Indian Wants the Bronx.* New York: Dramatists Play Service, 1967.

Hoskyns, Barney. *Beneath the Diamond Sky: Haight Ashbury, 1965–1970.* New York: Simon and Schuster, 1997.

Howe, Irving. *World of Our Fathers.* New York: Simon and Schuster, 1976.

Hughes, Langston. "Bop," in *The Best of Simple.* New York: Hill and Wang, 1961, 117–118.

———. "Key Chains with No Keys" (1943), in *Langston Hughes and the Chicago Defender: Essays on Race, Politics and Culture, 1942–62.* Ed. by Christopher C. De Santis. Urbana: University of Illinois Press, 1995.

Hunter, Evan. *A Matter of Conviction* (1959). New York: Giant Cardinal, 1961.

Hunter, Stephen. *Violent Screen: A Critic's 13 Years on the Front Lines of Movie Mayhem.* Baltimore: Bancroft Press, 1995.

Isherwood, Christopher. *My Guru and His Disciple.* New York: Farrar, Straus and Giroux, 1980.

Jacobson, Matthew Frye. *Whiteness of a Different Color: European Immigrants and the Alchemy of Race.* Cambridge, Mass.: Harvard University Press, 1999.

Jahn, Brian, and Tom Weber. *Reggae Island: Jamaican Music in the Digital Age.* New York: Da Capo, 1998.

Jameson, Frederic. *Postmodernism, or the Cultural Logic of Late Capitalism.* Durham, N.C.: Duke University Press, 1991.

Jenkins, Henry. *What Made Pistachio Nuts? Early Sound Comedy and the Vaudeville Aesthetic.* New York: Columbia University Press, 1992.

Jensen, Joan. *Passage from India: Asian Indian Immigrants in North America.* New Haven: Yale University Press, 1988.

Joselit, Jenna Weissman. *Our Gang: Jewish Crime and the New York Jewish Community, 1900–1940.* Bloomington: University of Indiana Press, 1983.

Kamenetz, Rodger. *The Jew in the Lotus: A Poet's Rediscovery of Jewish Identity in Buddhist India.* San Francisco: HarperSanFrancisco, 1995.

Kasinitz, Philip. *Caribbean New York: Black Immigrants and the Politics of Race.* Ithaca, N.Y.: Cornell University Press, 1992.

Kelley, Robin D. G. "The Riddle of the Zoot: Malcolm Little and Black Cultural

Politics during World War II," in *Race Rebels: Culture, Politics, and the Black Working Class*. New York: Free Press, 1994.

Kempton, Arthur. *Boogaloo: The Quintessence of American Popular Music*. New York: Pantheon, 2003.

Kenner, Rob. "Dancehall," in Light, 351–360.

Kim, Hye Kyung. "Indian Influence on American Costume from 1960 to 1975," dissertation, University of Maryland, 1990.

Kozol, Wendy. *Life's America*. Philadelphia: Temple University Press, 1994.

Kraus, Joe. "The Jewish Gangster: A Conversation across Generations," *American Scholar*, Winter, 1995, 53–65.

Kuper, Adam. *Changing Jamaica*. Boston: Routledge and Kegan Paul, 1976.

La Briola, John. "Bloc Party," in *Westword*, September 26, 2002 (found at http://westword.com/Issues/2002-09-26/music/music2_full.htm).

LaCapra, Dominick. *Writing History, Writing Trauma*. Baltimore: Johns Hopkins University Press, 2001.

Lacey, Robert. *Little Man: Meyer Lansky and the Gangster Life*. Boston: Little, Brown, 1991.

Laguerre, Michael. *Minoritized Space: An Inquiry into the Spatial Order of Things*. Berkeley: Institute of Governmental Studies Press and the Institute of Urban and Regional Development, University of California, 1999.

Landau, Jon. "Growing Young with Rock and Roll," *The Real Paper*, May 22, 1974, 20, 22.

Laurents, Arthur. *Original Story By: A Memoir of Broadway and Hollywood*. New York: Alfred A. Knopf, 2000.

Law, Lisa. *Flashing on the 60s*. San Francisco: Chronicle, 1997.

Lawrence, Greg. *Dance with Demons: The Life of Jerome Robbins*. New York: Berkley, 2001.

Lawrence, Jacob. *American Vaudeville* (1951). Hirschhorn Museum and Sculpture Garden, Smithsonian Institution, Washington, D.C.

Lears, T. J. Jackson. "From Salvation to Self-Realization: Advertising and the Therapeutic Roots of the Consumer Culture, 1880–1930," in *The Culture of Consumption: Critical Essays in American History 1880–1980*, 1–38. Ed. by Richard Wightman Fox and T. J. Jackson Lears. New York: Pantheon, 1983.

Leary, Timothy. 1983. *Flashbacks: An Autobiography*. New York: Putnam's, 1990.

Leonard, Karen. *Making Ethnic Choices: California's Punjabi Mexican Americans*. Philadelphia: Temple University Press, 1994.

Lhamon, W. T., Jr. *Raising Cain: Blackface Performance from Jim Crow to Hip Hop*. Cambridge, Mass.: Harvard University Press, 2000.

Light, Alan. *The Vibe History of Hip Hop*. New York: Three Rivers Press, 1999.

Ling, Amy, ed. *Yellow Light: The Flowering of Asian American Arts*. Philadelphia: Temple University Press, 1999.

Lipsitz, George. *Dangerous Crossroads: Popular Music, Postmodernism, and the Poetics of Place*. New York: Verso, 1994.

Lorey, David. E. *The U.S.-Mexican Border in the Twentieth Century*. Wilmington, Del.: Scholarly Resources, 1999.

Lowe, Lisa. *Immigrant Acts: On Asian American Cultural Politics*. Durham, N.C.: Duke University Press, 1996.

Lupton, Deborah. "The Embodied Computer User," in Bell and Kennedy, eds., 477–488.

Macks, Jon. *Fuhgeddaboutit: How to Badda Boom, Badda Bing, and Find Your Inner Mobster*. New York: Simon and Schuster, 2001.

MAD about the Sixties: The Best of the Decade by "The Usual Gang of Idiots." New York: Little, Brown, 1995.

Maira, Sunaina. *Desis in the House: Indian American Youth Culture*. Philadelphia: Temple University Press, 2002.

———. "Trance-Global-Nation: Orientalism, Cosmopolitanism, and Citizenship in Youth Culture," *Journal of Popular Music Studies,* Spring 2003 (15.1): 3–33.

Mandle, Jay. "Economic Development of the English-Speaking Caribbean and Relations with the United States," in Palmer, 53–62.

Manuel, Peter. "Representations of New York City in Latin Music," in *Island Sounds in the Global City: Caribbean Popular Music and Identity in New York,* 22–43. Ed. by Ray Allen and Lois Wilcken. Brooklyn: Institute for Studies in American Music, 1998.

Marcus, Greil. *Ranters and Crowd Pleasers: Punk in Pop Music, 1977–92*. New York: Doubleday, 1993.

Margarita, Sabrina. Interview with Rachel Rubin, July 23, 2001.

Marsh, Dave. *Born to Run: The Bruce Springsteen Story*. New York: Doubleday, 1979.

Maslin, Janet. "Review/Film: Sure, He Had His Faults, but the Man Had Vision!" *New York Times,* December 13, 1991.

Masson, Jeffrey Moussaieff. *My Father's Guru: A Journey through Spirituality and Disillusion*. New York: Addison-Wesley, 1993.

Mazón, Mauricio. *The Zoot Suit Riots: The Psychology of Symbolic Annihilation*. Austin: University of Texas Press, 1984.

McNamara, Eileen. "Writer's Point Lost on Amherst," *Boston Globe,* December 1, 1999, B1.

McWilliams, Carey. *North from Mexico: The Spanish Speaking People of the United States* (1949). New York: Praeger, 1969.

———. "Zoot-Suit Riots," *New Republic,* June 21, 1943, 18–20.

Mehta, Gita. *Karma Cola: Marketing the Mystic East* (1977). New York: Fawcett Columbine, 1990.

Melnick, Jeffrey. *A Right to Sing the Blues: African Americans, Jews, and American Popular Song*. Cambridge, Mass.: Harvard University Press, 1999.

Miller, Mark. "A Jamaican Invasion in West Virginia," *Newsweek*, March 28, 1988, 24.

Miller, Timothy. *The Hippies and American Values*. Knoxville: University of Tennessee Press, 1991.

Mills, C. Wright, Clarence Senior, and Rose Kohn Goldsen. *The Puerto Rican Journey: New York's Newest Migrants* (1950). New York: Russell and Russell, 1967.

Montoya, Jose. "El Louie" (1969), in *Information: 20 Years of Joda*. San Jose, Calif.: Chusma House, 1992.

Mordden, Ethan. *Coming Up Roses: The Broadway Musical in the 1950s*. New York: Oxford University Press, 1998.

Morgenthau, Tom et al. "The Drug Gangs," *Newsweek*, March 28, 1988, 20–27.

Mukherjee, Bharati. *Leave It to Me*. New York: Fawcett Columbine, 1997.

Mungo, Ray. *Famous Long Ago: My Life and Hard Times with Liberation News Service, at Total Loss Farm, and on the Dharma Trail*. New York: Citadel, 1990.

Nakamura, Lisa. *Cybertypes: Race, Ethnicity, and Identity on the Internet*. New York: Routledge, 2002.

———. "Race in/for Cyberspace," in Bell and Kennedy, eds., 712–720.

Neal, Larry. "Malcolm X—An Autobiography." In *Hoodoo Hollerin' Bebop Ghosts*. Washington, D.C.: Howard University Press, 1974.

Negrón-Muntaner, Frances, and Ramón Grosfoguel. *Puerto Rican Jam: Essays on Culture and Politics*. Minneapolis: University of Minnesota Press, 1997.

Nelson, Havelock. "DJ Kool Herc," in Light, 16–17.

Ngai, Mai. *Impossible Subjects Illegal Aliens and the Making of Modern America*. Princeton, N.J.: Princeton University Press, 2004.

Oboler, Suzanne. *Ethnic Labels, Latino Lives: Identity and the Politics of (Re)Presentation in the United States*. Minneapolis: University of Minnesota Press, 1995.

Okihiro, Gary. *Margins and Mainstreams: Asians in American History and Culture*. Seattle: University of Washington Press, 1994.

Onkey, Lauren. Personal Communication, November 14, 2003.

Ornitz, Samuel. *Haunch Paunch and Jowl: An Anonymous Autobiography*. New York: Boni and Liveright, 1923.

Orsi, Robert. "The Religious Boundaries of an Inbetween People: Street *Feste* and the Problem of the Dark-Skinned Other in Italian Harlem, 1920–1990," *American Quarterly* 44.3 (1992): 313–347.

Osofsky, Gilbert. *Harlem: The Making of a Ghetto. Negro New York, 1890–1930* (1965). 2nd ed. New York: Harper and Row, 1971.

Oumano, Elena. "Spliff Competition," *Village Voice* (villagevoice.com), February 2–8, 2000.

Pachucos, in *Information: 20 Years of Joda,* 137–145. San Jose, Calif.: Chusma House, 1992.

Padilla, Elena. *Up from Puerto Rico* (1958). New York: Columbia University Press, 1964.

Paine, Jeffery. *Father India: How Encounters with an Ancient Culture Transformed the Modern West.* New York: HarperCollins, 1998.

Paiz, Patricio. "En memoria de Arturo Tijerina," in *Aztlán and Viet Nam: Chicano and Chicana Experiences of the War,* 139–142. Ed. by George Mariscal. Berkeley: University of California Press, 1991.

Palmer, Ransford. *U.S.-Caribbean Relations: Their Impact on Peoples and Culture.* Westport, Conn.: Praeger, 1998.

Paz, Octavio. *Labyrinth of Solitude: Life and Thought in Mexico.* Trans. by Lysander Kemp, 1950. New York: Grove, 1961.

Penniman, Bruce. "When a School Decides There's No Place for 'West Side Story,'" *Christian Science Monitor,* December 14, 1999, 18.

People's Voice, vol. 1, nos. 1–35 (February 14–October 10, 1942), New York.

Perdomo, Willie. *Where a Nickel Costs a Dime.* New York: W. W. Norton, 1996.

Pérez, Richie. "From Assimilation to Annihilation: Puerto Rican Images in U.S. Films," in Rodríguez, 142–163.

Perry, Helen Swick. *The Human Be-In.* New York: Basic Books, 1970.

Pietri, Pedro. *Puerto Rican Obituary.* New York: Monthly Review, 1973.

Piña, Leslie, and Constance Korosec. *Fashion Fabrics: 1960s.* Atglen, Pa.: Schiffer, 1998.

Poirer, Richard. "Learning from the Beatles," in *Notes from the New Underground: An Anthology.* Ed. by Jesse Kornbluth. New York: Viking, 1968.

Potash, Chris. *Reggae, Rasta, Revolution: Jamaican Music from Ska to Dub.* New York: Schirmer, 1997.

Prashad, Vijay. *The Karma of Brown Folk.* Minneapolis: University of Minnesota Press, 2000.

———. "PropaGandhi Ahimsa in Black America" (found at http://www.little india.com/India/march02/ahimsa.thm).

Prothero, Stephen. "Mother India's Scandalous Swamis" (found at www.infinity foundation.com/mandala/h_es/he_es_prother_hindu.htm).

Puterbaugh, Parke, and James Henke. *I Want to Take You Higher: The Psychedelic Era, 1965–1969.* San Francisco: Chronicle, 1997.

Pynchon, Thomas. *Gravity's Rainbow* (1973). New York: Penguin, 1995.

[Ram Dass]. *Be Here Now* (1971). San Cristobal, N.M.: Hanuman Foundation, 1978.

Reimers, David. *Still the Golden Door: The Third World Comes to America.* New York: Columbia University Press, 1985.

Reynolds, Simon. *Generation Ecstasy: Into the World of Techno and Rave Culture.* Boston: Little, Brown, 1998.

Rivera, Raquel. *New York Ricans form the Hip Hop Zone.* New York: Palgrave, 2003.

Roberts, John Storm. *The Latin Tinge: The Impact of Latin American Music on the United States* (1979). New York: Oxford University Press, 1999.

Rockaway, Robert. *But—He Was Good to His Mother: The Lives and Crimes of Jewish Gangsters.* Jerusalem and New York: Gefen, 2000.

Rodríguez, Clara E., ed. *Latin Looks: Images of Latinas and Latinos in the U.S. Media.* Boulder, Colo.: Westview, 1997.

Roediger, David. *The Wages of Whiteness: Race and the Making of the American Working Class.* New York: Verso, 1996.

———. *Working toward Whiteness: How America's Immigrants Became White.* New York: Basic Books, 2005.

Rogin, Michael. *Independence Day, Or How I Learned to Stop Worrying and Love the Enola Gay.* London: British Film Institute, 1998.

———. *Blackface, White Noise: Jewish Immigrants in the Hollywood Melting Pot.* Berkeley: University of California Press, 1998.

Roszak, Theodore. *The Making of a Counterculture.* Garden City, N.Y.: Anchor, 1969.

Rubin, Rachel. "Filipino Babies and Eskimo Pies: Foreign Love in Postwar Country Music," paper delivered at International Association for the Study of Popular Music, 2002.

Runowicz, John. Personal communication, September 16, 2003.

Ruth, David. *Inventing the Public Enemy: The Gangster in American Culture, 1918–1934.* Chicago: University of Chicago Press, 1996.

Said, Edward. *Orientalism.* New York: Random House, 1979.

Salzman, Mark. *Lost in Place: Growing Up Absurd in Suburbia.* New York: Vintage, 1995.

Sanchez, Thomas. *The Zoot Suit Murders* (1978). New York: Vintage, 1991.

Sánchez Korrol, Virginia E. *From Colonia to Community: The History of Puerto Ricans in New York City* (1983). Berkeley: University of California Press, 1994.

Sanders, Ed. *The Family* (1971). New York: New American Library, 1989.

Sandoval-Sánchez, Alberto. *José, Can You See? Latinos on and off Broadway.* Madison: University of Wisconsin Press, 1999.

Sandoval-Sánchez, Alberto. "Puerto Rican Identity Up in the Air: Air Migration, Its Cultural Representations and Me 'Cruzando el Charco,'" in Negrón-Muntaner and Grosfoguel, 189–208.

———. "*West Side Story:* A Puerto Rican Reading of America," in Rodríguez, 164–179.

Santelli, Robert. *Aquarius Rising: The Festival Years.* New York: Dell, 1980.

Santiago, Esmeralda. *When I Was Puerto Rican.* New York: Vintage, 1993.

Sassen, Saskia. *Globalization and Its Discontents: Essays on the New Mobility of People and Money.* New York: New Press, 1998.

Satchidananda Sri Swami with Peter Max. *Beyond Words* (1997). Ed. by Lester Alexander. Buckingham, Va.: Integral Yoga Publications, 1992.

Schell, Orville. *Virtual Tibet: Searching for Shangri-La from the Himalayas to Hollywood.* New York: Henry Holt, 2001.

Schneider, Eric. *Vampires, Dragons, and Egyptian Kings: Youth Gangs in Postwar New York.* Princeton, N.J.: Princeton University Press, 1999.

Schulberg, Budd. *The Harder They Fall.* New York: Random House, 1990.

Seager, Richard Hughes. *Buddhism in America.* New York: Columbia University Press, 1999.

Shankar, Rajiv. Foreword to *A Part, Yet Apart: South Asians in Asian America.* Ed. by Lavina Dhingra Shankar and Rajini Srikanth. Philadelphia: Temple University Press, 1998.

Shankar, Ravi. "Fresh Air," interview on NPR, November 17, 1999.

———. *My Music, My Life.* New York: Simon and Schuster, 1968.

———. *Raga Mala* (1997). New York: Welcome Rain, 1999.

Shilts, Randy. *And the Band Played On: Politics, People, and the AIDS Epidemic.* New York: St. Martin's, 1987.

Shorris, Earl. *Latinos: A Biography of the People.* New York: W. W. Norton, 1992.

Shridharani, Krishnalal. *My India, My America.* New York: Duell, Sloan and Pearce, 1941.

Shukla, Sandhya. *India Abroad: Diasporic Cultures of Postwar America and England.* Princeton, N.J.: Princeton University Press, 2003.

Silber, Nina. *The Romance of Reunion: Northerners and the South, 1865–1900.* Chapel Hill: University of North Carolina Press, 1993.

Singer, David. "The Jewish Gangster: Crime as *Unzer Shtik,*" *Judaism,* Winter 1974, 6–16.

Sinha, Mrinalini. Introduction to Katherine Mayo, *Mother India* (1927). Ann Arbor: University of Michigan Press, 1998.

Sklar, Robert. *City Boys.* Princeton, N.J.: Princeton University Press, 1992.

Smethurst, James. *The Black Arts Movement: Literary Nationalism in the 1960s and 1970s.* Chapel Hill: University of North Carolina Press, 2005.

Smith, Judith. Personal communication, July 10, 2003.

————. *Visions of Belonging: Family Stories, Popular Culture, and Postwar Democracy, 1940–1960*. New York: Columbia University Press, 2004.

Smucker, Tom. "Reverse Crossover," *Village Voice,* September 2–8, 2000, online at www.villagevoice.com.

Sollors, Werner. *Beyond Ethnicity: Consent and Descent in American Culture.* New York: Oxford University Press, 1986.

————, ed. *The Invention of Ethnicity.* New York: Oxford University Press, 1991.

Song, Min. "Pakhar Singh's Argument with Asian America: Color and the Structure of Race Formation," in *A Part, Yet Apart: South Asians in Asian America,* 79–102. Ed. by Lavina Dhingra Shankar and Rajini Srikanth. Philadelphia: Temple University Press, 1998.

Spector, Ronnie. *Be My Baby.* New York: Harmony Books, 1990.

Stancell, Steven. *Rap Whoz Who: Performers, Producers, Promoters.* New York: Schirmer, 1996.

Stegner, Wallace, and the editors of *Look. One Nation.* Boston: Houghton Mifflin, 1945.

Stephens, Gregory. *On Racial Frontiers: The New Culture of Frederick Douglass, Ralph Ellison, and Bob Marley.* New York: Cambridge University Press, 1999.

Sterling, Bruce. "Short History of the Internet" (1993). Available at http://www.library.yale.edu/div/instruct/internet/history.htm

Stolzoff, Norman. *Wake the Town and Tell the People: Dancehall Culture in Jamaica.* Durham, N.C.: Duke University Press, 2000.

Stratton, Jon. "Buffy the Vampire Slayer: What Being Jewish Has to Do with It." *Television and New Media* 6, no. 2 (May 2005): 176–199.

Suntree, Susan. *Rita Moreno.* New York: Chelsea House, 1991.

Sutton, Constance. "The Caribbeanization of New York City and the Emergence of a Transnational Socio-Cultural System," in Sutton and Chaney, 15–30.

Sutton, Constance, and Elsa Chaney. *Caribbean Life in New York City: Sociocultural Dimensions.* New York: Center for Migration Studies of New York, 1987.

Swartley, Ariel. "The Wild, The Innocent, and the E Street Shuffle," in Greil Marcus, *Stranded: Rock and Roll for a Desert Island,* 49–57. New York: Random House: 1979.

Szwed, John. "The Real Old School," in Light, 3–11.

Taylor, Timothy. *Global Pop: World Music, World Markets.* New York: Routledge, 1997.

Thomas, Deborah. *Modern Blackness: Nationalism, Globalization, and the Politics of Culture in Jamaica.* Durham, N.C.: Duke University Press, 2004.

Toop, David. *Rap Attack 2: African Rap to Global Hip Hop.* New York: Serpent's Tail, 1991.

Torres, Andrés, and José E. Velázquez. *The Puerto Rican Movement: Voices from the Diaspora.* Philadelphia: Temple University Press, 1998.

Tse, Holly. Interview with Rachel Rubin, July 19, 2001.

Tuan, Mia. *Forever Foreigners or Honorary Whites? The Asian Ethnic Experience Today.* New Brunswick, N.J.: Rutgers University Press, 1998.

Tweed, Thomas, and Stephen Prothero, eds. *Asian Religions in America: A Documentary History.* New York: Oxford University Press, 1999.

"28 Zoot Suiters Seized on Coast after Clashes with Service Men," *New York Times,* June 7, 1943.

Ueda, Reed. *Postwar Immigrant America: A Social History.* New York: Bedford/St. Martin's, 1994.

Valdez, Vincent. *Kill the Pachuco Bastard!* (2001). Collection of Cheech and Patti Marin, reproduced in *Chicano Visions: American Painters on the Verge.* Ed. Cheech Marin. Boston: Little, Brown, 2002.

Wagenheim, Kal, and Olga Jiménez de Wagenheim. *The Puerto Ricans: A Documentary History* (1994). Princeton, N.J.: Markus Wiener, 1999.

Wakefield, Dan. *Island in the City: Puerto Ricans in New York.* New York: Corinth, 1959.

Ward, Curtis. "The Future of U.S. Immigration Policy," in Palmer, 75–85.

Warner, Jay. *The Billboard Book of American Singing Groups: A History, 1940–1990.* New York: Billboard, 1992.

Warshow, Robert. "The Gangster as Tragic Hero" (1948). Reprinted in *The Immediate Experience.* New York: Atheneum, 1970.

Waters, Mary. *Black Identities: West Indian Immigrant Dreams and American Realities.* Cambridge, MA: Harvard University Press, 2001.

Weber, Bruce. "Reggae Rhythms Speak to an Insular Tribe," *New York Times,* National, Sunday (nytimes.com), September 19, 1999.

Weinstein, Deena, and Michael A. Weinstein. "Net Game Cameo," in Bell and Kennedy, eds., 210–215.

Whalen, Carmen Teresa. *From Puerto Rico to Philadelphia: Puerto Rican Workers and Postwar Economies.* Philadelphia: Temple University Press, 2001.

White, Shane, and Graham White. *Stylin': African American Expressive Culture from Its Beginnings to the Zoot Suit.* Ithaca, N.Y.: Cornell University Press, 1998.

Williams, Mary E. *Readings on* West Side Story. San Diego: Greenhaven, 2001.

Wong, Kristina. Interview with Rachel Rubin, July 18, 2001.

The WPA Guide to New York City: The Federal Writers' Project Guide to 1930s New York (1939). New York: Pantheon Books, 1982.

Yanez, Rene. 1977. *Pachuco and Pachuca*, in *Chicano Art: Resistance and Affirmation, 1965–1985*, 264. Ed. by Richard Griswold del Castillo, Teresa McKenna, and Yvonne Yarbro-Bejarano. Wight Art Gallery, University of California, Los Angeles, 1991.

Yang, Jeff, Dina Gan, Terry Hong, and the staff of *A*. Magazine. *Eastern Standard Time: A Guide to Asian Influence on American Culture*. New York: Houghton Mifflin, 1997.

Yogananda, Paramahansa. *Autobiography of a Yogi* (1946). New York: Self-Realization Fellowship, 1993.

SELECTED ZINES

The nature of both zine publishing and Internet publishing is fairly ephemeral. In some cases, the address will have changed or the zine may no longer exist.

Angry Little Asian Girl (e-zine; www.angrylittleasiangirl.com)

Asian American Revolutionary Movement E-Zine (e-zine; www.aamovement.net)

AsiaZine (e-zine; www.asiazine.com)

Bagong Pinay (e-zine; www.newfilipina.com)

Bamboo Girl (paper zine)

Banana Café (e-zine, www.bananacafe.ca/0203/0203-16.htm)

Big Bad Chinese Mama (e-zine; www.bigbadchinesemama.com)

Blast@explode.com (e-zine; blast@explode.com)

Dead Fish (e-zine; www.deadfish.com)

Destroy All Monsters (e-zine; www.destroy-all-monsters.com)

Evolution of a Race Riot (paper zine)

Exoticize This! (also called *Exoticize My Fist!*) (e-zine; http://members.aol.com/Critchicks/)

Gas 'n' Go (paper zine)

Geek the Girl (e-zine; www.nodeadtrees.com/ezines/geekgirl)

generationrice (e-zine; www.generationrice.com)

Giant Robot (paper zine)

Gidra (e-zine; www.gidra.net)

Half-Korean (e-zine; www.halfkorean.net)

Hi-Yaa! (e-zine; www.hi-yaa.com/index2.html)

Il Stix (e-zine; www.ilstix.com)

Koe (paper zine)

Moons in June (paper zine)

Oriental Whatever (paper zine)

Riot Grrrl Review (paper zine)
Robot Power (paper zine)
Shoyu (e-zine; www.shoyuzine.tripod.com/shoyu2010/)
slander (e-zine; www.worsethanqueer.com)
Slant (paper zine)
Tennis and Violins (paper zine)
Yellow Kitty (paper zine)

MUSIC

"Boddhisatva" (Steely Dan, *Countdown to Ecstasy,* 1973).
"Born in the U.S.A." (Bruce Springsteen, *Live in New York City,* 2001).
The Concert for Bangladesh (Various Artists, 1971).
"Gimme No Crack" (Shinehead, *Unity,* 1988).
Gypsy Punks: Underdog World Strike (Gogol Bordello, 2005).
"Jamaican in New York" (Shinehead, *Sidewalk University,* 1992).
J.U.F. (Gogol Bordello vs. Tamir Muskat, 2004).
Kids from Foreign (Born Jamericans, 1994).
"Lamento Borincano" (1929; Rafael Hernández, *Lamento Borincano—Early Puerto Rican Music: 1916–1939,* 2001).
Lamento Borincano—Early Puerto Rican Music: 1916–1939 (2001).
"My Island" (1973; Paulette Williams, *Trojan "Tighten Up" Box Set,* 2002).
"Rocking in America" (The Meditations, *For the Good of Man,* 1989).
"Rum and Coca Cola" (1943; Lord Invader, *Calypso Calaloo,* 1993).
"Running from Jamaica" (1976; The Meditations, *Deeper Roots,* 1994).
"Sons of He" (Burning Spear, *Calling Rastafari,* 1999).
"Statue of Liberty" (Burning Spear, *Calling Rastafari,* 1999).
"Swami Everykinanda" (Tuli Kupferberg, *Tuli & Friends,* 1989).
"Territorial Pissings" (Nirvana, *Nevermind,* 1991).
"Thank U" (Alanis Morissette, *Supposed Former Infatuation Junkie,* 1998).
The Wild, the Innocent, and the E Street Shuffle (Bruce Springsteen, 1973).
"Wild West Indians" (Reggae Cowboys, *Rock Steady Rodeo,* 1999).
"World's Fair" (1964; The Skatalites, *Foundation Ska,* 1997).
"Yo Vuelvo a mi Bohío" (1951; El Jíbaro de Adjuntas, *Lamento Borincano—Early Puerto Rican Music: 1916–1939,* 2001).
"Zoot Suit Riot" (Cherry Poppin' Daddies, *Zoot Suit Riot,* 1998).

TELEVISION AND FILM

Alien Nation. Dir. Graham Baker. Twentieth-Century Fox, 1988.

American Me. Dir. Edward James Olmos. Universal Pictures, 1992.

Analyze That! Dir. Harold Ramis. Warner Brothers, 1999.

Analyze This! Dir. Harold Ramis. Warner Brothers, 2002.

The Big Combo. Dir. Joseph Lewis. Allied Artists Pictures Corporation, 1955.

Billy Bathgate. Dir. Robert Benton. Touchstone Pictures, 1991.

Blind Alley. Dir. Charles Vidor. Columbia Pictures, 1939.

"The Boogie Woogie Man Will Get You (If You Don't Watch Out)." Dir. James "Shamus" Culhane. Universal Pictures: 1943.

Buffy the Vampire Slayer (TV series). Created by Joss Whedon, 1997–2003.

Bugsy. Dir. Barry Levinson. TriStar/Desert Vision, 1991.

Chappaqua. Dir. Conrad Rooks. Regional/Hunter, 1967.

"Coal Black and De Sebben Dwarfs." Dir. Carl W. Stalling. Warner Brothers, 1943.

The Concert for Bangladesh. Dir. Saul Swimmer. Twentieth-Century Fox, 1972.

The Dark Mirror. Dir. Robert Siodmak. International Pictures, 1946.

Eight Men Out. Dir. John Sayles. Orion, 1988.

A Force of Evil. Dir. Abraham Polonsky. Enterprise/MGM, 1948.

The Godfather. Dir. Francis Coppola. Paramount, 1972.

"Goldilocks and the Three Jivin' Bears." Dir. I. Freleng. Warner Brothers, 1944.

Grosse Point Blank. Dir. George Armitage. Caravan Pictures, 1997.

"The Hams That Couldn't Be Cured." Dir. Walter Lantz. Walter Lantz Productions, 1942.

Independence Day. Dir. Roland Emmerich. Twentieth-Century Fox, 1996.

The Jazz Singer. Dir. Alan Crosland. Warner Brothers, 1927.

Lansky. Dir. John McNaughton. HBO, 1999.

Let 'Em Have It. Dir. Sam Wood. Reliance Pictures/United Artists, 1935.

Life and Debt. Dir. Stephanie Black. New Yorker Films, 2001.

Little Caesar. Dir. Mervyn LeRoy. Warner Brothers, 1930.

Men in Black II. Dir. Barry Sonnenfeld. Sony Pictures, 2002.

Monterey Pop. Dir. D. A. Pennebaker. Fair Enterprises, 1968.

"Mother Goose." Dir. Bill Tytla. Famous Studios, 1947.

1941. Dir. Stephen Spielberg. Columbia Pictures, 1979.

Once Upon a Time in America. Dir. Sergio Leone. Warner Brothers/Embassy International/PSO International, 1984.

The Petrified Forest. Dir. Archie Mayo. Warner Brothers, 1936.

The Public Enemy. Dir. William Wellman. Warner Brothers, 1931.

Raga. Dir. Howard Worth. Apple Films, 1971.

Scarface. Dir. Howard Hawks and Richard Rosson. United Artists, 1932.

The Sopranos. Series created by David Chase. HBO, 1999–present.

Stormy Weather. Dir. Andrew Stone. Twentieth-Century Fox, 1943.

"Tin Pan Alley Cats." Directed by Carl Stalling. Warner Brothers, 1943.

West Side Story. Dir. Robert Wise and Jerome Robbins. United Artists, 1961.

Who Killed Roger Rabbit? Dir. Robert Zemeckis. Touchstone Pictures, 1988.

Wiseguy. Series created by Stephen J. Cannell. Episode title: "Independent Operator."

Woodstock. Dir. Michael Wadleigh. Warner Brothers, 1970.

The Young Savages. Dir. John Frankenheimer. United Artists, 1961.

"Zoot Cat." Dir. William Hanna and Joseph Barbera. MGM, 1944.

Zoot Suit. Dir. Luis Valdez. Universal Pictures, 1981.

WEBSITES

www.thesmokinggun.com/capeman/capeman.html

www.electricearl.com/dws/eternals.html

www.home.earthlink.net/~oleander1/countdo.htm

www.purelyrics.com/index.php?lyrics=itxlckkp

www.multiracial.com/government/thind.html

www.infinityfoundation.com/mandala/h_es/h_es_proth_hindu.htm

www.lib.berkeley.edu/SSEAL/echoes/chapter4/chapter4.html

www.ilw.com/lawyers/colum_article/articles/2003,0512-smith.shtm

www.manbehinddthedoll.com

www.sequoiarecords.com/902.sthml

www.bluesaccess.com/No_25/butter.html

www.aejv.com/max-bio.htm

www.bsnpubs.com/buddah/buddahstory.html

www.guitargonauts.com/pick-46.html

www.mcny.org/collections/abbott/a148-a.htm

www.bobmarley.com/songs/songs.cgi?sheriff

www.jayquan.com /charliea.htm

www.cocaine-facts.org/pages/jamaica_traffickers.html

www.jamaica-gleaner.com/gleaner/20010717/cleisure/cleisure2.html

www.naid.sppsr.ucla.edu/ny64fair/map-docs/buildingfair.htm

www.pacificnet.net/~jaweb/lou-b-01.html

www.reggaecowboys.com

www.social.chass.ncsu.edu/wyrick/debclass/Revers.htm

www.westsidestory.com/site/leve12/archives/bibliography/herald1.html

www.imdb.com/name/nm0000217

INDEX

Note: Locators in italics indicate figures.

ABOUT THE AUTHORS

Rachel Rubin is Associate Professor of American Studies at the University of Massachusetts Boston. She is author of *Jewish Gangsters of Modern Literature,* co-editor of *American Popular Music: New Approaches to the Twentieth Century,* and editor of *A House Is Not a Home,* by Polly Adler.

Jeffrey Melnick is Associate Professor of American Studies at Babson College. He is author of *A Right to Sing the Blues: African Americans, Jews, and American Popular Song* and *Black-Jewish Relations on Trial: Leo Frank and Jim Conley in the New South,* and co-editor of *American Popular Music: New Approaches to the Twentieth Century* and *Race and the Modern Artist.*